College Vocabulary

An Introduction

ELLIOTT L. SMITH

Ferris State University

ST. MARTIN'S PRESS
New York

Senior Editor: Mark Gallaher
Development Editor: Andrea R. Guidoboni
Project Editor: Joyce Hinnefeld
Text Design: Leon Bolognese
Cover Design: Darby Downey

Library of Congress Catalog Card Number: 88-63041

432
fedcb

For information, write:
St. Martin's Press, Inc.
175 Fifth Avenue
New York, NY 10010

ISBN: 0-312-01615-8

ACKNOWLEDGMENT

Definition of *pandemic* from *Webster's New World Dictionary*, Second College Edition. Copyright © 1986 by Simon and Schuster, Inc. Reprinted by permission from *Webster's New World Dictionary*.

To the Instructor

The goal of any vocabulary text is to provide students with a "user-friendly" structure for improving their understanding and use of words. This is the intent of *College Vocabulary*, and its structures have been classroom-tested for many years.

The text is divided into five chapters. The first chapter, "The Structure of Words," focuses on roots, prefixes, suffixes, and phonics to explain how words are formed, or "composed," and pronounced. The second and third chapters, "Words from Roots I" and "Words from Roots II," teach students how to unlock the meanings of new words through an understanding of Latin and Greek roots. Chapters 4 and 5, "Words with Prefixes" and "Words with Suffixes," present a more thorough treatment of prefixes and suffixes, building on the base established in Chapter 1. Supplementary exercises featuring additional roots and derivatives appear at the end of Chapter 2 and Chapter 3. These exercises are for students or instructors who wish to work beyond the basic scope of the book.

Usage is the primary strategy of instruction throughout *College Vocabulary*. For example, in the two chapters featuring Latin and Greek roots (together), students are given the opportunity to do just about everything that can be done with the words being taught. Each of the thirty-six exercise sequences that make up these chapters begins with a brief introduction explaining the connection between the featured root or roots and the list of defined derivatives that follows. The word list includes both pronunciations and part-of-speech indications, and the definitions are carefully tailored to reinforce the kinship between the featured roots and the words being taught. Pronunciations are also given in the introduction for those sample derivatives that may be new words to some students. Students then "handle" these same words in four exercises: (1) true-false, (2) definition replacement, (3) fill-in and part-of-speech identification, and (4) matching. To increase the student's exposure to a broader variety of roots, a bonus root is provided at the conclusion of each sequence, and one or two derivatives of the bonus root appear in all the exercises of the sequence.

The thirty-two exercise sequences in the prefix and suffix chapters, although briefer, provide an added sentence completion exercise after every fourth sequence. These completion exercises are designed to help students begin the process of moving new words from the level of recognition to the level of usage. Additionally, these chapters provide students with the opportunity to list a few sample words of their own containing the prefixes or suffixes featured in the individual sequences.

Throughout *College Vocabulary*, words specifically taught in early sequences of exercises are used as incidental words in later sequences—for reinforcement. The reverse is also true. Words to be specifically taught in later sequences occasionally appear as incidental words in earlier sequences. Students can be instructed that when they encounter an unfamiliar word (not being taught), they should look it up in the index and then turn to the "future" sequence where the word is fully presented. By doing this, students familiarize themselves with the index and also regularly preview parts of the book yet to come. Also at the back of the text is an answer section with answers to the exercises for the odd-numbered sequences, thus allowing the book to be used both auto-tutorially and in a classroom setting.

The Instructor's Manual to accompany *College Vocabulary* includes the following: (1) both general guidelines and specific suggestions for classroom use, (2) seventeen quizzes covering the entire text, one quiz for every four exercise sequences, (3) seventeen alternate quizzes that the instructor can modify, (4) answers to the exercises for the even-numbered sequences, and (5) answers to the supplementary exercises following the roots chapters and to the introductory exercises in the prefix and suffix chapters. All quizzes may be reproduced for classroom use.

Acknowledgments

I am grateful to the reviewers who assisted me in the development of this text: Vivian Brown, Laredo Junior College; Eric W. Reitz, Catonsville Community College; Cindy Thompson, Northeast Louisiana University; and Elizabeth Wahlquist, Brigham Young University. I would also like to thank the following people at St. Martin's: Ed Tiefenthaler, regional sales manager; Susan Anker, editor-in-chief; Mark Gallaher, English editor; Andrea R. Guidoboni, development editor; Joyce Hinnefeld, project editor; Mary Aldridge, copy editor; and Andrew Goldwasser, proofreader.

Elliott L. Smith

Contents

Chapter

The Structure of Words

Words are actually brief compositions. The parts of these compositions are called *roots, prefixes,* and *suffixes.* The following list demonstrates how words are assembled or composed:

prefix		root		suffix		word
ad-	+	miss	+	-ible	=	admissible
bi-	+	lingu	+	-al	=	bilingual
con-	+	sequ	+	-ence	=	consequence
ex-	+	clam	+	-ation	=	exclamation
hyper-	+	act	+	-ive	=	hyperactive
in-	+	anim	+	-ate	=	inanimate
re-	+	curr	+	-ent	=	recurrent
super-	+	son	+	-ic	=	supersonic
sub-	+	mar	+	-ine	=	submarine
tele-	+	vis	+	-ion	=	television

But words are not always so neatly composed of one prefix, one root, and one suffix. Sometimes they do not have a prefix or suffix. Sometimes they include more than one prefix or suffix. Occasionally, they may even have two roots. The following list demonstrates the variety in word composition. As in the first list, the prefixes are followed by hyphens, and the suffixes are preceded by hyphens. The roots are in italics.

benediction: *bene* + *dict* + -ion
bicentennial: bi- + *cent* + *enni* + -al
carnivorous: *carni* + *vor* + -ous
circumscribe: circum- + *scribe*
dictionary: *dict* + -ion + -ary
discomfort: dis- + com- + *fort*
fraternalism: *fratern* + -al + -ism
inadmissible: in- + ad- + *miss* + -ible
pseudoartistic: pseudo- + *art* + -ist + -ic
unimportant: un- + im- + *port* + -ant

Roots, prefixes, and suffixes are the semantic (sə-MAN-tik) elements of words; that is, they are the elements that give a word its meaning. Roots, prefixes, and suffixes have their own separate meanings and can be looked up individually in a dictionary. The individual meanings of roots, prefixes, and suffixes suggest the overall meanings of the

PRONUNCIATION KEY

a	(ask, cat, brat)	ŋ	(link, anger, sing)
ay	(ape, hate, way)	o	(audio, fall, corn)
ah	(bar, father, on)	ow	(ocean, clover, show)
au	(out, doubt, lousy, cow)	oo	(book, pull, poor)
b	(bite, fable, fib)	oi	(oil, joint, coy)
ch	(chest, catcher, church)	p	(pun, grapple, trap)
d	(dog, needle, sod)	r	(run, sport, fear)
e	(elf, bed, care)	s	(sin, center, wrestle, class)
ee	(equal, heat, honey)	sh	(shoe, ambition, smash)
ə	(about, agent, pencil, lemon, circus)	t	(town, rattle, cat)
		th	(think, ether, truth)
f	(flag, after, fluff, phone)	t͡h	(this, either, lathe)
g	(go, haggle, dog)	u	(up, hut, burn, deter)
h	(her, ahead, home)	uw	(ooze, lose, fool, shoe)
hw	(while, when, nowhere)	v	(van, shovel, save)
i	(if, kit, mirror)	w	(we, away, swerve)
iy	(ice, kite, deny)	y	(yes, onion, lawyer)
j	(jump, agile, judge)	yu	(bureau, curable, pure)
k	(kiss, cake, shaken)	yuw	(unity, youth, mute, skew)
l	(low, fellow, level)	z	(zink, dazzle, maze)
m	(me, camel, mum)	zh	(pleasure, measure, vision)
n	(no, annul, fan)		

words they compose. The following list includes the meanings of the prefixes, roots, and suffixes in several words:

atheist
a- (without) + *the* (God) + *-ist* (a person who)

carnivorous
carni (flesh) + *vor* (to eat) + *-ous* (characterized by)

incredible
in- (not) + *cred* (to believe) + *-ible* (able to be)

recurrent
re- (again) + *curr* (to run) + *-ent* (showing)

supersonic
super- (above) + *son* (sound) + *-ic* (like)

In addition to meaning, words also have sound. When we "sound" a word, we pronounce it. The study of word pronunciation is called *phonics*. The pronunciation key on the accompanying page shows the phonic alphabet used throughout *College Vocabulary*.

The purpose of a phonic alphabet is to spell words out in such a way that you can learn to pronounce them through their spelling. The same sounds are consistently represented by the same characters. Traditional English spelling does not do this. In the following list, note the many different ways that traditional spelling presents the *sh* sound. Also note that the phonic alphabet spells the sound only one way.

English Spelling	*Phonic Spelling*
cons*c*ience	(KAHN-shən)
ma*ch*ine	(mə-SHEEN)
man*s*ion	(MAN-shən)
men*t*ion	(MEN-shən)
mis*s*ion	(MISH-ən)
nau*se*ous	(NO-shəs)
o*ce*an	(OW-shən)
*p*sh*aw	(SHO)
*sch*ist	(SHIST)
*sh*ow	(SHOW)
spe*ci*al	(SPESH-əl)
*s*ugar	(SHOOG-ər)
tis*su*e	(TISH-uw)

Traditional spelling also spells parts of words the same way when they are pronounced in different ways. Note the *ough* grouping in the following list:

English Spelling	Phonic Spelling
cough	(KOF)
plough	(PLAU)
though	(T͡HOW)
through	(THRUW)
tough	(TUF)

In addition to always spelling the same sounds with the same characters, the phonic alphabet also presents three levels of stress. The strongest, or primary, stress is indicated by CAPITAL LETTERS; the secondary stress is indicated by *italics*; and the third, or tertiary (TUR-shee-*er*-ee), stress, which is almost no stress at all, is indicated by ordinary lowercase letters. The following list contains words that demonstrate these stress patterns:

English Spelling	Phonic Spelling
agriculture	(AG-rə-*kul*-chər)
contemporary	(kən-TEM-pə-*rer*-ee)
dictionary	(DIK-shə-*ner*-ee)
historical	(his-TOR-i-kəl)
hyperactive	(*hiy*-pər-AK-tiv)
installment	(in-STOL-mənt)
magazine	(MAG-ə-*zeen*)
photographic	(*fow*-tə-GRAF-ik)
vocabulary	(vow-KAB-yə-*ler*-ee)
zodiac	(ZOW-dee-*ak*)

Note that the inverted *e* (ə), which is called a *schwa*, never occurs in a syllable with either primary or secondary stress.

To check your understanding of the pronunciation key, write the traditional spelling of the following words given in the phonic alphabet:

1. (AK-rə-*bat*) _____

2. (BRIY-bə-ree) _____

3. (*mis*-ə-SIP-ee) _____

4

4. (KAU·ərd·lee) _____

5. (STIY·rə-*fowm*) _____

6. *pen*·ə·SIL·in) _____

7. (AL·fə-*bet*) _____

8. (KRIS·məs) _____

9. (*ow*·shə·NAHG·rə·fee) _____

10. (i·TUR·nə·tee) _____

11. (ri·VAHL·viŋ) _____

12. (kən·FYUW·zhən) _____

13. (byuw·TISH·ən) _____

14. (KAHM·yə-*niz*·əm) _____

15. (*pik*·chə·RESK) _____

16. (ə·LAU·əns) _____

17. (IN·stiŋkt) _____

18. (in-*siy*·klə·PEE·dee·ə) _____

19. (BUT·ər-*fliy*) _____

20. (liŋ·GWEE·nee) _____

21. (JAN·yə-*wer*·ee) _____

22. (*yur*·ə·PEE·ən) _____

23. (dis·PLEZH·ər) _____

24. (HWIS·əl) _____

25. (in·JOI·ə·bəl) _____

26. (bi·KEE·nee) _____

27. (ə-MER-ə-kə-*niz*-əm) _____

28. (HWIP-*lash*) _____

29. (i-LEK-shən) _____

30. (*yuw*-nə-VUR-sə-tee) _____

The answers are (1) *acrobat*, (2) *bribery*, (3) *Mississippi*, (4) *cowardly*, (5) *Styrofoam*, (6) *penicillin*, (7) *alphabet*, (8) *Christmas*, (9) *oceanography*, (10) *eternity*, (11) *revolving*, (12) *confusion*, (13) *beautician*, (14) *communism*, (15) *picturesque*, (16) *allowance*, (17) *instinct*, (18) *encyclopedia*, (19) *butterfly*, (20) *linguine*, (21) *January*, (22) *European*, (23) *displeasure*, (24) *whistle*, (25) *enjoyable*, (26) *bikini*, (27) *Americanism*, (28) *whiplash*, (29) *election*, and (30) *university*.

Chapter

Words from Roots I

Derivatives are words formed from other words or word parts. For example, the word *phonetics* (fə-NET-iks), meaning "the study of speech sounds and how they are written in combinations," is a derivative of the Greek root *phon,* meaning "sound." Other modern English derivatives of the same root include *microphone, phonics, phonograph, saxophone, stereophonic, symphony,* and *telephone.*

This chapter and the next focus on modern English words that are derivatives of Latin and Greek roots. Learning a number of these roots offers you a very efficient way of improving your vocabulary. There are two reasons for this. First, more than half of all the words in the English language are derived from Latin or Greek. Second, many English words may be derived from a single root. For example, if you know that the Latin root *fid,* or *fed,* means "faith" or "trust" and you can recognize the root in English words, you have a start at understanding the meaning of each of the following derivatives:

af*fid*avit	con*fide*	dif*fid*ence
bona *fide*	con*fid*ence	dif*fid*ent
con*fed*eracy	con*fid*ent	dif*fid*ently
con*fed*erate	con*fid*ential	*fed*eracy
con*fed*eration	con*fid*entiality	*fed*eral
con*fid*ant	con*fid*entially	*fed*eralism
con*fid*ante	con*fid*ing	*fed*eralist

*fede*ralistic	*fide*ism	in*fide*l
*fede*ralize	*fide*ist	in*fide*lity
*fede*rally	*fide*istic	mala *fide*
*fede*rate	*fide*lity	per*fid*ious
*fede*ration	*fidu*cial	per*fid*iously
*fede*rative	*fidu*ciary	per*fid*y

This chapter consists of twenty sequences of exercises. Begin each sequence by reading the introductory paragraph. This paragraph explains the root or roots featured in the sequence. Next, study the list of defined words. These are the ten words taught in the sequence. Any word marked by an asterisk (*) is a derivative of the *bonus root,* which is presented at the end of the sequence. Take the time to pronounce each word as it is presented in the phonic alphabet.

When you are familiar with the word list, go on to the four exercises: (1) true-false, (2) definition replacement, (3) fill-in and part-of-speech identification, and (4) matching. The ten words from the original word list are to be used in each of the exercises. In the true-false exercise, simply answer with *T* or *F.* In the definition replacement exercise, write in the blank the word defined within the brackets. In the fill-in and part-of-speech identification exercise, write the appropriate word in the blank within each sentence and then indicate that word's part of speech (*a* for adjective, *adv* for adverb, *n* for noun, and *v* for verb) in the blank at the beginning of the sentence. In the matching exercise, match the words with their definitions. Before beginning the exercises, familiarize yourself with the bonus root at the end of the sequence. You will probably be able to recall the meaning of the bonus root just as well as you do those of the featured roots.

As you read the introductory paragraph to each sequence, do not be bothered by the fact that some roots have more than one spelling. For example, the first root discussed has five possible spellings: *ann, anni, annu, enn,* and *enni.* But all of these spellings mean "year." Variation in spelling happens most often with roots from Latin verbs or Greek roots that add an *o* or *y* when combining with other word parts. Such variant spellings of roots are called *combining forms.*

At the conclusion of the chapter are three supplementary roots and derivatives exercises. These exercises present additional roots not taken up in the chapter. If your instructor assigns them, or if you decide to work them on your own, fill in the blanks after each root and sample derivative(s) with three additional derivatives. You may want to check a college-level dictionary to make sure that the derivatives you put in the blanks are accurate. The specific part of a dictionary word entry that you will want to check is called the *etymology* (*et-ə-*MAHL-*ə-*jee), which explains the word's origin and development, working backward in time. Although dictionaries vary somewhat, the etymology usually appears within boldface brackets, either just before or just after the definition. The following is a sample entry from *Webster's New World Dictionary*, Second College Edition:

pan·dem·ic (pan dem′ik) *adj.* [< LL. *pandemus* < Gr. *pandēmos* < *pan,* all (see PAN-) + *dēmos,* the people: see DEMOCRACY] prevalent over a whole area, country, etc.; universal; general; specif., epidemic over a large region: said of a disease—*n.* a pandemic disease

From this entry, you can see that *pandemic* includes two Greek roots: *pan,* meaning "all," and *dem,* meaning "people."

Words from Roots (1)

The root *ann* or *enn* comes from the Latin word *annus,* meaning "year." Thus, any word containing this root will have something to do with the idea of a year or years. For example, an *anniversary* is a yearly celebration of an important event. Likewise, the word *annual* means "happening or taking place yearly." It may also denote a book or magazine that is published once a year, or a plant that lives for only one year or one growing season. The root may also be spelled *anni, annu,* or *enni.*

WORD LIST

1. *ann*als (AN-əlz), *n*: a written record of events presented in a year-by-year, or chronological, order

2. *ann*uity (ə-NUW-ə-tee), *n*: a yearly or regular payment of a fixed amount of money that is paid as a result of an earlier investment, or the original investment contract itself

3. bi*enni*al (biy-EN-ee-əl), *a*: happening every two years or lasting for two years; *n,* an event that occurs every second year, or a plant that bears fruit, flowers, or seed in the second year

4. cent*enni*al (sen-TEN-ee-əl), *n*: the celebration of a one-hundredth anniversary; *a,* related to the celebration of a one-hundredth anniversary; happening once in a hundred years or lasting a hundred years

*5. *greg*arious (grə-GER-ee-əs), *a*: literally, living in flocks or herds; fond of being with other people

6. mill*enni*um (mə-LEN-ee-əm), *n*: a period of a thousand years; a time of peace and great prosperity

7. per *ann*um (pər-AN-əm), *adv*: by the year or annually

8. per*enni*al (pə-REN-ee-əl), *a*: year after year; throughout the years; *n,* a plant that blooms annually

---

a (fat); ay (fate); ah (far); au (doubt); ch (church); e (elf, bed, care); ee (equal); ə (about); hw (while); i (fit); iy (kite); ŋ (link, sing); o (audio, corn); ow (ocean); oo (book); oi (oil); sh (shoe, ambition); th (think); u (up, deter); uw (ooze); y (yes, onion); yu (bureau, cure); yuw (youth, unity); zh (pleasure)

11

9. semi*annual* (*sem*-i-AN-yə-wəl), *a*: occurring every half year

10. super*annuated* (*suw*-pər-AN-yə-*way*-tid), *a*: worn-out or retired, as from age or years of use and hard work; obsolete or outdated

TRUE-FALSE

_____ 1. The president of the United States receives a fixed salary *per annum*.

_____ 2. A *biennial* plant usually blooms twice a year, in the spring and in the fall.

_____ 3. Americans celebrate Thanksgiving *semiannually*.

_____ 4. *Gregarious* individuals are generally sociable.

_____ 5. *Superannuated* ideas are brand-new, modern, and up-to-date.

_____ 6. A film entitled *The Annals of World War II* will likely include an account of the Japanese attack on Pearl Harbor, which occurred on December 7, 1941.

_____ 7. A team that is a *perennial* contender for the championship is a team that is close to the top year after year.

_____ 8. An *annuity* is a single cash payment.

_____ 9. A *centennial* celebration can occur only once in a hundred years.

_____ 10. A *millennium* is an extended period of bloody warfare.

DEFINITION REPLACEMENT

_____ 1. A weapons agreement with the Soviet Union does not necessarily mean that the [*a time of peace and prosperity*] will follow.

_____ 2. In the modern world, a given technology can become [*obsolete or outdated*] in a very brief period of time.

_____ 3. The company holds its [*happening every two years*] picnic at the county park.

12

_____ 4. From the mid-fifties through the early sixties, the Boston Celtics were the [*year after year*] champions of the Eastern Conference of the National Basketball Association.

_____ 5. Because Hawaii became a state in 1959, the [*one-hundredth anniversary*] of the event will be celebrated in 2059.

_____ 6. I am able to go to college only because of a substantial [*a regular payment of a fixed sum of money*] left me by my aunt's estate.

_____ 7. My roommate says that when he becomes rich and famous, his diaries will be looked at as important [*a year-by-year written record*] of our times.

_____ 8. My homeowner's insurance has become so expensive that I am forced to make [*occurring every half year*] payments.

_____ 9. Sheep are [*living in flocks*] creatures.

_____ 10. Some major league baseball players today receive salaries in excess of $1 million [*by the year*].

FILL-IN AND PART-OF-SPEECH IDENTIFICATION

_____ 1. John's parents own a _____ farm. The place has been in the family for a hundred years.

_____ 2. This plant is a _____. It blooms every other year.

_____ 3. Not a very _____ individual, I prefer to live alone in the mountains.

_____ 4. The naval museum had on display models of hundreds of _____ battleships.

_____ 5. According to the sales representative, this comprehensive policy will pay me an _____ of $750 a month when I retire.

_____ 6. I am a _____ procrastinator when it comes to doing my income tax return each April.

_____ 7. When I received my college degree, I thought I had achieved a personal _____. But I was wrong; the real battles of life were just beginning.

13

_____ 8. We searched the early _____ of city government in the hope of finding some mention of our ancestors.

_____ 9. In the spring and fall, my sister and I go on our _____ shopping trips to Chicago.

_____ 10. Today, a salary of $30,000 _____ is barely enough to take care of a family.

MATCHING

_____ 1. centennial   a. annually

_____ 2. superannuated   b. a regular fixed payment of money

_____ 3. perennial   c. obsolete

_____ 4. annals   d. fond of being with other people

_____ 5. millennium   e. happening every two years

_____ 6. semiannual   f. year after year

_____ 7. annuity   g. the celebration of a one-hundredth anniversary

_____ 8. gregarious   h. every six months

_____ 9. per annum   i. a written record chronologically arranged

_____ 10. biennial   j. a time of peace and prosperity

BONUS ROOT

greg (flock, herd, group): aggregate, aggregation, antisegregationist, congregate, congregation, congregational, congregative, desegregate, desegregation, egregious, segregate, segregation, segregationist, segregative

Words from Roots (2)

The root *loc,* from the Latin word *locus,* means "place." *Local* problems are problems connected with a particular place or area, rather than with the whole country. A *locomotive* is the engine that moves a train from one place to another. The combining form of this root is *loco.*

WORD LIST

1. al*loc*ate (AL-ə-*kayt*), *v*: to place aside or set apart for a specific purpose, as money or time for later use

✶ 2. dis*loc*ate (DIS-low-*kayt,* dis-LOW-*kayt*), *v*: to put something out of its normal place or position

3. *loc*alism (LOW-kə-*liz*-əm), *n*: an expression or manner typical of a specific place

✶ 4. *loc*ality (low-KAL-ə-tee), *n*: a general area, place, or neighborhood

✶ 5. *loc*alize (LOW-kə-*liyz*), *v*: to limit to a particular place or region; to determine the specific place of origin; to collect or gather in one place

6. *loco*motion (*low*-kə-MOW-shən), *n*: movement from one place to another, or the power making such movement possible

7. *loc*us (LOW-kəs), *n*: a specific point or place; the central point, as of some activity

✶8. *medi*ate (MEE-dee-*ayt*), *v*: to (try to) resolve differences between parties who are in disagreement, as by placing oneself in the middle between them.

✶9. *medi*ocrity (*mee*-dee-AHK-rə-tee), *n*: the state or quality of being ordinary or mediocre; a person of average ability

10. re*loc*ate (ree-LOW-*kayt*), *v*: to move to a new place, especially a new residence or section of the country

---

a (f*a*t); ay (f*a*te); ah (f*a*r); au (d*ou*bt); ch (*ch*ur*ch*); e (*e*lf, b*e*d, c*a*re); ee (*e*qual); ə (*a*bout); hw (*wh*ile); i (f*i*t); iy (k*i*te); ŋ (li*n*k, si*n*g); o (*au*dio, c*o*rn); ow (*o*cean); oo (b*oo*k); oi (*oi*l); sh (*sh*oe, ambi*ti*on); th (*th*ink); u (*u*p, det*e*r); uw (*oo*ze); y (*y*es, on*i*on); yu (b*u*reau, c*u*re); yuw (*y*outh, *u*nity); zh (plea*s*ure)

15

TRUE-FALSE

_____ 1. One's smile occupies the central *locality* of the face.

_____ 2. If I *relocate* my house and home, I move to another place.

_____ 3. A *localism* is a figure of speech used to put someone down.

_____ 4. To *allocate* money is to waste it.

_____ 5. A city's public transportation system often provides several different means of *locomotion*.

_____ 6. A *locus* is a noisy little insect that infests the hills of southern West Virginia about every seven years.

_____ 7. To *mediate* differences between angry people is to try to bring them to a compromise.

_____ 8. To *dislocate* a bone is to carefully season it with salt and garlic before cooking.

_____ 9. Nothing is more outstanding than *mediocrity.*

_____ 10. When a problem has been *localized,* it becomes more widespread.

DEFINITION REPLACEMENT

_____ 1. Unless we can [*to limit to a particular place*] the problem, a solution will be very difficult.

_____ 2. The exact [*a specific point or place*] of the signal for help has not yet been pinpointed.

_____ 3. In pioneer times, the horse was a principal source of [*movement from one place to another*].

_____ 4. [*The quality of being ordinary*] characterizes the play of many people on the tennis court.

16

_____ 5. When in college, you must [*to place aside for specific use*] enough time for study.

_____ 6. Where I grew up, people used the [*an expression typical of a specific place*] "crick" for "creek."

_____ 7. For no particular reason, the college wants to [*to move to a new place*] the student center on the edge of campus.

_____ 8. If you [*to put something out of its normal place*] your thumb, believe me, you will know it.

_____ 9. No one has been asked to [*to resolve differences between parties*] the labor dispute.

_____ 10. The [*a general area*] where I lived when I was a child is now occupied by a huge shopping mall.

FILL-IN AND PART-OF-SPEECH IDENTIFICATION

_____ 1. The entire _____ of the campus was once a thousand-acre farm.

_____ 2. The campus _____ for students native to the area is "townies."

_____ 3. How can one _____ the differences between two people who refuse to agree about anything?

_____ 4. Everyone agrees that the village should _____ more funds for library acquisitions.

_____ 5. The precise _____ of the disturbance was a trailer park north of town.

_____ 6. Some people think that the _____ of many American products has allowed higher-quality foreign goods to gain a foothold in our markets.

_____ 7. If you _____ a shoulder, you can expect to be out of the lineup for several weeks.

_____ 8. An automobile's _____ is provided by the engine.

_____ 9. Because of recurrent floods, the county should _____ the bridge on higher ground.

_____ 10. By closing a few of its more distant stores, the company can _____ its marketing efforts.

MATCHING

_____ 1. localize   a. the power making movement possible

_____ 2. mediate   b. to set apart for a specific purpose

_____ 3. localism   c. to move to a new place

_____ 4. allocate   d. a general area or place

_____ 5. dislocate   e. to resolve differences between disagreeing parties

_____ 6. relocate   f. the central point, as of some activity

_____ 7. locomotion   g. to collect or gather in one place

_____ 8. locus   h. the quality of being mediocre

_____ 9. mediocrity   i. an expression used in a specific place

_____ 10. locality   j. to put something out of its normal place

BONUS ROOT

medi (middle): immediacy, immediate, media, median, mediator, medieval, medieval-ism, medievalist, mediocre, Mediterranean

Words from Roots (3)

The root *bio,* from the Greek word *bios,* means "life." Typical modern English derivatives of this root include *biology,* the science of living plants and animals; *biography,* the story of a person's life; and *antibiotic* (*an*-ti-biy-AHT-ik), a chemical substance that fights disease by killing living microorganisms.

WORD LIST

1. auto*bio*graphy (*o*-tə-biy-AH-grə-fee), *n*: the story of a person's life written by the subject

2. *bio*degradable (*biy*-ow-di-GRAY-də-bəl), *a*: capable of decaying naturally, as by processes exacted by other living organisms, and being reabsorbed into the environment

3. *bio*feedback (*biy*-ow-FEED-*bak*), *n*: a technique, using electronic devices, wherein an unconscious or involuntary bodily (life) process—such as heartbeat—is brought under the control of the conscious mind

4. *bio*genesis (*biy*-ow-JEN-ə-sis), *n*: the development of life from previously existing and similar life forms, rather than from nonliving matter

5. *bio*mass (BIY-ow-*mas*), *n*: the total amount of living matter in a specific area, volume, or habitat

6. *bio*nics (biy-AHN-iks), *n*: the technology of designing and making instruments modeled after the structure of living organisms

7. *bio*psy (BIY-*ahp*-see), *n*: the removal of a small amount of living tissue from the body for examination, as in a medical diagnosis of a disease; *v,* to perform such a procedure

8. *bio*sphere (BIY-ə-*sfir*), *n*: that part of the earth, from the crust out into the atmosphere, where life exists

*9. *cycl*ical (SI-kli-kəl), *a*: happening or moving in cycles; recurring at regular intervals

a (f*a*t); ay (f*a*te); ah (f*a*r); au (d*ou*bt); ch (*ch*ur*ch*); e (*e*lf, b*e*d, c*a*re); ee (*e*qual); ə (*a*bout); hw (*wh*ile); i (f*i*t); iy (k*i*te); ŋ (li*n*k, si*ng*); o (*au*dio, c*o*rn); ow (*o*cean); oo (b*oo*k); oi (*oi*l); sh (*sh*oe, ambi*ti*on); th (*th*ink); u (*u*p, de*te*r); uw (*oo*ze); y (*y*es, on*i*on); yu (b*u*reau, c*u*re); yuw (*y*outh, *u*nity); zh (plea*s*ure)

10. sym*biotic* (*sim*-bi-AHT-ik), *a*: living together, as two types of organisms, to the benefit of both; mutually beneficial

TRUE-FALSE

_____ 1. *Biofeedback* may be accurately defined as "food for thought."

_____ 2. We humans live in the earth's *biosphere.*

_____ 3. The *biomass* of a jungle is substantial.

_____ 4. *Cyclical* events occur only once.

_____ 5. Only you can write your *autobiography.*

_____ 6. A *biopsy* is usually thought of as a method of fertilization.

_____ 7. Raising someone from the dead is called *biogenesis.*

_____ 8. *Symbiotic* relationships are of a mutual nature.

_____ 9. That which is *biodegradable* never decays.

_____ 10. From *bionics,* scientists may create humanlike implements.

DEFINITION REPLACEMENT

_____ 1. By the process of [*the development of life from other living things*], new life forms evolve from older ones.

_____ 2. The ultimate achievement of [*the technology of making lifelike implements*] might be the creation of an android.

_____ 3. You could hardly call warfare a [*mutually beneficial*] activity.

_____ 4. By reading your [*the story of a person's life written by the subject*], I can learn a lot about you.

_____ 5. Physicians often do a [*the examination of living tissue removed from the body*] to determine whether or not a patient has a serious disease.

_____ 6. The seasons of the year are [*recurring at regular intervals*].

_____ 7. Being [*decaying naturally*], fallen trees gradually rot on the forest floor.

_____ 8. The [*the total amount of living matter*] in a single glass of water may be great.

_____ 9. Outer space is not a part of our planet's [*the part of the earth where life exists*].

_____ 10. By using [*a technique for controlling involuntary life processes*], you may be able to reduce your blood pressure.

FILL-IN AND PART-OF-SPEECH IDENTIFICATION

_____ 1. Among other things, marriage is a _____ relationship, one from which both partners gain benefits.

_____ 2. You are wrong when you say that _____ includes the notion of life springing from something not alive.

_____ 3. Planet X-173, located in the ninth quadrant, was a dead planet and thus had no area of living organisms corresponding to the earth's _____.

_____ 4. Although she insisted that it was fiction, the book was really the author's _____, her life story.

_____ 5. Happily, the _____ revealed that the swollen tissue was not malignant.

_____ 6. "I am the product of advanced _____," said the robot, speaking in an eerie monotone.

_____ 7. The problem with many of these chemicals is that they are not _____ _____; they do not break down naturally in the ground.

_____ 8. My down moods, I have finally learned, are _____; they come and go like the phases of the moon.

21

_____ 9. The _____ of a swamp would likely be much greater than that of a desert.

_____ 10. Maxwell became a fanatic over _____; he wanted to reduce his heartbeat to forty beats per minute.

MATCHING

_____ 1. autobiography

_____ 2. bionics

_____ 3. biogenesis

_____ 4. biosphere

_____ 5. biomass

_____ 6. biodegradable

_____ 7. cyclical

_____ 8. symbiotic

_____ 9. biopsy

_____ 10. biofeedback

a. decaying naturally and harmlessly in the environment

b. to perform an examination on living tissue

c. a technology that makes lifelike devices

d. happening at recurrent intervals

e. a technique for controlling involuntary bodily functions

f. that part of the earth containing life

g. the development of life from other life forms

h. mutually beneficial

i. all living matter in a particular area

j. the story of a person's life written by the subject

BONUS ROOT

cycl(o) (circle, wheel): bicycle, cyclic, cycloid, cyclone, Cyclops, cyclorama, cyclotron, encyclical, encyclopedia, encyclopedic, motorcycle, tricycle, unicycle

Words from Roots (4)

Both the Latin root *mem(or)* and the Greek root *mne* mean "to remember." To *memorize* information is to commit it to memory. Anything described as *memorable* is worth remembering. A *memorial* service serves to help us remember a person or an event. However, if we are suffering from *amnesia* (am-NEE-zhə), we are unable to remember certain things.

WORD LIST

1. a*mne*sty (AM-nəs-tee), *n*: literally, a forgetting, as in the granting of a general pardon for some offense

2. com*memor*ate (kə-MEM-ə-rayt), *v*: to honor the memory of something or someone, as in a ceremony or celebration

3. *mem*ento (mi-MEN-tow), *n*: anything that serves as a reminder; an object that makes one remember; a souvenir

4. *mem*ento mori (mi-MEN-tow MOR-ee), *n*: any reminder of death, as a skull and crossbones on a bottle of poison

5. *mem*oirs (MEM-*wahrz*), *n*: autobiographical writings detailing events from one's past; personal accounts of remembered occurrences

6. *memor*abilia (*mem*-ər-ə-BIL-ee-ə), *n*: a collection of things worth remembering, as from a specific time in the past

7. *memor*andum (*mem*-ə-RAN-dəm), *n*: a short note intended to jog the memory—often shortened to "memo"

8. *mne*monics (nee-MAHN-iks), *n*: any system or technique intended to improve or assist the memory; *mne*monic (nee-MAHN-ik), *a*: intended to improve the memory

*9. *mori*bund (MOR-ə-*bund*), *a*: near death, or deathlike; coming to an end; without the vitality of life

---

a (f*a*t); ay (f*a*te); ah (f*a*r); au (d*ou*bt); ch (*ch*ur*ch*); e (*e*lf, b*e*d, c*a*re); ee (*e*qual); ə (*a*bout); hw (*wh*ile); i (f*i*t); iy (k*i*te); ŋ (li*n*k, si*ng*); o (*au*dio, c*o*rn); ow (*o*cean); oo (b*oo*k); oi (*oi*l); sh (*sh*oe, ambi*ti*on); th (*th*ink); u (*u*p, det*er*); uw (*oo*ze); y (*y*es, on*i*on); yu (b*u*reau, c*u*re); yuw (*you*th, *u*nity); zh (plea*s*ure)

*10. post*mortem* (*powst*-MOR-təm), *n*: a careful examination of something that has died; *a*, occurring after death

TRUE-FALSE

_____ 1. To many, a cemetery is a *memento mori*.

_____ 2. A *memorandum* is normally taken with a glass of water to help one forget about the day's disappointments.

_____ 3. A *memento* can bring back fond memories.

_____ 4. An *amnesty* is a declaration of guilt.

_____ 5. It is impossible to perform a *postmortem* on someone who is alive.

_____ 6. *Memoirs* are always fictional.

_____ 7. A collection of *memorabilia* will likely arouse one's memory of some past situation.

_____ 8. A *moribund* appearance suggests health and vigor.

_____ 9. *Mnemonic* devices are supposed to improve the memory.

_____ 10. To *commemorate* a past success is to try to forget it.

DEFINITION REPLACEMENT

_____ 1. On the fourth Thursday in November, Americans [*to honor the memory of*] the first Thanksgiving.

_____ 2. A short course in [*techniques to improve the memory*] can help most people become better students.

_____ 3. Reading the senator's [*autobiographical writings*] was almost like reliving her life.

_____ 4. The [*a careful examination of something that has died*] revealed that the patient had been taking drugs.

_____ 5. Your diploma will be an important [*an object that makes one remember*] of your college years.

_____ 6. There was no [*a general pardon*] for the convicted smugglers.

_____ 7. A vampire in need of a refill will likely have a [*deathlike*] appearance.

_____ 8. Stanley has a lot of [*a collection of things worth remembering*] from the fifties.

_____ 9. The [*a short note intended to jog the memory*] omitted the time of the meeting.

_____ 10. To the person who has lost a friend in an automobile accident, a wrecked car can be a [*a reminder of death*].

FILL-IN AND PART-OF-SPEECH IDENTIFICATION

_____ 1. If your cause is not actually dead, it is clearly _____.

_____ 2. The campus veterans' club is gathering _____ from World War II for a display at the local American Legion hall.

_____ 3. Most of the anti-drug advertisements on television include a _____, a reminder of the fatal consequences of taking drugs.

_____ 4. Judith uses clever _____ devices to help her remember information for tests.

_____ 5. Was there ever an official _____ granted to the men who went to Canada to avoid the draft during the Vietnam War?

_____ 6. I am so absentminded that I need a written _____ to remind me where to go to work each day.

_____ 7. Grimly, the students gathered around the posted examination scores as if attending a _____.

_____ 8. This model of the Eiffel Tower is a _____ of my trip to Paris.

_____ 9. Each Christmas, Christians _____ the birth of Jesus.

_____ 10. The retired general's _____ included many interesting stories about both the Korean and Vietnam wars.

MATCHING

_____ 1. memento   a. the granting of a general pardon

_____ 2. postmortem   b. techniques for improving the memory

_____ 3. memorabilia   c. a souvenir

_____ 4. amnesty   d. without the vitality of life

_____ 5. memorandum   e. to honor the memory of

_____ 6. memento mori   f. autobiographical writings

_____ 7. moribund   g. a short note to jog the memory

_____ 8. memoirs   h. a collection of things worth remembering

_____ 9. mnemonics   i. a careful examination of something that has died

_____ 10. commemorate   j. a reminder of death

BONUS ROOT

mor(t), _mori_ (death): amortization, amortize, immortal, immortality, mortal, mortality, mortgage, mortician, mortification, mortify, mortuary, rigor mortis

Words from Roots (5)

The Latin root *cur,* from the verb *currere,* means "to run." The root also appears as *curr, curs,* or *course.* The *current* of a river runs in a certain direction. The letters of *cursive* writing are joined and thus run together. A *course* of study or *curriculum* runs along toward its conclusion, a degree.

WORD LIST

1. con*course* (KAHN-*kors*), *n*: a running or flowing together; a large open area, as in a building, where crowds gather or pass through; a broad thoroughfare

2. con*current* (kən-KUR-ənt), *a*: running together, in the sense of occurring at the same time; acting together or cooperating

3. *cour*ier (KOOR-ee-ər, KUR-ee-ər), *n*: originally, a messenger who ran with an urgent message; any person, agency, or service that carries mail; a tour guide

4. *curs*ory (KUR-sə-ree), *a*: running over quickly with little attention to detail; hasty or superficial

5. dis*curs*ive (dis-KUR-siv), *a*: running or wandering from topic to topic; rambling or digressive

6. in*cur* (in-KUR), *v*: literally, to run toward, and thus to bring (something bad) upon oneself; to become liable or subject to

7. in*curs*ion (in-KUR-zhən), *n*: a running into, and thus a sudden (brief) raid or invasion

8. pre*curs*or (pri-KUR-sər), *n*: a person or event that runs before; a forerunner, harbinger, or predecessor

9. re*current* (ri-KUR-ənt), *a*: running back, and thus returning again and again; intermittent

*10. *tox*ic (TAHK-sik), *a*: relating to or caused by a toxin or poison; poisonous

---

a (fat); ay (fate); ah (far); au (doubt); ch (church); e (elf, bed, care); ee (equal); ə (about); hw (while); i (fit); iy (kite); ŋ (link, sing); o (audio, corn); ow (ocean); oo (book); oi (oil); sh (shoe, ambition); th (think); u (up, deter); uw (ooze); y (yes, onion); yu (bureau, cure); yuw (youth, unity); zh (pleasure)

TRUE-FALSE

_____ 1. *Concurrent* incidents happen at the same time.

_____ 2. A *discursive* lecture is short and to the point.

_____ 3. Someone too young to swear is called a *precursor*.

_____ 4. A *courier* service delivers mail.

_____ 5. An *incursion* is a sudden raid on or invasion of territory.

_____ 6. Consuming large amounts of *toxic* substances generally makes a person more healthy.

_____ 7. To *incur* someone's anger is to bring it upon yourself.

_____ 8. A *cursory* examination of the facts is a superficial one.

_____ 9. *Recurrent* ideas are always modern and up-to-date.

_____ 10. A *concourse* is a class offered by a dishonest instructor.

DEFINITION REPLACEMENT

_____ 1. Although we have made only a [*hasty or superficial*] investigation, things look pretty good.

_____ 2. The changing leaves of autumn are always a [*a forerunner or harbinger*] of winter.

_____ 3. The east [*an area where crowds pass through*] extended from the main lobby of the airport to the check-in counter.

_____ 4. As usual, it was impossible to follow the instructor's [*rambling or digressive*] lecture.

_____ 5. The third [*a sudden invasion*] into the small nation brought a military response of substantial magnitude.

_____ 6. We think the infection was caused by a [*containing poison*] dye in my sock.

_____ 7. Economic recessions are a [*returning again and again*] phenomenon of the capitalistic system.

_____ 8. Population growth and starvation are [*occurring at the same time*] problems in many underdeveloped nations.

_____ 9. If you [*to bring upon yourself*] the displeasure of the boss, you may as well look for another job.

_____ 10. Our [*a tour guide*] was a walking encyclopedia of information about every spot we visited.

FILL-IN AND PART-OF-SPEECH IDENTIFICATION

_____ 1. Leonard's analysis of the situation was _____ at best, nonsensical for the most part.

_____ 2. Once again, the _____ was late delivering the package.

_____ 3. In the long run, the _____ into Afghanistan proved to be a mistake for the Soviet Union.

_____ 4. The elevated _____ almost collapsed under the weight of so many people.

_____ 5. High and low tides are _____; they happen again and again.

_____ 6. Even the most _____ review of this document will tell you that it was hastily prepared.

_____ 7. If you _____ the suspicion of one member of the family, you will be on thin ice with the whole clan.

_____ 8. The chickens were made ill by a _____ chemical in their food.

_____ 9. A high fever, especially in the tropics, is often a _____ of a serious illness.

_____ 10. When inflation and unemployment are _____, the nation experiences tough economic times.

MATCHING

_____ 1. recurrent   a. a service that carries messages

_____ 2. cursory   b. returning again and again

_____ 3. precursor   c. wandering off the topic; rambling

_____ 4. courier   d. to bring upon oneself

_____ 5. incursion   e. hasty or superficial

_____ 6. concurrent   f. a broad thoroughfare

_____ 7. incur   g. a sudden raid or invasion

_____ 8. concourse   h. containing poison

_____ 9. discursive   i. occurring at the same time

_____ 10. toxic   j. a forerunner, harbinger, or predecessor

BONUS ROOT

tox (poison): antitoxin, detoxify, intoxicated, toxemia, toxicant, toxicity, toxicogenic, toxicology, toxicosis, toxin, toxoplasmosis

Words from Roots (6)

The Greek root *path,* and its combining forms *patho* and *pathy,* mean "feeling," "suffering," or "disease." To experience *sympathy* is to feel something for another person. A *pathogen* (PATH-ə-jən) is a microorganism, such as a virus, that causes disease. And a *psychopath* (SIY-kə-*path*) is an unstable person suffering from a mental disorder.

WORD LIST

1. anti*pathy* (an-TIP-ə-thee), *n*: a strong and deep feeling of dislike; hatred

2. a*pathy* (AP-ə-thee), *n*: a total lack of emotion, interest, feeling, or concern; indifference

*3. *belli*cose (BEL-ə-*kows*), *a*: eager to quarrel or fight; hostile or warlike

4. cardiomyo*pathy* (*kahr*-dee-ow-miy-AHP-ə-thee), *n*: *cardio* (heart) + *myo* (muscle) + *pathy* (disease), and thus a disease of the heart muscles, usually chronic and progressive

5. em*pathy* (EM-pə-thee), *n*: the ability to participate completely in another person's feelings and emotions; the feeling itself

6. *path*etic (pə-THET-ik), *a*: arousing feelings of pity and sometimes contempt; pitiful

7. *patho*logical (*path*-ə-LAHJ-i-kəl), *a*: resulting from or caused by disease; compulsive

8. *patho*logist (pə-THAHL-ə-jəst), *n*: a physician who specializes in the diagnosis of disease

9. *path*os (PAY-*thahs*), *n*: the emotional quality, as in a literary work or musical composition, that arouses pity, sorrow, or compassion; the feeling itself

10. tele*pathy* (tə-LEP-ə-thee), *n*: thought communication (over some distance) between two or more people

---

a (*f*at); ay (*f*ate); ah (*f*ar); au (*d*oubt); ch (*church*); e (*e*lf, b*e*d, c*a*re); ee (*e*qual); ə (*a*bout); hw (*wh*ile); i (*f*it); iy (k*i*te); ŋ (li*nk*, si*ng*); o (*au*dio, c*o*rn); ow (*o*cean); oo (b*oo*k); oi (*oi*l); sh (*sh*oe, ambi*ti*on); th (*th*ink); u (*u*p, det*er*); uw (*oo*ze); y (*y*es, on*i*on); yu (b*u*reau, c*u*re); yuw (*you*th, *u*nity); zh (plea*s*ure)

TRUE-FALSE

_____ 1. Although *cardiomyopathy* is a rather grand medical term, it can be easily understood by breaking it down into its three component parts.

_____ 2. *Empathy* is the exercise of isolating oneself from other people.

_____ 3. *Pathos* usually produces wild laughter.

_____ 4. A *bellicose* individual could hardly be described as apathetic.

_____ 5. *Pathological* liars are likely to be motivated by impulses over which they have little control.

_____ 6. More often than not, you love people for whom you feel *antipathy*.

_____ 7. A *pathologist* is an expert in *telepathy*.

_____ 8. *Cardiomyopathy* is a progressive disease of the heart.

_____ 9. A *pathetic* act may produce feelings of contempt in those who witness it.

_____ 10. A state of *apathy* usually arises from a situation of extreme happiness.

DEFINITION REPLACEMENT

_____ 1. Most parents feel [*a sharing in the emotions of others*] for another couple whose child has mysteriously vanished.

_____ 2. Although no one else knew, the identical twins often used [*thought transference*] to communicate.

_____ 3. I admit that my [*a deep feeling of dislike*] for all governments sympathetic to communism sometimes clouds my thinking.

_____ 4. A [*compulsive*] thief, Fred mistakenly stole his own car.

_____ 5. The resident cardiologist maintained that too much cholesterol in the diet can result in [*a disease of the heart muscles*].

_____ 6. Stories filled with [*compassionate pity and sorrow*] often make us cry—at least when we are alone.

_____ 7. The job of a [*a physician who diagnoses diseases*] can sometimes be joyful.

_____ 8. Historians are often amazed by the population's general [*a total lack of interest*] about issues related to our nation's most important traditions.

_____ 9. The villain's [*pitiful and contemptuous*] plea for sympathy displeased most of the audience.

_____ 10. The ambassador's opposition to [*hostile and warlike*] pronouncements seemed appropriate for an opening speech to a peace conference.

FILL-IN AND PART-OF-SPEECH IDENTIFICATION

_____ 1. The heart specialist said that _____ can be caused by many things, such as poor diet, lack of exercise, and cigarette smoking.

_____ 2. Jan considers _____ a sort of psychic ventriloquism.

_____ 3. Personally, I find the annual slaughter of innocent animals during deer season a pitiful and _____ exercise in primitive behavior.

_____ 4. We were surprised by the lack of _____ between the two boxers after the fight. They seemed like old friends.

_____ 5. The last act of the play was so filled with _____ that many people in the audience wept.

_____ 6. _____ actions often provoke _____ responses; that is, hostility begets hostility.

_____ 7. Marvin's compulsive telling of tall tales must be _____. Surely he is sick.

_____ 8. Most people experience some degree of _____ when they see their fellow human beings suffering needlessly.

_____ 9. It is inappropriate to call a _____ a medical fortune-teller.

_____ 10. Judging by the poor attendance at home football games, school spirit seems to have been replaced by a general _____ among both students and faculty. No one seems to care.

MATCHING

_____ 1. pathetic

_____ 2. pathos

_____ 3. antipathy

_____ 4. pathological

_____ 5. cardiomyopathy

_____ 6. telepathy

_____ 7. pathologist

_____ 8. apathy

_____ 9. empathy

_____ 10. bellicose

a. a total lack of feeling or interest

b. caused by disease or compulsion

c. eager to fight or quarrel

d. causing pity and sometimes contempt

e. thought transference

f. a strong and deep hatred

g. the emotional quality of sorrow or compassion

h. the ability to share another's feelings

i. a physician who specializes in the diagnosis of disease

j. a chronic disease of the heart muscles

BONUS ROOT

bel, bell(i) (war): antebellum, bellicosity, belligerence, belligerency, belligerent, postbellum, rebel, rebellion, rebellious, rebelliousness

Words from Roots (7)

The meaning of the Latin root *spec(t)* or *spic* can be seen in the verbs *spectare*, meaning "to behold" or "to look," and *specere,* meaning "to see." This root has many modern English derivatives. A *spectator* is an onlooker. We look through *spectacles* hoping to behold the world more clearly. To *respect* is to look at with regard and esteem. A person under *suspicion* is looked at with distrust. A *specimen* (SPES·ə·mən) is something looked at as an example of its kind.

WORD LIST

1. a*spect* (AS·*pekt*), *n*: the way something looks when seen from a specific view; a particular appearance, as one of several possible; a phase

2. au*spic*ious (o·SPISH·əs), *a*: looking good, as for the future; promising; fortunate; successful

3. con*spic*uous (kən·SPIK·yə·wəs), *a*: easily seen; attracting attention because of unusual or remarkable qualities

*4. con*vene* (kən·VEEN), *v*: to come together, as for a general or common purpose; to cause to come together; to assemble

5. de*spic*able (DES·pik·ə·bəl, di·SPIK·ə·bəl), *a*: looked down on, as with contempt; deserving to be despised; mean

6. intro*spec*tion (*in*·trə·SPEK·shən), *n*: a looking into one's own thoughts and feelings; self-analysis

7. retro*spect* (RE·trə·*spekt*), *n*: a looking back, as to review or examine something that has occurred in the past

8. *spec*ious (SPEE·shəs), *a*: looking reasonable, correct, or logical at first glance, but later proving otherwise; not genuine

9. *spec*ter, *spec*tre (SPEK·tər), *n*: a vision, whether real or imagined; a ghost of terrifying aspect or any object of fear or dread

---

a (f*a*t); ay (f*a*te); ah (f*a*r); au (d*ou*bt); ch (*ch*urch); e (*e*lf, b*e*d, c*a*re); ee (*e*qual); ə (*a*bout); hw (*wh*ile); i (f*i*t); iy (k*i*te); ŋ (li*n*k, si*ng*); o (*au*dio, c*o*rn); ow (*o*cean); oo (b*oo*k); oi (*oi*l); sh (*sh*oe, ambi*ti*on); th (*th*ink); u (*u*p, de*te*r); uw (*oo*ze); y (*y*es, on*i*on); yu (b*u*reau, c*u*re); yuw (*y*o*u*th, *u*nity); zh (plea*s*ure)

10. *speculate* (SPEK-yə-*layt*), *v*: to look at a situation, often in advance, in an effort to figure out what will happen; to ponder or consider

TRUE-FALSE

_____ 1. *Conspicuous* flaws are ones that can be easily seen.

_____ 2. A *specter* is an eyewitness to an important occurrence.

_____ 3. To *convene* a meeting is to cancel it on short notice.

_____ 4. *Specious* evidence is the most valid type of evidence.

_____ 5. An *aspect* is a secret message.

_____ 6. That which is thought about in *retrospect* has already taken place.

_____ 7. A *despicable* individual is a person deserving of praise.

_____ 8. To *speculate* is to try to look at or ponder in advance.

_____ 9. An *auspicious* occasion will likely be a promising one.

_____ 10. When we engage in *introspection,* we usually tell others our most secret thoughts.

DEFINITION REPLACEMENT

_____ 1. The committee voted not to [*to come together*] again.

_____ 2. For such a [*deserving to be despised*] crime, the accused was sentenced to prison.

_____ 3. No one was convinced by such a [*not genuine*] argument.

_____ 4. From time to time, all of us [*to try to figure out*] about the future.

_____ 5. The morning sun revealed the castle in its most beautiful [*a particular appearance*].

_____ 6. Through [*a looking into one's own thoughts*], you can become better acquainted with yourself.

_____ 7. The [*a dreaded vision*] of looming death frightens most people, at least a little.

_____ 8. From such an [*promising for the future*] beginning, everyone expected great things.

_____ 9. Events are often understood more clearly in [*a looking back on something in the past*].

_____ 10. The building was [*attracting attention as a result of unusual qualities*] because of its old-fashioned design.

FILL-IN AND PART-OF-SPEECH IDENTIFICATION

_____ 1. Everyone agreed that a bright green tuxedo would be a pretty _____ _____ outfit at a wedding.

_____ 2. Because hindsight is always twenty-twenty, it often pays to look at things in ___ _____.

_____ 3. Your stealing money from the collection plate was _____. It was a contemptible act.

_____ 4. In my nightmare the _____ of the devil was standing just beyond the foot of my bed.

_____ 5. I had never before looked at this _____, or phase, of the problem.

_____ 6. All but the mentally blind will see right through such _____ logic.

_____ 7. The study group will _____ on the second Monday in January, and three times a week after that.

_____ 8. No stranger to _____, my cousin often practices self-analysis.

_____ 9. I never _____ about other people's futures, and about my own only now and then.

_____ 10. I would hardly call losing our first three games an _____ beginning to the season. To the contrary, things looked very bleak.

MATCHING

_____ 1. introspection   a. promising good things for the future

_____ 2. conspicuous   b. to ponder or consider

_____ 3. retrospect   c. easily seen; unusual

_____ 4. auspicious   d. a ghost of terrifying aspect

_____ 5. specious   e. mean and contemptible

_____ 6. convene   f. a specific view or appearance of something

_____ 7. specter   g. seemingly genuine but not so

_____ 8. aspect   h. self-analysis or self-examination

_____ 9. speculate   i. a looking back or reviewing

_____ 10. despicable   j. to assemble for a common purpose

BONUS ROOT

ven(e), vent (to come): advent, adventitious, adventure, adventurer, adventuresome, adventurous, adventurousness, circumvent, circumvention, convenience, convenient, convent, convention, conventional, event, eventful, eventual, eventuate, inconvenience, inconvenient, intervene, intervention, interventionism, interventionist, invent, invention, inventive, prevent, prevention, preventive, revenue, souvenir, venture, venturesome, venturous, venturousness

Words from Roots (8)

The Latin root *mit(t)*, *miss*, or *mise* comes from the verb *mittere* or *missus*, meaning "to send." To *submit* a proposal is to send it to the appropriate person, who will then take it under consideration. To *dismiss* employees is to send them away. A *mission* is a task that someone is sent to perform, and a *transmittal* involves sending something, such as a *message*, over some distance.

WORD LIST

1. de*mise* (di-MIYZ), *n*: a state of having been sent away or down, and thus death

2. e*miss*ary (EM-ə-*ser*-ee), *n*: a person or group sent on an important, and sometimes secret, mission

3. *emit* (i-MIT), *v*: to send out; to discharge; to utter

4. inter*mitt*ent (*in*-tər-MIT-ənt), *a*: sent between intervals, and thus stopping and starting; periodic; recurrent

5. *missive* (MIS-iv), *n*: a written message that is sent somewhere; a letter—often used poetically

6. pre*mise*, pre*miss* (PRIM-is), *n*: a basic statement sent before, as one that is later developed or proven; a beginning position; *v*, to make such a statement

*7. rein*carn*ation (*ree*-in-kahr-NAY-shən), *n*: a thing that is once again in the flesh or reborn; a coming back into being, although perhaps in a different (bodily) form

8. re*miss* (ri-MIS), *a*: careless, negligent, or lax in the performance of some duty, task, or responsibility

9. re*mission* (ri-MISH-ən), *n*: a sending back, in the sense of a pardon or forgiveness, as for crimes or sins; a lessening or disappearance of symptoms

10. re*mitt*ance (ri-MIT-əns), *n*: money sent back, as through the mail; the sending of such money

---

a (f*a*t); ay (f*a*te); ah (f*a*r); au (d*ou*bt); ch (*ch*urch); e (*e*lf, b*e*d, c*a*re); ee (*e*qual); ə (*a*bout); hw (*wh*ile); i (f*i*t); iy (k*i*te); ŋ (li*n*k, si*ng*); o (*au*dio, c*o*rn); ow (*o*cean); oo (b*oo*k); oi (*oi*l); sh (*sh*oe, ambi*ti*on); th (*th*ink); u (*u*p, de*te*r); uw (*oo*ze); y (*y*es, on*i*on); yu (b*u*reau, c*u*re); yuw (*you*th, *u*nity); zh (plea*s*ure)

TRUE-FALSE

_____ 1. Progress that is *intermittent* is likely to be uneven.

_____ 2. A wilted flower is called a *reincarnation*.

_____ 3. A *missive* is intended to be read.

_____ 4. To send a *remittance* is to send money.

_____ 5. A *demise* is a new beginning.

_____ 6. When a disease is in *remission*, its symptoms have worsened.

_____ 7. A government *emissary* can expect to do a good bit of traveling.

_____ 8. A *premise* is a logical conclusion to an argument.

_____ 9. To be *remiss* is to be careless or negligent.

_____ 10. To *emit* a noise is to muffle it.

DEFINITION REPLACEMENT

_____ 1. These big boats [*to send out*] too much noise for a small lake surrounded by private homes.

_____ 2. If your [*a beginning position*] is false, your conclusion will also be open to question.

_____ 3. I am asking the court for a [*a pardon or forgiveness*] of my debts, considerable though they may be.

_____ 4. When an idea has reached its [*death*], people no longer believe it.

_____ 5. Susan claims that she is the [*something reborn in the flesh*] of Cleopatra and that she is in her seventh life.

_____ 6. The company claimed that my [*money sent through the mail*] had not arrived in time for the advertised special.

_____ 7. Even though the showers were only [*stopping and starting*], the picnic was called off.

_____ 8. Because I have been [*negligent and lax*] in my studies, I am not looking forward to exam week.

_____ 9. My girlfriend sent me a sweet [*a written letter*] telling me that she loved me.

_____ 10. Christianity teaches that Jesus was God's [*someone sent on an important mission*] to humankind.

FILL-IN AND PART-OF-SPEECH IDENTIFICATION

_____ 1. Your _____, that most students are incapable of doing college-level work, gets your argument into trouble right at the start.

_____ 2. Our cause has reached an early _____; no one supports us anymore. We're dead in the water.

_____ 3. My premise is that there should never be _____ of guilt for the taking of innocent life.

_____ 4. The president has again sent an _____ to the Soviet Union to try to set up talks on nuclear disarmament.

_____ 5. Even though my income tax _____ was lost in the mail, the IRS says that I owe a penalty for late payment.

_____ 6. These new units _____ a strange and piercing sound that can be heard outside the building.

_____ 7. The article claimed that many married couples are _____ in performing their roles as parents. They are not responsible parents.

_____ 8. If your support of our position is _____, we never know whether you are going to be for us or against us.

_____ 9. If I believed in such things, I would say that my history instructor is the

_____ of Genghis Khan. He is the tyrant reborn in the flesh.

_____ 10. I received a welcome _____ from the IRS telling me that the government owed me money.

MATCHING

_____ 1. emit

_____ 2. remiss

_____ 3. demise

_____ 4. remittance

_____ 5. reincarnation

_____ 6. intermittent

_____ 7. emissary

_____ 8. remission

_____ 9. missive

_____ 10. premise

a. someone sent on an important mission

b. a written (and mailed) message

c. something reborn in the flesh

d. the state of death

e. a pardon or forgiveness

f. careless or negligent

g. to send out or discharge

h. money sent through the mail

i. a beginning statement or position

j. stopping and starting at intervals

BONUS ROOT

carn (flesh, meat): carnage, carnal, carnality, carnation, carnify, carnival, carnivore, carnivorous, chili con carne, incarnate

Words from Roots (9)

The root *ped* is a curious one; sometimes it means "foot," and sometimes it means "child." Why? Because it is actually two roots. English has made use of both the Latin word *pedis*, meaning "foot," and the Greek word *paidos*, meaning "child." *Pedals* are operated with the feet, and a *quadruped* (KWAHD-rə-*ped*) is an animal with four feet. However, a *pediatrician* (pee-dee-ə-TRISH-ən) is a physician who specializes in the treatment of children, not feet.

WORD LIST

1. ex*ped*ient (ik-SPEE-dee-ənt), *a*: literally, with one's foot unentangled; appropriate or useful to a purpose; opportune or convenient; *n*, a means to an end; a device constructed for an emergency; a makeshift

2. ex*ped*ite (EK-spə-*diyt*), *v*: to get one's foot unentangled, and thus to speed up the process of; to hasten or quicken

3. im*ped*iment (im-PED-ə-mənt), *n*: something that entangles the foot, and thus any obstruction or hindrance

4. ortho*ped*ics (or-thə-PEE-diks); *n*: literally, the straightening of a child; the branch of surgery that corrects bone, joint, and muscle deformities

5. *ped*agogue (PED-ə-*gahg*), *n*: one who leads a child, and thus a teacher; a dogmatic teacher

6. *ped*antic (pi-DAN-tik), *a*: like a teacher who is often too concerned with the details of learning

7. *ped*estrian (pə-DES-tree-ən), *n*: someone on foot, and thus an ordinary or common person; *a*, without cleverness, interest, or imagination

*8. *pyr*omaniac (*piy*-rə-MAY-nee-*ak*), *n*: one who has an irresistible impulse to start fires

*9. *pyr*otechnics (*piy*-rə-TEK-niks), *n*: the art of making or displaying fireworks; any brilliant display, particularly a performance

---

a (fat); ay (fate); ah (far); au (doubt); ch (church); e (elf, bed, care); ee (equal); ə (about); hw (while); i (fit); iy (kite); ŋ (link, sing); o (audio, corn); ow (ocean); oo (book); oi (oil); sh (shoe, ambition); th (think); u (up, deter); uw (ooze); y (yes, onion); yu (bureau, cure); yuw (youth, unity); zh (pleasure)

10. sesqui*pedal*ian (*ses*-kwə-pə-DAY-lee-ən), *a*: literally, a foot-and-a-half long, and thus very long; *n*, a long word (an intentionally humorous usage)

TRUE-FALSE

_____ 1. To *expedite* a process is to make it go more slowly.

_____ 2. *Pedagogues* are sometimes *pedantic*.

_____ 3. An *orthopedic* surgeon treats only elderly people.

_____ 4. Americans normally enjoy elaborate displays of *pyrotechnics* on Halloween and Thanksgiving.

_____ 5. The word *cardiomyopathy* could appropriately be called a *sesquipedalian*.

_____ 6. *Pyromaniacs* are compulsive users of air conditioning.

_____ 7. An *expedient* solution is not the same thing as a permanent solution.

_____ 8. If a *pedagogue* loves anything, it is teaching.

_____ 9. An individual with *pedestrian* tastes is a person who will be satisfied with only the best of everything.

_____ 10. A speech *impediment* sometimes hinders pronunciation.

DEFINITION REPLACEMENT

_____ 1. My English instructor, although likable enough, is a hard-nosed [*a dogmatic teacher*].

_____ 2. Never make the mistake of lending your lighter to a [*a person with a compulsion to start fires*].

_____ 3. It was more [*opportune or convenient*] to fire the unskilled workers than to train them.

_____ 4. The word *sesquipedalian* is itself an example of a [*a very long word*].

_____ 5. Such a [*too concerned with the details of learning*] approach to the study of poetry turned many students off.

_____ 6. Is there any way we can [*to speed up the process of*] the distribution of mail throughout the company?

_____ 7. [*A brilliant display of fireworks*] and the Fourth of July go together like fried chicken and potato salad.

_____ 8. Poor reading skills are always an [*something that obstructs*] to learning.

_____ 9. That which is [*ordinary or common*] may be thought of as the opposite of that which is high and refined.

_____ 10. A specialist in [*the branch of surgery that corrects bone deformities*], Dr. Rothchild knows all there is to know about compound fractures.

FILL-IN AND PART-OF-SPEECH IDENTIFICATION

_____ 1. _____ has to do with the repair of broken bones, not the correction of misspelled words.

_____ 2. If enjoying a cheeseburger is _____, then I will admit to an ordinary taste in food.

_____ 3. Jan maintains that Congress will never _____ the process whereby a bill becomes the law of the land. She says it will always be slow and methodical.

_____ 4. If you tuned in late, you missed the _____ of the first inning; both teams scored nine runs.

_____ 5. Many "how-to" books are written by self-proclaimed _____ who would teach us to do ordinary things that most people can do well enough on their own.

_____ 6. A _____ normally indulges in arson for kicks, not for profit.

_____ 7. The speaker began with an epigram: "If nothing succeeds like success, then nothing is as _____ as expediency."

45

_____ 8. The debate could only be described as _____; it went on much longer than it should have.

_____ 9. The _____ instructor, always making a point of teaching, often takes the joy out of learning.

_____ 10. The constant bickering between labor and management was the biggest _____ to progress in the negotiations.

MATCHING

_____ 1. sesquipedalian   a. excessively concerned with the details of learning

_____ 2. expedite   b. a hindrance

_____ 3. pyromaniac   c. a very long word

_____ 4. pyrotechnics   d. a makeshift or convenience

_____ 5. orthopedics   e. a firebug

_____ 6. pedantic   f. to quicken the progress of

_____ 7. pedagogue   g. any brilliant display

_____ 8. expedient   h. a dogmatic teacher

_____ 9. pedestrian   i. one who is on foot, and thus common

_____ 10. impediment   j. the branch of surgery that deals with bone deformities

BONUS ROOT

pyr(o) (fire): pyracantha, pyre, Pyrex, pyrexia, pyrochemical, pyrocondensation, pyrogenic, pyromancy, pyromania, pyrophobia, pyrosis, pyrotechnic

Words from Roots (10)

Another root with two meanings is *sol,* which may mean either "sun" or "alone." *Solar* energy comes from the sun. A *solo* is a song sung by one person, not by the sun. A *solipsist* (SAHL-əp-sist) is a person who thinks that in the final analysis the individual can really know and experience only the self. This philosophical position is called *solipsism* (SAHL-əp-siz-əm). And anything related to or characteristic of the notion is said to be *solipsistic* (sahl-əp-SIS-tik).

WORD LIST

1. de*sol*ate (DES-ə-lit), *a:* without inhabitants or visitors; deserted or abandoned; (DES-ə-*layt*), *v:* to lay waste or deprive of inhabitants; to forsake or abandon

*2. pro*voke* (prə-VOWK), *v:* to call forth, as anger, irritation, or excitement; to annoy or stir up

3. *sol*arium (sə-LER-ee-əm), *n:* a room, often glass-enclosed, that offers maximum exposure to the sun, as where people rest when being treated for an illness

4. *sol*arize (SOW-lə-*riyz*), *v:* to expose, or overexpose, to sunlight; to convert the heating and cooling system of a house or building to sun power

5. *sol*iloquy (sə-LIL-ə-kwee), *n:* the act of speaking to oneself; lines in a play spoken inwardly by a character rather than to other characters

6. *sol*itaire (SAHL-ə-*ter*), *n:* originally, a hermit or recluse; a single gem, as a diamond, set by itself; a card game played by one person

7. *sol*itary (SAHL-ə-*ter*-ee), *a:* without companions; alone; lonely; single

8. *sol*itude (SAHL-ə-*tuwd*), *n:* the state of being alone, but not necessarily lonely; an isolated place

9. *sol*stice (SAHL-stis), *n:* the time of year when the sun is either farthest north or south of the equator, resulting in the longest or shortest day of the year; literally

---

a (fat); ay (fate); ah (far); au (doubt); ch (church); e (elf, bed, care); ee (equal); ə (about); hw (while); i (fit); iy (kite); ŋ (link, sing); o (audio, corn); ow (ocean); oo (book); oi (oil); sh (shoe, ambition); th (think); u (up, deter); uw (ooze); y (yes, onion); yu (bureau, cure); yuw (youth, unity); zh (pleasure)

means "sun stands still," as the sun seems to occupy almost the same spot in the noon sky for several days before and after each solstice

*10. *voci*ferous (vow-SIF-ər-əs), *a*: literally, carrying a loud voice, and thus noisy, vehement, or clamorous

TRUE-FALSE

_____ 1. In a *solarium,* one might get a good tan.

_____ 2. A *vociferous* reply will likely be quite noisy.

_____ 3. If you cheat at *solitaire,* you fool only yourself.

_____ 4. To *solarize* something is to expose it to the sun.

_____ 5. The winter *solstice* occurs on Saint Patrick's Day.

_____ 6. *Solitude* is a *vociferous* response to provocation.

_____ 7. To *provoke* anger is to quiet it.

_____ 8. A *soliloquy* is an argument among several people.

_____ 9. A hermit lives a *solitary* life.

_____ 10. To *desolate* a landscape is to make it more fruitful.

DEFINITION REPLACEMENT

_____ 1. The village was [*without inhabitants or deserted*] following the earthquake.

_____ 2. For his part in the show, Fred performed a famous [*lines spoken by a solitary character as if to himself*] from one of Shakespeare's plays.

_____ 3. The longest day of the year occurs at the summer [*the time when the sun is farthest north of the equator*].

_____ 4. My uncle lived a [*without companions*] life on a desert island.

_____ 5. The team players were given a [*noisy, vehement, and clamorous*] cheer as they boarded the bus.

_____ 6. Discretion would suggest that you not [*to call forth anger*] a hungry lion.

_____ 7. If we [*to convert to heating and cooling by sun power*] the house, we can reduce our utility bills.

_____ 8. Occasionally, everyone needs a little [*the state of being alone*].

_____ 9. I passed the afternoon playing [*a card game played by one person*].

_____ 10. Fran uses the family [*a glass-enclosed room exposed to the sun*] as a greenhouse.

FILL-IN AND PART-OF-SPEECH IDENTIFICATION

_____ 1. If you _____ the film for any length of time, it will be ruined.

_____ 2. A book as carefully written as this will _____ much thought and discussion.

_____ 3. At the very top of the tree perched a single bird singing a _____ tune to the morning.

_____ 4. Christmas follows the winter _____ by only a few days.

_____ 5. A clamor of _____ support for the candidate arose spontaneously throughout the hall.

_____ 6. Crazy Harry stood in the woods and delivered a poetic _____ to the birds in the trees.

_____ 7. _____ can sometimes be hard to come by in the hustle and bustle of a big city.

_____ 8. We now know that the moon is a _____ and solitary place; nothing lives or grows there.

_____ 9. Believe it or not, there is a card game called double _____ that can be played by two people.

_____ 10. Because the glass captures the sun's heat, the _____ is a very warm place even in winter.

MATCHING

_____ 1. provoke   a. noisy and clamorous

_____ 2. solitaire   b. a speech made to oneself

_____ 3. vociferous   c. an isolated place or setting

_____ 4. solarize   d. a glass-enclosed sun room

_____ 5. solitude   e. to call forth excitement

_____ 6. desolate   f. a single gem set by itself, as in a ring

_____ 7. solstice   g. without companions; lonely

_____ 8. solarium   h. to expose to sunlight

_____ 9. solitary   i. the longest or shortest day of the year

_____ 10. soliloquy   j. to lay waste

BONUS ROOT

voc, voke (voice, to call): advocacy, advocate, avocation, convocation, equivocal, equivocate, evocative, evoke, invocation, invoke, irrevocable, provocation, provocative, revocable, revocation, revoke, vocabulary, vocal, vocalist, vocalize, vocation

Words from Roots (11)

The Greek root *arch* is another with two meanings—perhaps two groups of meanings. One has to do with power, and means "chief," "leader," or "ruler," as in *monarch*, the sole ruler, or *architect*, the chief builder. The other has to do with time, and means "first," "old," or "ancient," as in *archaic* (ahr-KAY-ik), meaning "ancient" or "old-fashioned." Actually, both meanings include the notion of "first"—first in power or first in time. The combining form *archy* occurs in words employing the "power" meaning.

WORD LIST

1. an*arch*ist (AN-ər-kist), *n*: a person who wants no leader or believes that all forms of government are bad because they interfere with individual liberty; one who engages in activities to destroy all forms of government

2. *arch*aeology, *arch*eology (*ahr*-kee-AHL-ə-jee), *n*: the scientific study of ancient peoples and their cultures, including excavations to retrieve tools, implements, and other artifacts

3. *arch*aism (AHR-kee-*iz*-əm, ahr-KAY-*iz*-əm), *n*: an archaic word, phrase, or expression, as "gaol" for "jail"; any behavior or practice long out-of-date, as the costumes worn by the Amish in Pennsylvania

4. *arch*enemy (AHRCH-EN-ə-mee), *n*: the chief or principal enemy; traditionally, the devil or Satan; the most substantial foe

5. *arch*etype (AHR-kə-*tiyp*), *n*: an original (first) or ancient model or pattern from which later copies are made or occur; a perfect example of a type or group

6. *arch*ives (AHR-*kiyvz*), *n*: records, often public, of an organization that go back to its beginning; the building that houses such records

7. hier*archy* (HIY-ə-*rahr*-kee), *n*: the layered system of rule in an organization; graded ranks of authority or the people who occupy them; pecking order

---

a (*f*at); ay (*f*ate); ah (*f*ar); au (*d*oubt); ch (*ch*urch); e (*e*lf, b*e*d, c*a*re); ee (*e*qual); ə (*a*bout); hw (*wh*ile); i (f*i*t); iy (k*i*te); ŋ (li*n*k, si*n*g); o (*a*udio, c*o*rn); ow (*o*cean); oo (b*oo*k); oi (*oi*l); sh (*sh*oe, ambi*ti*on); th (*th*ink); u (*u*p, de*te*r); uw (*oo*ze); y (*y*es, on*i*on); yu (b*u*reau, c*u*re); yuw (*y*outh, *u*nity); zh (plea*s*ure)

8. olig*arch*y (AHL-ə-*gahr*-kee), *n*: a form of government in which the power to rule is confined to a few people; the group that exercises such authority

9. patri*arch* (PAY-tree-*ahrk*), *n*: the father who is ruler of a family or tribe; the founder of something, as a business, colony, or religion

*10. sine*cure* (SIY-nə-*kyoor*, SIN-ə-*kyoor*), *n*: literally, a position without care, and thus a comfortable job requiring little work or responsibility

TRUE-FALSE

_____ 1. Christianity teaches that Satan is the *archenemy*.

_____ 2. George Washington is one of the *patriarchs* of the United States.

_____ 3. An *anarchist* is a person who thinks the government is always right.

_____ 4. A *hierarchy* can exist even in a chicken coop.

_____ 5. Historians often catch a rash called *archives*.

_____ 6. A *sinecure* is a position of great responsibility.

_____ 7. *Archaeology* is the study of modern architecture.

_____ 8. An *archetype* is an original or ancient model.

_____ 9. In an *oligarchy,* all people have equal power and authority.

_____ 10. A garment in the latest design is called an *archaism.*

DEFINITION REPLACEMENT

_____ 1. The [*a layered system of authority*] of this corporation has become far too complicated.

_____ 2. Traditionally, Christianity regards God as the [*the father or founder*] of the universe.

_____ 3. [*The scientific study of ancient peoples*] teaches us much about our ancient ancestors.

_____ 4. It is sometimes difficult to distinguish between the terrorist and the philosophical [*a person who opposes all forms of government*].

_____ 5. In recent times, cancer seems to have become the [*the chief or principal enemy*] of good health.

_____ 6. After thirty years, my uncle was given a [*a position requiring little work*] on the board of directors.

_____ 7. Alas, politeness is today regarded as an [*any behavior long out-of-date*] by many vulgar people.

_____ 8. In the village [*public records of the past*], we found the record of the marriage of our great-grandparents.

_____ 9. Even in a country as democratic as the United States, something of an [*a form of government in which power is held by a few people*] still exists.

_____ 10. For many people, Adolf Hitler remains the twentieth century's [*a perfect model or example*] of a political villain.

FILL-IN AND PART-OF-SPEECH IDENTIFICATION

____ 1. There is probably no _____, no ancient model, of a person who wants to do nothing in life but work.

____ 2. Some people view the vice presidency as a _____, a largely ceremonial position with little real responsibility.

____ 3. My roommate wants to major in _____. She thinks anything under two thousand years old is a fad.

____ 4. The president of this company regards himself as an institutional _____

_____. He thinks of himself as everyone's godfather.

____ 5. I think my history instructor is a closet _____; he seems to hate any type of authority.

53

_____ 6. Procrastination is my _____. Almost every day that devil forces me to put off doing what I should be doing.

_____ 7. This corporation is really an _____. It is ruled by the president and a small group of vice presidents.

_____ 8. Can you imagine what sorts of drawings probably exist in the _____ _____ of *Mad* magazine?

_____ 9. I would say that your wearing knickers to class is something of an _____.

_____ 10. Even among small children playing together in the schoolyard, there is often a _____ of dominance, a pecking order.

MATCHING

_____ 1. sinecure   a. a person who dislikes all forms of government

_____ 2. hierarchy   b. a small ruling group

_____ 3. archetype   c. records that go back to the distant past

_____ 4. archaism   d. the study of ancient peoples and cultures

_____ 5. oligarchy   e. a well-paying position requiring little work or responsibility

_____ 6. anarchist

_____ 7. archives   f. a perfect example of something

_____ 8. archenemy   g. a dreadful foe or devil

_____ 9. archaeology   h. a founder or father

_____ 10. patriarch   i. graded ranks of authority

    j. anything long out-of-date

BONUS ROOT

cur(e) (care): accuracy, accurate, curable, curative, curator, cure, curiosity, curious, inaccuracy, inaccurate, incurable, insecure, insecurity, manicure, pedicure, procure, secure, security

Words from Roots (12)

The root *min*, because it comes from several Latin words, also has more than one meaning. First, it can mean "less," "little," or "small." The *minimum* amount is the smallest amount, a *minority* is less than a majority, and a *miniature* poodle is smaller than a regular poodle. But *min* can also mean "to project" or "to threaten." Thus, that which is *prominent* projects outward, and a *menacing* expression is a threatening one.

WORD LIST

1. di*min*ish (də-MIN-ish), *v*: to make or become smaller or less

2. di*min*ution (*dim-ə-*NYUW-shən), *n*: the act, process, or instance of diminishing or being diminished

3. e*min*ent (EM-ə-nənt), *a*: rising or towering above others; prominent or projecting; outstanding, noteworthy, or remarkable

4. im*min*ent (IM-ə-nənt), *a*: likely to happen at any moment; impending, or threatening to occur

5. *min*acious (mi-NAY-shəs), *a*: possessing or displaying menacing or threatening qualities; *min*atory (MIN-ə-*tor*-ee)

6. *min*uscule (MIN-ə-*skyuwl*), *a*: very small, either in size or amount; tiny; minute

7. *min*utia (mə-NUW-shee-ə), plural, *min*utiae (mə-NUW-shi-ee), *n*: a single small, unimportant, or trivial detail; in the plural form, unimportant details collectively

*8. *ortho*dox (OR-thə-*dahks*), *a*: upright, in the sense of conforming to established or proper beliefs, teachings, or customs; conventional

*9. *ortho*graphy (or-THAHG-rə-fee), *n*: the practice of spelling according to standard or accepted rules

10. pro*min*ontory (PRAHM-ən-*tor*-ee), *n*: a peak or high ridge of land that juts out into a sea or other body of water

---

a (f*a*t); ay (f*a*te); ah (f*a*r); au (d*ou*bt); ch (*ch*urch); e (*e*lf, b*e*d, c*a*re); ee (*e*qual); ə (*a*bout); hw (*wh*ile); i (f*i*t); iy (k*i*te); ŋ (li*n*k, si*ng*); o (*au*dio, c*o*rn); ow (*o*cean); oo (b*oo*k); oi (*oi*l); sh (*sh*oe, ambi*ti*on); th (*th*ink); u (*u*p, de*te*r); uw (*oo*ze); y (*y*es, oni*o*n); yu (b*u*reau, c*u*re); yuw (*you*th, *u*nity); zh (plea*s*ure)

TRUE-FALSE

_____ 1. *Orthography* is the study of correct pronunciation.

_____ 2. *Minacious* and *minatory* have the same meaning.

_____ 3. An *imminent* event is a very important one.

_____ 4. New and unconventional teachings are usually considered *orthodox*.

_____ 5. *Minutiae* are trivial in nature.

_____ 6. A *minuscule* quantity is an infinite quantity.

_____ 7. To *diminish* is to make more menacing.

_____ 8. A *promontory* can be seen from some distance.

_____ 9. An *eminent* person is one who is about to happen.

_____ 10. The *diminution* of one's reputation leaves it reduced.

DEFINITION REPLACEMENT

_____ 1. Elizabeth is an [*conventional*] Democrat.

_____ 2. An [*outstanding or noteworthy*] academician spoke at the commence-
ment.

_____ 3. We decided to build the house on a [*a high ridge*] overlooking the
sea.

_____ 4. English [*standard spelling rules*] is not always consistent with conventional pronunciation.

_____ 5. My progress in the science class was [*tiny or minute*] at best.

_____ 6. The spring sun will [*to make less*] the amount of snow on the
ground.

_____ 7. It is the [*trivial details*] of daily life that take up so much of my time.

_____ 8. The villain's performance was so [*minatory*] that the children in the audience were frightened.

_____ 9. When the drums stopped, everyone knew that the announcement was [*likely to happen at any moment*].

_____ 10. A few inches of additional insulation will result in a [*the process of diminishing*] of outside noise.

FILL-IN AND PART-OF-SPEECH IDENTIFICATION

_____ 1. Will someone please tell us how we can substantially _____ the amount of violence in the world?

_____ 2. The American Medical Association does not view acupuncture as an _____ _____ method of treatment.

_____ 3. The island's south _____ was a chalk cliff and could be seen for miles on a moonlit night.

_____ 4. Whether you call them minatory or _____, the gestures were still quite threatening.

_____ 5. Cleaning the house, preparing meals, cutting the grass, and ironing clothes may be considered everyday _____ by some people, but I enjoy them; they give me a sense of accomplishment.

_____ 6. The _____ of my cousin's mental ability was caused by drug abuse. He is now almost like a child.

_____ 7. Where I live, frequent lightning in the northwest always means that a storm is

_____.

_____ 8. Compared to that of my professors, my knowledge seems to be _____ _____, very tiny indeed.

_____ 9. My music instructor considers himself an _____ authority, but few people have heard of him outside the conservatory.

_____ 10. English _____ is based primarily on word meaning rather than on pronunciation.

MATCHING

_____ 1. orthodox

_____ 2. minutia

_____ 3. diminish

_____ 4. promontory

_____ 5. minacious

_____ 6. minuscule

_____ 7. diminution

_____ 8. imminent

_____ 9. eminent

_____ 10. orthography

a. the act, process, or instance of being diminished

b. very small, tiny, or minute

c. outstanding, noteworthy, or remarkable

d. conventional

e. a high peak or ridge

f. a trivial detail

g. the practice of spelling words according to standard rules

h. threatening to occur

i. to make or become smaller or less

j. minatory

BONUS ROOT

orth(o) (straight, upright): orthodontics, orthodontist, orthodoxy, orthogenesis, orthographer, orthographic, orthopedic, orthopedics, orthoscopic, unorthodox

Words from Roots (13)

Just as one root can have two meanings, two roots can have the same or similar meanings. For example, both the Greek root *geo* and the Latin root *terr* mean "earth." *Geology* is the study of the physical characteristics of the earth and its history. A *geodesic* (*jee-ə-DES-ik*) dome is a structure with a roof curvature like that of the earth. A *territory* is a specific area of the earth. A *terrace* is a flat mound of earth with sloping sides. And a *terrier* is a small dog originally so named because it was bred to burrow into the ground after small game.

WORD LIST

1. apo*gee* (AP-ə-*jee*), *n*: the point at which something orbiting the earth is farthest from the earth; the farthest or highest point

2. disin*ter* (*dis*-in-TUR), *v*: to remove from the earth, specifically from a grave or tomb; to revive or bring to light again

3. *geo*centric (*jee*-ow-SEN-trik), *a*: earth-centered; related to the notion that the earth is the center of the universe

4. *geo*politics (*jee*-ow-PAHL-ə-tiks), *n*: the study of geography and politics in combination, particularly how various factors of geography influence governmental policies; the interrelationship of geography and politics; *geo*political (*jee*-ow-pə-LIT-i-kəl), *a*: having to do with geopolitics

5. peri*gee* (PER-ə-*jee*), *n*: the point at which something orbiting the earth is nearest to the earth; the lowest or nearest point

*6. pre*sent*iment (pri-ZEN-tə-mənt), *n*: an advance feeling that something is going to happen; a premonition or foreboding

*7. *sens*ory (SEN-sər-ee), *a*: related to feeling or experiencing things through the senses

8. sub*terr*anean (*sub*-tə-RAY-nee-ən), *a*: beneath the surface of the earth; hidden or secret; *n*, a creature living underground

---

a (fat); ay (fate); ah (far); au (doubt); ch (church); e (elf, bed, care); ee (equal); ə (about); hw (while); i (fit); iy (kite); ŋ (link, sing); o (audio, corn); ow (ocean); oo (book); oi (oil); sh (shoe, ambition); th (think); u (up, deter); uw (ooze); y (yes, onion); yu (bureau, cure); yuw (youth, unity); zh (pleasure)

9. *terr*arium (tə-RER-ee-əm), *n*: an enclosure of glass or plastic containing a garden of small plants and sometimes animals

10. *terr*estrial (tə-RES-tree-əl), *a*: of the earth, as opposed to the heavens; worldly or common; land-dwelling rather than aquatic or water-dwelling; *n,* an inhabitant of the earth

TRUE-FALSE

_____ 1. It is possible to experience a *presentiment* in a dream.

_____ 2. Astronomers today tell us that the solar system is *geocentric.*

_____ 3. Sparkling water from a spring deep in the earth is called *perigee.*

_____ 4. Cats are *subterranean* creatures.

_____ 5. A *terrarium* generally contains a variety of small plants.

_____ 6. An orbiting satellite is closer to the earth at its *apogee* than at its *perigee.*

_____ 7. We humans are *terrestrial* beings.

_____ 8. The eyes and ears are *sensory* organs.

_____ 9. Wars can be caused by *geopolitical* disagreements between nations.

_____ 10. To *disinter* is to vote down by a large margin.

DEFINITION REPLACEMENT

_____ 1. The experiment was intended to get a [*related to the senses*] response.

_____ 2. Experts say that acid rain is doing great [*of the earth*] damage to the planet.

_____ 3. At its [*the highest point in orbit*], the satellite could not be seen from the ground.

_____ 4. Pam had a momentary [*a feeling that something is going to happen*] that she would win the lottery.

_____ 5. Rand is growing a small rubber tree in his [*a glass enclosure containing a garden*].

_____ 6. The police decided to [*to remove from the ground*] the body of the victim and perform an autopsy.

_____ 7. The [*beneath the surface of the earth*] passageway led us safely out of the dungeon.

_____ 8. The peace treaty included several [*combining geography and politics*] considerations.

_____ 9. At its orbital [*the nearest point*], we signaled the spaceship to return to earth.

_____ 10. The drawings we found proved that our ancestors believed in a [*earth-centered*] universe.

FILL-IN AND PART-OF-SPEECH IDENTIFICATION

_____ 1. You have to understand the _____ of the region to make any sense of the conflict.

_____ 2. We keep our nuclear missiles stored in _____ silos, ready to respond on command.

_____ 3. Addison's _____ that the university would award him a scholarship came true.

_____ 4. In a way, a _____ is a miniature earth under glass.

_____ 5. In a _____ cosmos, human beings seem less insignificant than they do otherwise.

_____ 6. The candidate's campaign reached its _____ just before she was discovered to have mob connections. From there, everything went downhill.

_____ 7. A roasting turkey can make a strong _____ impression on a hungry stomach.

_____ 8. My guru says that the first _____ did not evolve; they immigrated from somewhere else in the universe.

_____ 9. Richard Nixon's _____ as a political leader occurred when he was forced to resign the presidency.

_____ 10. We must _____ the leaking drums; they contain toxic materials and will contaminate the groundwater.

MATCHING

_____ 1. geocentric   a. to remove from the ground

_____ 2. presentiment   b. a "little earth" under glass

_____ 3. apogee   c. related to the senses

_____ 4. terrarium   d. a premonition or foreboding

_____ 5. subterranean   e. of the earth

_____ 6. sensory   f. the highest point, as in orbit

_____ 7. terrestrial   g. the lowest point, as in orbit

_____ 8. geopolitics   h. earth-centered

_____ 9. perigee   i. beneath the surface of the earth

_____ 10. disinter   j. the combination of geography and politics

BONUS ROOT

sens, sent (to feel): consensus, consent, consentience, consentient, dissension, dissent, dissenter, dissentient, dissentious, insensible, insensitive, insensitivity, insentience, insentient, resent, resentful, resentment, scent, sensation, sensational, sensitive, sensitize, sensual, sensuous, sentience, sentient, sentiment, sentimental

Words from Roots (14)

The combining form *neo* comes from the Greek word *neos,* meaning "new." Similarly, the Latin root *nov* comes from the word *novus,* also meaning "new." *Neo* appears at the beginnings of words. *Neon,* for example, literally meaning "a new gas," is an inert and colorless gas used in electric lights. The *neolithic* (*nee-ə-*LITH·ik) period in human history is the New Stone Age, when polished stone implements were first developed, and *neocolonialism* (*nee-*ow-kə-LOW-*nee-ə*l-*iz-*əm) refers to a revival of colonial principles of government. A *nova,* although meaning literally "a new star," is actually a star that suddenly puts out a new burst of brilliance; a *novel* idea is a new and perhaps strange idea.

WORD LIST

1. in*nov*ation (*in-ə-*VAY·shən), *n:* (the act or process of introducing) something new and different; an improvement

2. *neo*logism (nee-AHL-ə-*jiz-*əm), *n:* a new word or an old word used in a new way, as *disinformation,* meaning "a lie"

3. *neo*natal (*nee-*ow-NAYT·əl), *a:* related to or affecting an infant, especially during the early months of life

4. *neo*phyte (NEE-ə-*fiyt*), *n:* a new convert, as to a religion, and thus a beginner or novice

5. *neo*teric (*nee-ə-*TER·ik), *a:* of recent origin, and thus new or modern; *n,* a modern person, or one willing to accept new ideas and practices, and perhaps without sufficient reflection

6. *nov*antique (NOWV-an-*teek*), *a:* new and old at the same time; *n,* an idea or object that is simultaneously modern and yet old or from the past

7. *nov*elty (NAHV-əl·tee), *n:* the quality of newness or freshness; anything that is new and fresh; a clever little article, often cheaply made

---

a (*fat*); ay (*fate*); ah (*far*); au (*doubt*); ch (*church*); e (*elf, bed, care*); ee (*equal*); ə (*about*); hw (*while*); i (*fit*); iy (*kite*); ŋ (*link, sing*); o (*audio, corn*); ow (*ocean*); oo (*book*); oi (*oil*); sh (*shoe, ambition*); th (*think*); u (*up, deter*); uw (*ooze*); y (*yes, onion*); yu (*bureau, cure*); yuw (*youth, unity*); zh (*pleasure*)

8. *novice* (NAHV·is), *n*: a person new at any task or activity; a beginner or neophyte

*9. *placate* (PLAY·*kayt*), *v*: literally, to please; to calm another's anger; to appease or pacify

10. *renovate* (REN·ə·*vayt*), *v*: to make (appear) new and fresh again; to renew or restore

TRUE-FALSE

_____ 1. The same person may be both a *neophyte* and a *novice*.

_____ 2. In extreme cases, a *neoteric* may be accused of neolatry, the virtual worship of all things new and trendy.

_____ 3. The primary purpose of a *novelty* is to bore.

_____ 4. *Innovations* are usually intended to be improvements.

_____ 5. To *renovate* a building is to take it down and rebuild it from the ground up.

_____ 6. Experience is what the *novice* and *neophyte* lack.

_____ 7. Old-fashioned ceiling fans used to circulate air through an air-conditioned building might be considered *novantique*.

_____ 8. A *neologism* is a new spelling of an old word.

_____ 9. Sometimes only a few kind words will *placate* an angry heart.

_____ 10. *Neonatal* care takes place before the baby is born.

DEFINITION REPLACEMENT

_____ 1. We now know that the [*related to a newborn infant*] period is very important to a child's later development.

_____ 2. Only at a cost of millions can we [*to renew or restore*] this old ferryboat.

_____ 3. Our interest in personal computers is yet [*of recent origin*].

64

_____ 4. You should not expect a [*a beginner or neophyte*] to play as well as an experienced professional.

_____ 5. A technological [*something new and improved*] may result in people losing their jobs.

_____ 6. How [*new and old at the same time*] is a computer that prints out in Gothic script!

_____ 7. The tribe believes it can [*to appease or pacify*] the gods by sacrificing a sheep.

_____ 8. Today we could hardly call *astrodome* a [*a new word*].

_____ 9. A doll that wets its diaper is no longer a [*a new or clever object*], even to small children.

_____ 10. Even though I am an academic [*a beginner or novice*], I spend many hours in the college library.

FILL-IN AND PART-OF-SPEECH IDENTIFICATION

_____ 1. As far as I am concerned, the greatest _____ in sports telecasting is the instant replay. What an improvement!

_____ 2. Without public funding, we can never _____ the Old Jail and make it look as it did a hundred years ago.

_____ 3. Alex is a _____, a novice, on the electronic keyboard, yet she is doing quite well.

_____ 4. For a while, those little yellow signs in car windows that said such things as "Masochist Riding in Trunk" were a _____, but no one has them now.

_____ 5. You cannot _____ the fury of a storm by dreaming of blue skies.

_____ 6. *Fisherperson* is a _____ that I am having a little trouble getting used to, even when I am out on the lake with one.

_____ 7. Although almost fifty, I am still a _____ at life, a neophyte, and I do not think the situation is going to change very much in the years to come.

_____ 8. _____ diseases, those likely to occur in the first months after birth, are on the increase.

_____ 9. Nothing could be more _____ than a laser reproduction of a Norman cathedral—the old coupled with a new technology.

_____ 10. Even the magazines agree that yuppies are this age's _____, people infatuated with anything that smacks of newness.

MATCHING

_____ 1. neophyte

_____ 2. innovation

_____ 3. renovate

_____ 4. placate

_____ 5. novice

_____ 6. novelty

_____ 7. novantique

_____ 8. neonatal

_____ 9. neoteric

_____ 10. neologism

a. a new word or an old word used in a new way

b. a cheap little item, although perhaps clever in its manufacture

c. a novice

d. a modern person

e. to restore to a like-new condition

f. an improvement or advancement

g. to appease or pacify

h. that which combines the old and new

i. a neophyte

j. immediately after birth

BONUS ROOT

plac (to please): complacence, complacency, complacent, complacently, implacable, placable, placation, placative, placatory, placebo, placid, placidity, placidly, placidness

Words from Roots (15)

Not only do the Latin roots *fin* and *termin* both mean "end," "limit," or "boundary," but defining modern English derivatives of either root often requires using derivatives of the other. For example, to *exterminate* an infestation of insects is to *finish* the creatures off. Likewise, to *determine* the meaning of a word is to *define* it. To *finalize* an agreement is to bring it to its *terminus* (TUR-mə-nəs)—that is, its end or goal.

WORD LIST

1. af*fin*ity (ə-FIN-ə-tee), *n*: a close relationship or attraction; a natural liking or sympathy; a connection

2. de*fin*itive (di-FIN-ə-tiv), *a*: that sets or settles limits or boundaries in an accurate, reliable, and authoritative way; decisive or conclusive

3. *fin*ale (fi-NAL-ee, fi-NAH-lee), *n*: a grand ending or conclusion, as of a performance

4. *fin*ite (FIY-niyt), *a*: limited or bordered by time or by any measurement

5. in*fin*ite (IN-fə-nit), *a*: without end, bounds, or limits; endless

6. in*termin*able (in-TURM-ə-nə-bəl), *a*: seeming to have no end; tiresomely long; protracted

7. *termin*al (TUR-mə-nəl), *a*: at or near the end; ending; near death or causing death; *n*, a computer station, train station, or airport—all at the end of some type of line

8. *termin*ate (TUR-mə-nayt), *v*: to bring to an end or conclusion; to end or stop; to kill; to fire

9. *termin*ology (*tur*-mə-NAHL-ə-jee), *n*: the vocabulary or terms used in a particular occupation or field of study, which literally define the limits or boundaries of that occupation or field of study

---

a (f*a*t); ay (f*a*te); ah (f*a*r); au (d*ou*bt); ch (*ch*ur*ch*); e (*e*lf, b*e*d, c*a*re); ee (*e*qual); ə (*a*bout); hw (*wh*ile); i (f*i*t); iy (k*i*te); ŋ (li*n*k, si*ng*); o (*a*udio, c*o*rn); ow (*o*cean); oo (b*oo*k); oi (*oi*l); sh (*sh*oe, ambi*ti*on); th (*th*ink); u (*u*p, det*er*); uw (*oo*ze); y (*y*es, on*i*on); yu (b*u*reau, c*u*re); yuw (*y*o*u*th, *u*nity); zh (plea*s*ure)

*10. *vac*uous (VAK-yə-wəs), *a*: empty, in the sense of being devoid of meaning, intelligence, or interest; lacking serious content; stupid

TRUE-FALSE

_____ 1. An orchestral *finale* comes at the end of the performance.

_____ 2. An *interminable* discussion ends almost before it begins.

_____ 3. The earth has *infinite* resources of every kind.

_____ 4. A *vacuous* remark is devoid of serious meaning.

_____ 5. To have an *affinity* for science is to hate science.

_____ 6. A *terminal* illness usually ends in complete recovery.

_____ 7. To *terminate* a discussion is to bring it to an end.

_____ 8. *Definitive* statements are generally incomplete and inaccurate.

_____ 9. The purpose of *terminology* is to bring confusion to a particular field of study.

_____ 10. We humans are *finite* creatures.

DEFINITION REPLACEMENT

_____ 1. The lecture about student apathy toward important social issues seemed [*tiresomely long*].

_____ 2. Both of my suitemates have an [*a natural liking*] for mathematics.

_____ 3. Medical [*the vocabulary of an occupation*] is not as intimidating to patients as it once was.

_____ 4. Even a supercomputer has a [*limited to a measurement*] capacity for storing information.

_____ 5. In a true democracy, you cannot [*to end or stop*] free expression.

_____ 6. The [*decisive and conclusive*] history of the twentieth century will not be written for a long time.

_____ 7. How can such a [*empty of serious content*] novel become a national bestseller?

_____ 8. On a clear winter night, the stars seem [*without limit*] in number.

_____ 9. The old [*a train station*] has been restored and is now a nice restaurant.

_____ 10. Unfortunately, we left before the evening's [*a grand conclusion*].

FILL-IN AND PART-OF-SPEECH IDENTIFICATION

_____ 1. You will hear no _____ platitudes from this speaker; her remarks will be serious and meaningful.

_____ 2. Computer _____ is virtually a foreign language to the uninitiated.

_____ 3. The earth contains only a _____ store of fossil fuels. One day they will be gone.

_____ 4. Fritz suffered a nearly _____ case of good humor; he almost died laughing.

_____ 5. Neoterics have an _____ for change; they just naturally adjust to that which is new.

_____ 6. These _____ arguments sometimes run late into the night.

_____ 7. The _____ of the *1812 Overture* is often accompanied by the firing of cannons.

_____ 8. When we _____ employees, we do not shoot them; we just fire them.

_____ 9. When we are young, life seems _____; but later we realize that we have only a finite measure of it.

_____ 10. The _____ ruling on this case will come only from the Supreme Court.

MATCHING

_____ 1. infinite   a. a close attraction or natural sympathy

_____ 2. terminate   b. near death or causing death

_____ 3. affinity   c. endless

_____ 4. interminable   d. the vocabulary of an occupation or field of study

_____ 5. vacuous   e. a grand end or conclusion

_____ 6. definitive   f. lacking meaning or intelligence

_____ 7. terminology   g. limited by time or measurement

_____ 8. finite   h. tiresomely long

_____ 9. terminal   i. to end, stop, kill, or fire

_____ 10. finale   j. accurate, reliable, and authoritative

BONUS ROOT

vac (empty): evacuate, evacuation, evacuee, vacancy, vacant, vacate, vacation, vacational, vacuity, vacuum

Words from Roots (16)

Both the Greek root *pan* and the Latin root *omni* mean "all." *Pantheism* (PAN-thee-*iz*-ən) is the notion that God exists in all things, or actually is all things. In John Milton's *Paradise Lost,* the capital of Hell is called *Pandemonium* (pan-də-MOW-nee-əm), the abode of all demons. Today, of course, we use the word to mean a general scene of noisy disorder. An *omnidirectional* (ahm-ni-də-REK-shən-əl) signal is one that goes out in all directions, and an *omnibus* (AHM-nə-bəs) is a public carriage that transports all people. Today we have shortened it to *bus.*

WORD LIST

1. *omni*potent (ahm-NIP-ə-tənt), *a*: possessing unlimited power or authority; all-powerful

2. *omni*present (*ahm*-ni-PREZ-ənt), *a*: present in all places at the same time

3. *omni*scient (ahm-NISH-ənt), *a*: all-knowing; possessing infinite knowledge

4. *omni*vorous (ahm-NIV-ər-əs), *a*: eating both animal and vegetable matter; consuming everything available, as with the mind

5. *pan*acea (pan-ə-SEE-ə), *n*: a (supposed) remedy for all problems; a cure-all

6. *pan*chromatic (*pan*-krow-MAT-ik), *a*: sensitive to all visible colors

7. *pan*demic (pan-DEM-ik), *a*: occurring over a wide geographical area and affecting a large percentage of the population; universal; *n,* a disease occurring over such a wide area

8. *pan*oply (PAN-ə-plee), *n*: a full set of armor, and thus any complete protective covering; any splendid, impressive, or magnificent array

9. *pan*orama (*pan*-ə-RAM-ə, *pan*-ə-RAH-mə), *n*: a wide and unbroken view in all directions; a complete or total view

---

a (fat); ay (fate); ah (far); au (doubt); ch (church); e (elf, bed, care); ee (equal); ə (about); hw (while); i (fit); iy (kite); ŋ (link, sing); o (audio, corn); ow (ocean); oo (book); oi (oil); sh (shoe, ambition); th (think); u (up, deter); uw (ooze); y (yes, onion); yu (bureau, cure); yuw (youth, unity); zh (pleasure)

71

*10. traj*ect*ory (trə-JEK-tə-ree), *n*: the curved path of an object hurtling through space, as a missile or comet

TRUE-FALSE

_____ 1. *Omnivorous* animals are so called because they eat all the time.

_____ 2. That which is *pandemic* affects a wide area.

_____ 3. A *trajectory* is a type of electrical circuit.

_____ 4. There are probably no true *panaceas*.

_____ 5. *Panchromatic* film is most often used to take black-and-white pictures.

_____ 6. A *panoramic* view is broad and unobstructed.

_____ 7. One can be an *omnivorous* reader without eating books.

_____ 8. The president of the United States is *omnipotent*.

_____ 9. A knight in full *panoply* is ready for battle.

_____ 10. Theoretically at least, God is both *omnipresent* and *omniscient*.

DEFINITION REPLACEMENT

_____ 1. After watching the evening news, one might think that folly and destruction are [*in all places at the same time*].

_____ 2. Hunger is a [*occurring over a wide geographical area*] problem throughout the underdeveloped countries of the world.

_____ 3. From the top of the hill we could see the [*a complete view*] of the valley below.

_____ 4. My garbage disposal is an [*consuming everything*] piece of technology.

_____ 5. The normal human eye is [*sensitive to all visible colors*].

_____ 6. The [*the path of a hurled object*] of the spinning Frisbee was almost flat for a time.

_____ 7. My grandmother thought that chicken soup was a quick [*a remedy for all problems*] for everything that ailed a child.

_____ 8. In this company at least, the chairman of the board is [*possessing unlimited authority*].

_____ 9. The villain was saved by a well-planned [*a protective covering*] of lies and half-truths.

_____ 10. Supercomputers may be smart, but they are not [*all-knowing*].

FILL-IN AND PART-OF-SPEECH IDENTIFICATION

_____ 1. In a world of many equally powerful nations, none will be _____, or all-powerful.

_____ 2. My uncle's goat is _____; the creature eats everything that does not eat him.

_____ 3. Just because you are good at trivia games does not mean that you are _____; you do not know everything.

_____ 4. _____ film should be stored in the refrigerator; otherwise it loses its sensitivity to color.

_____ 5. An all-out nuclear war will result in nothing short of a _____, a death plague throughout the world.

_____ 6. The use of computers in the classroom is no _____ for all the problems plaguing American education.

_____ 7. A rocket's _____ depends on many things, one of which is the thrust at launch.

_____ 8. To understand the full _____ of European history requires years of reading and study, maybe a lifetime.

_____ 9. To the believer, God is both _____ and omniscient, everywhere and all-knowing.

_____ 10. A _____ of snow covered the plowed field, protecting it until the spring thaw.

MATCHING

_____ 1. panorama   a. all-powerful

_____ 2. omniscient   b. a protective covering

_____ 3. panoply   c. a full and unobstructed view

_____ 4. trajectory   d. present in all places at once

_____ 5. panchromatic   e. a cure-all

_____ 6. omnipotent   f. eating both meat and vegetables

_____ 7. omnivorous   g. all-knowing

_____ 8. omnipresent   h. the curved path of an object hurtling through space

_____ 9. pandemic   i. sensitive to all visible colors

_____ 10. panacea   j. epidemic over a very large area

BONUS ROOT

ject, jac, jet (to throw): abject, abjection, adjacent, adjective, conjectural, conjecture, dejected, dejection, ejaculate, ejaculation, eject, ejection, inject, injection, interject, interjection, jet, jetsam, jettison, jetty, project, projection, reject, rejection

Words from Roots (17)

Both the Greek root *graph(y)* or *gram* and the Latin root *scrib(e)* or *script* mean "to write." An *autograph* is written in one's own hand and is one's own signature. A *monogram* is a written design combining the initials of a name. On public walls we often find crude writings called *graffiti*. And *choreography* (kor-ee-AHG-rə-fee) includes the written notations of the sequence of movements in a dance. Likewise, a *scribe* is someone who copies *manuscripts*—that is, handwritten documents. To *scribble* is to write carelessly, and a *prescription* is a physician's written directions for the preparation and use of a medicine.

WORD LIST

1. ana*gram* (AN-ə-*gram*), *n*: a word or phrase constructed from another by writing the letters of the first in a different order, as *live* and *evil*

2. a*scribe* (ə-SKRIYB), *v*: literally, to write to, and thus to attribute to a specific person, source, cause, or origin; to assign as an attribute; to give credit

3. calli*graphy* (kə-LIG-rə-fee), *n*: the art of beautiful handwriting; penmanship

4. epi*gram* (EP-ə-*gram*), *n:* a brief and often witty, satirical, or paradoxical saying, as "If speech is silver, silence is golden."

5. *graph*ic (GRAF-ik), *a*: written in vivid and realistic detail

6. mono*graph* (MAHN-ə-*graf*), *n*: a paper, article, or book written on a single (scholarly) subject

7. nonde*script* (*nahn*-di-SKRIPT), *a*: unremarkable, not easy to describe because of a lack of noteworthy characteristics or qualities; *n*, a person or thing not easy to describe because of this lack

8. post*script* (POWST-*script*), *n*: literally, to write after, and thus additional information added after the conclusion of a letter, article, book, etc.

---

a (f*a*t); ay (f*a*te); ah (f*a*r); au (d*ou*bt); ch (*ch*urch); e (*e*lf, b*e*d, c*a*re); ee (*e*qual); ə (*a*bout); hw (*wh*ile); i (f*i*t); iy (k*i*te); ŋ (li*n*k, si*ng*); o (*a*udio, c*o*rn); ow (*o*cean); oo (b*oo*k); oi (*oi*l); sh (*sh*oe, ambi*ti*on); th (*th*ink); u (*u*p, de*te*r); uw (*oo*ze); y (*y*es, on*i*on); yu (b*u*reau, c*u*re); yuw (*y*outh, *u*nity); zh (plea*s*ure)

9. trans*scribe* (tran-SKRIYB), *v*: literally, to write over or across, and thus to write out in full or to make a written copy; to record

*10. *vivacity* (vi-VAS-ǝ-tee), *n*: a general liveliness or animation of disposition

TRUE-FALSE

_____ 1. An *epigram* may make a clever point.

_____ 2. A letter usually begins with a *postscript*.

_____ 3. *Nondescript* individuals are easy to forget.

_____ 4. An *anagram* is a short poem designed to be read from right to left.

_____ 5. To *transcribe* your roommate's history notes is to copy them.

_____ 6. More often than not, *graphic* descriptions are vague and imprecise.

_____ 7. To *ascribe* innocence is to deny innocence.

_____ 8. *Vivacity* is a quality of lively and animated individuals.

_____ 9. A *monograph* is written on a single topic.

_____ 10. *Calligraphy* is skill at sending or receiving long telegrams.

DEFINITION REPLACEMENT

_____ 1. "If money cannot buy happiness, neither can poverty" was the speaker's opening [*a brief and witty saying*].

_____ 2. The speaker's appearance was about as [*without noteworthy characteristics*] as his lecture.

_____ 3. Why [*to attribute to*] genius to anything so obviously ordinary?

_____ 4. The novel's descriptive passages were so [*written in vivid and realistic detail*] that I read them with one eye closed.

_____ 5. Alas, my love tossed my missive away without reading the [*information added after the conclusion*].

_____ 6. The title of Samuel Butler's novel *Erewhon* is an [*a word constructed by rearranging another*] of the word *nowhere*.

_____ 7. Too much [*a liveliness or animation of disposition*], even in a friend, can become annoying after a while.

_____ 8. I cannot [*to make a written copy of*] these notes; the handwriting is illegible.

_____ 9. [*The art of beautiful handwriting*] does not have a chance against electronic typewriters and word processors.

_____ 10. The other day I read an interesting [*a scholarly article on a single topic*] on the ability of some animals to think and reason.

FILL-IN AND PART-OF-SPEECH IDENTIFICATION

_____ 1. Finally, even the judge objected to the witness's overly _____ description of the crime.

_____ 2. If I _____ everything that takes place on the six-week literary tour of England, I will not have time to do anything else.

_____ 3. The role requires a young person of great _____, not a brooding individual too gloomy to get out of bed.

_____ 4. If I am forced to read one more _____ on the subject of how poorly prepared American high school graduates are for college, I'm going to drop out of school.

_____ 5. My English instructor, who has a little saying ready for every occasion, sprinkles her lectures with catchy _____.

_____ 6. You simply cannot _____ a sane motive to such a brutal act.

_____ 7. An epigram on a tombstone sometimes serves as the _____ to an entire life.

_____ 8. The _____ in these old manuscripts suggests a scribe of great talent and patience.

_____ 9. The usual collection of _____ characters showed up to audition for the bit part; none had enough talent worth remarking.

_____ 10. The word *cask* is an easy _____ of the word *sack,* but *carthorse* is a more complicated one of the word *orchestra.*

MATCHING

_____ 1. calligraphy   a. a clever and sometimes paradoxical saying

_____ 2. nondescript   b. written information appearing after a conclusion

_____ 3. epigram   c. written in vivid and realistic detail

_____ 4. transcribe   d. a general liveliness or animation of disposition

_____ 5. monograph   e. the art of beautiful handwriting

_____ 6. postscript   f. to make a written copy

_____ 7. ascribe   g. a word constructed by rearranging another word

_____ 8. vivacity   h. lacking noteworthy characteristics

_____ 9. anagram   i. a scholarly article on a single subject

_____ 10. graphic   j. to attribute or give credit to

BONUS ROOT

viv, vit (to live): convivial, revivify, survive, vital, vitality, vitamin, vivacious, vivid, vivify

Words from Roots (18)

Although regard for the self may seem excessive in what has been called the "me generation," the notion of self is as old as human history. The Latin root meaning "self" is *ego,* as in *egotism,* meaning "excessive self-interest." The Greek root meaning "self" is *auto,* as in *autograph, automatic, automobile,* and *autobiography.*

WORD LIST

1. alter *ego* (OL·tər EE·gow), *n*: literally, another self; another aspect of oneself; a constant companion

*2. a*manu*ensis (ə-*man*-yə-WEN-sis), *n*: originally, a slave with secretarial duties; one who takes dictation rapidly, thus using the hands; an intentionally humorous usage meaning a secretary

3. *auto*bahn (OT-ə-*bahn*), *n*: a high-speed expressway (for automobiles) in Germany

4. *auto*mation (*o*-tə-MAY-shən), *n*: an entire system of manufacturing using self-operating machinery

5. *auto*maton (o-TAHM-ə-*tahn*), *n*: a self-acting apparatus; a machine programmed to perform the same task over and over; a robot; a person who behaves in a very mechanical way

6. *auto*nomous (o-TAHN-ə-məs), *a*: self-governing, as a nation; functioning independently of outside interference or control

7. *ego*centric (*ee*-gow-SEN-trik), *a*: always placing oneself at the center; assuming oneself to be the norm for all human experience; *n,* an egocentric person

8. *ego*tist (EE-gə-tist), *n*: an individual characterized by self-conceit, self-interest, and a disregard for others

*9. e*man*cipate (i-MAN-sə-*payt*), *v*: to set free from bondage or slavery, and thus to unhand

---

a (fat); ay (fate); ah (far); au (doubt); ch (church); e (elf, bed, care); ee (equal); ə (about); hw (while); i (fit); iy (kite); ŋ (link, sing); o (audio, corn); ow (ocean); oo (book); oi (oil); sh (shoe, ambition); th (think); u (up, deter); uw (ooze); y (yes, onion); yu (bureau, cure); yuw (youth, unity); zh (pleasure)

10. non*ego* (nahn-EE-gow), *n*: everything that is not part of the self; the external world; *a*, not of the self

TRUE-FALSE

_____ 1. *Automation* is often an element of modern technology.

_____ 2. To *emancipate* is to bury deep in the ground.

_____ 3. The United States of America has long been an *autonomous* nation.

_____ 4. One's *alter ego* is usually thought of as one's greatest enemy.

_____ 5. The *nonego* world is the world outside or beyond oneself.

_____ 6. *Egocentric* individuals think mostly of others.

_____ 7. Taking dictation should be the forte of an *amanuensis*.

_____ 8. An *egotist* will likely be considered conceited by other people.

_____ 9. Most motorists drive very slowly on an *autobahn*.

_____ 10. Scholars and philosophers are usually regarded as *automatons*.

DEFINITION REPLACEMENT

_____ 1. In the United States, the individual states are not [*self-governing*] little countries.

_____ 2. This job requires an [*a mechanical robot*] rather than a human being.

_____ 3. Tom considers his identical twin to be his [*another self*], not his sibling.

_____ 4. Eventually, most of us realize that the [*not of the self*] world is large and complex.

_____ 5. The true [*an individual interested only in himself or herself*] cares little about the feelings of others.

_____ 6. Jokingly, Susan sometimes calls her administrative assistant her [*a slave with secretarial duties*].

_____ 7. Few of us ever really [*to set free*] ourselves from our past experiences.

_____ 8. The [*a high-speed expressway*] is no place to ride a donkey cart.

_____ 9. Industrial [*a system of self-operating machinery*] often throws skilled people out of work.

_____ 10. To some degree, we are all [*self-centered*].

FILL-IN AND PART-OF-SPEECH IDENTIFICATION

_____ 1. Because of the high speeds, there are seldom minor accidents on the _____.

_____ 2. How does one _____ oneself from the slavery of egotism?

_____ 3. My psychology instructor called insecurity the _____ of aggressiveness.

_____ 4. Because of the complexity of modern society, it is virtually impossible for an individual to be a completely _____ person, independent of all others.

_____ 5. After spending millions of dollars on _____, the company closed down the factory because it was too expensive to operate.

_____ 6. It is difficult for the _____ even to admit the existence of the nonego world.

_____ 7. Working twenty years on an assembly line can make an _____ of almost anyone.

_____ 8. All of life over which I have no control or cannot understand is part of the _____.

_____ 9. Should calling a secretary an _____ be accompanied by an increase in salary?

_____ 10. Does the fact that I think the universe was created for my personal amusement make me _____?

MATCHING

_____ 1. automation   a. a robot that does one task over and over

_____ 2. egotist   b. an entirely self-interested person

_____ 3. autonomous   c. literally, another self

_____ 4. amanuensis   d. to set free, as from bondage

_____ 5. nonego   e. a complete system of automatic machinery

_____ 6. autobahn   f. assuming oneself to be the norm for everything

_____ 7. emancipate   g. a person skilled at taking dictation

_____ 8. alter ego   h. the external world

_____ 9. egocentric   i. functioning independently of outside control

_____ 10. automaton   j. a high-speed expressway

BONUS ROOT

man(u) (hand): manacles, mandate, mandatory, maneuver, manicure, manifest, manifesto, manipulation, manual, manufacture, manuscript

Words from Roots (19)

As we have cities today, so did the Greeks and Romans. Furthermore, many of our words relating to notions about cities are derivatives of the Greek root *poli,* or *polis,* and the Latin root *urb,* both of which mean "city." The *police* maintain law and order in the city. A *metropolis* is the main city of a region. If you live in the *suburbs,* you live near a city. An *interurban* bus travels between two or more cities.

WORD LIST

1. cosmo*poli*tan (*kahz*-mə-PAHL-ə-tən), *a:* possessing the polish or wisdom of wide experience, as might be gained from visiting many cities; not provincial; *n,* a person or thing possessing these characteristics

2. in*urb*ane (*in*-ər-BAYN), *a:* not citified, and thus unsophisticated, crude, or un-polished; uncouth

3. megalo*polis* (*meg*-ə-LAHP-ə-ləs), *n:* an extremely large urban area including several cities

4. metro*poli*tan (*me*-trə-PAHL-ə-tən), *a:* including the entire area and population of a large central city plus surrounding areas or suburbs; *n,* a person who lives in such an area and exhibits manners and attitudes characteristic of a city dweller

5. *poli*tic (PAHL-ə-tik), *a:* shrewd, crafty, and wise, especially in looking after one's own interests—as the citizen of a city is more clever than a bumpkin; *v,* to campaign, as for a political party

6. sub*urb*an (sə-BUR-bən), *a:* characteristic of the outskirts of a big city or life in such an area, and thus (sometimes) semicultured, pretentious, or even a little phony

*7. syn*onym*ous (si-NAHN-ə-məs), *a:* having the same or nearly the same meaning as something else, as another word; equivalent to

8. *urb*anite (UR-bə-*niyt*), *n:* a person who lives in a city, especially in the center of the city

---

a (fat); ay (fate); ah (far); au (doubt); ch (church); e (elf, bed, care); ee (equal); ə (about); hw (while); i (fit); iy (kite); ŋ (link, sing); o (audio, corn); ow (ocean); oo (book); oi (oil); sh (shoe, ambition); th (think); u (up, deter); uw (ooze); y (yes, onion); yu (bureau, cure); yuw (youth, unity); zh (pleasure)

9. *urb*anity (ur-BAN-ə-tee), *n*: a mix of qualities suggesting polish, sophistication, and courteousness

10. *urb*anize (UR-bə-*niyz*), *v*: to make like a city, or to assume ways of living typical of a city

TRUE-FALSE

_____ 1. A *cosmopolitan* person has been around a bit.

_____ 2. This same individual will likely possess a degree of *urbanity*.

_____ 3. The Pacific Ocean is a large *metropolitan* area.

_____ 4. A *suburban* area is not actually within the city.

_____ 5. Synonyms have *synonymous* meanings.

_____ 6. Most *urbanites* make their living by farming.

_____ 7. To *urbanize* an area is to pull down all the buildings and plant a forest.

_____ 8. *Inurbane* manners are extremely polished and refined.

_____ 9. That which is *politic* is shrewd and even crafty.

_____ 10. A mountain village is usually thought of as a *megalopolis*.

DEFINITION REPLACEMENT

_____ 1. Uncontrolled population growth will eventually [*to make like a city*] the entire country.

_____ 2. It was not very [*shrewd or wise*] of the candidate to tell an off-color joke at the rally.

_____ 3. I apologized for my [*unsophisticated or crude*] behavior; I suppose I forgot where I was.

_____ 4. The expressions *freedom fighters* and *terrorists* are hardly [*having the same meaning*] terms.

_____ 5. A thoroughgoing [*one who lives in the center of a city*], my roommate does not like the rural campus.

_____ 6. Kim attended a large [*characteristic of the outskirts of a big city*] high school near Detroit.

_____ 7. The entire northeastern part of the country may soon become one giant [*an urban area including several cities*].

_____ 8. The [*of the central city and surrounding suburbs*] police arrived on the scene and quickly quieted the disturbance.

_____ 9. The speaker's extreme [*polish and sophistication*] made many of the local people in the audience feel like hicks.

_____ 10. Such a [*possessing the wisdom of wide experience*] point of view suggests a life that has included much travel.

FILL-IN AND PART-OF-SPEECH IDENTIFICATION

_____ 1. The speaker's racist remark was worse than _____; it revealed an attitude suggesting that he thought he had sprung from superior ancestry.

_____ 2. Mavis is such a confirmed _____ that she plays a tape of city traffic to go to sleep by.

_____ 3. The words *cosmopolitan* and *metropolitan* are not _____; there are important differences in their meanings.

_____ 4. London is not just one city; it is many cities, a _____.

_____ 5. Josh is such a political hack; he will _____ for anyone nominated by his party.

_____ 6. Such a _____ individual naturally prefers the cultural variety of a metropolitan area over the sometimes meager offerings of the hinterlands.

_____ 7. Let's not _____ our national parks; we need to keep a little wilderness—to have a place to park our motor homes.

_____ 8. Guests on television talk shows sometimes pretend an _____, a sophistication, that they do not really possess.

_____ 9. The greater _____ area of cities like Boston and Chicago includes the surrounding towns and suburbs.

_____ 10. People who grow up in suburbia often develop _____ tastes and attitudes.

MATCHING

_____ 1. megalopolis   a. a person of wide experience and polish

_____ 2. urbanity   b. including both the central city and suburbs

_____ 3. suburban   c. one who lives in the center of a city

_____ 4. synonymous   d. not citified; crude

_____ 5. urbanize   e. to campaign, as for a political party

_____ 6. metropolitan   f. a mix of polish, sophistication, and courteousness

_____ 7. urbanite   g. having the same meaning

_____ 8. cosmopolitan   h. to make into a city

_____ 9. politic   i. characteristic of the outskirts of a big city

_____ 10. inurbane   j. a large city made up of several cities

BONUS ROOT

onym, onoma (name): acronym, anonymity, anonymous, antonym, homonym, matronymic, metonymy, onomatopoeia, patronymic, pseudonym, synonym

Words from Roots (20)

As new and fresh as love may seem when first encountered, the experience is an ancient one. The Greek root meaning "to love" is *phil*. It also has other forms: *phila, phile, philo,* and *philia. Philadelphia* is the city of brotherly love. An *Anglophile* is a person who loves all things connected with England. A *philodendron (fil-ə-DEN-drən)* is a climbing plant so named because it seems to love the tree on which it grows; it also has heart-shaped leaves. The Latin root meaning "to love" is *am(at)*. An *amateur* is a person who engages in some activity for love rather than for money. An *amorous* glance does not go unnoticed because the eyes suggest fondness—or even more.

WORD LIST

1. *am*iable (AY·mee·ə·bəl), *a*: literally, lovable; generally pleasant, friendly, and nice to be around

2. *am*ity (AM·ə·tee), *n*: friendly and peaceful relations, as between nations; friendship

3. Anglo*philia* (aŋ·glə·FIL·ee·ə), *n*: an affection or extreme admiration for anything connected with England

4. biblio*phile* (BIB·lee·ə·*fiyl*), *n*: an individual who loves books, especially for their design and appearance; a book collector

5. en*am*ored (in·AM·ərd), *a*: in love with, usually in a passive sense; captivated by

6. *phil*anderer (fi·LAN·dər·ər), *n*: an individual who engages in many casual love affairs

7. *phil*anthropy (fi·LAN·thrə·pee), *n*: a love of humankind in general; the desire to be helpful to others, and actions that reflect this desire, as the funding of humanitarian projects

8. *phil*atelist (fi·LAT·ə·list), *n*: one who loves stamps, especially postage stamps; an expert in the study of postage stamps, postmarks, and so on

---

a (fat); ay (fate); ah (far); au (doubt); ch (church); e (elf, bed, care); ee (equal); ə (about); hw (while); i (fit); iy (kite); ŋ (link, sing); o (audio, corn); ow (ocean); oo (book); oi (oil); sh (shoe, ambition); th (think); u (up, deter); uw (ooze); y (yes, onion); yu (bureau, cure); yuw (youth, unity); zh (pleasure)

9. *philo*sophical (*fil-ə-SAHF-i-kəl*), *a*: characteristic of a love for wisdom and reasoning; systematically thoughtful, sometimes to a fault; contemplative

*10. *prime*val (priy-MEE-vəl), *a*: of or related to the earliest times or ages; existing at or since the beginning; primal or primitive

TRUE-FALSE

_____ 1. A *bibliophile* is literally in love with books.

_____ 2. A *philanderer* takes love affairs very seriously.

_____ 3. *Anglophilia* is a quality of an *Anglophile*.

_____ 4. Among friends, there usually exists a degree of *amity*.

_____ 5. *Primeval* impulses are always *philanthropic*.

_____ 6. Real *philanthropy* should grow out of a love for one's fellow creatures.

_____ 7. An *amorous* glance is probably more loving than an *amiable* one.

_____ 8. Letter carriers are usually called *philatelists*.

_____ 9. *Philosophical* discussions involve the suggestion of a love for wisdom on the part of the participants.

_____ 10. To be *enamored* of someone is to despise the person.

DEFINITION REPLACEMENT

_____ 1. An Anglophile, Elizabeth has become [*captivated by*] of all things English.

_____ 2. Of an [*pleasant and friendly*] disposition, my cousin is nice to be around.

_____ 3. My aunt is a dedicated [*one who loves stamps*]; her house is filled with books of old postage stamps.

88

_____ 4. AIDS has made life risky for the [*one who engages in casual love affairs*].

_____ 5. Although the debate was quite [*reflecting a love for wisdom*], I did not think it made much sense.

_____ 6. There is little [*peacefulness or friendship*] between these two old antagonists.

_____ 7. Just because I have an interest in our [*related to the earliest times*] instincts does not mean that I want to live a primitive life-style.

_____ 8. Although a [*one who loves books*], Robert actually reads very little.

_____ 9. [*The funding of humanitarian projects*] should not be indulged in for show, but because one has a genuine interest in the welfare of others.

_____ 10. [*A fondness for all things English*] plays an important part in the marketing of English products abroad.

FILL-IN AND PART-OF-SPEECH IDENTIFICATION

_____ 1. Do not become _____ of alcohol; it will prove a false friend.

_____ 2. If the impulse to fight wars is _____, we are still primitive beings.

_____ 3. The planet could do with more _____, and less hostility, among its peoples.

_____ 4. Slum landlords cannot be accused of _____; indeed, they do not seem to care about anyone.

_____ 5. Quite often, the person running a bookstore is a _____.

_____ 6. It is impossible to be _____ about the topic of war when one is caught in the middle of a bloody battle.

_____ 7. Margaret's _____ has reached the point that she now pretends an English accent.

_____ 8. A true _____ even knows the chemical compounds used in the glue on the backs of postage stamps.

_____ 9. The Arnolds are such an _____ couple; they can make friends with anyone, even total strangers.

_____ 10. A lifelong _____, Neville seems incapable of a permanent relationship with a woman.

MATCHING

_____ 1. amity

_____ 2. philanthropy

_____ 3. enamored

_____ 4. philosophical

_____ 5. Anglophilia

_____ 6. philatelist

_____ 7. primeval

_____ 8. bibliophile

_____ 9. philanderer

_____ 10. amiable

a. in love with; captivated by

b. a fondness for all things English

c. friendly and peaceful relations, as between nations

d. a stamp collector

e. one who engages in many casual love affairs

f. existing since the beginning

g. reflecting a love of wisdom and reasoning

h. generally pleasant, friendly, and nice to be around

i. a love of humankind in general

j. a book collector

BONUS ROOT

prim, prin (first): primacy, prima donna, primal, primate, prime, primitive, primogenitor, primogeniture, primordial, prince, princess, principal, principality

Supplementary Roots and Derivatives Exercise (1)

1. *aqua, aque* (water): aquatic, _____, _____, _____

2. *aster, astr(o)* (star): astronomy, _____, _____, _____

3. *cent* (hundred): percent, _____, _____, _____

4. *civ* (citizen): civilian, _____, _____, _____

5. *dec* (ten): decade, _____, _____, _____

6. *domin* (master, to rule): dominate, _____, _____, _____

7. *fer* (to carry, to bear): transfer, _____, _____, _____

8. *gam* (marriage): bigamist, _____, _____, _____

9. *grad, gress* (to step, to walk): gradual, digression, _____, _____, _____

10. *jur* (to take an oath): perjury, _____, _____, _____

11. *labor* (to work): elaborate, _____, _____, _____

12. *mod* (measure, manner): moderate, modesty, _____, _____, _____

13. *morph* (form): amorphous, _____, _____, _____

14. *par* (equal): comparable, _____, _____, _____

15. *phob(ia)* (to fear): claustrophobia, _____, _____, _____

16. *scop(e)* (to look, to see): telescopic, _____, _____,

_____

17. *sign* (sign, seal, mark): signature, _____, _____,

_____

18. *techn* (art, skill): technique, _____, _____, _____

19. *volv, volu* (to roll): revolve, evolution, _____, _____,

_____

20. *zo* (animal): zodiac, _____, _____, _____

Supplementary Roots and Derivatives Exercise (2)

1. *aer(o)* (air): aerobatics, _____, _____, _____

2. *ambul* (to walk): ambulatory, _____, _____, _____

3. *cad, cid, cas* (to fall): cadence, incident, casualty, _____, _____,

_____

4. *cosm(o)* (universe, order): cosmos, _____, _____,

_____

5. *dent* (tooth): indentation, _____, _____, _____

6. *doc(t)* (to teach): indoctrinate, _____, _____, _____

7. *flu(x)* (to flow): fluent, influx, _____, _____,

_____

8. *frag, fract* (to break): fragment, fracture, _____, _____,

_____

9. *hydr(o)* (water): dehydrated, _____, _____, _____

10. *lith(o)* (stone): lithograph, _____, _____, _____

11. *magn* (great): magnify, _____, _____, _____

12. *mov, mot, mob* (to move): movable, motivate, immobile, _____,

_____, _____

13. *nav* (ship, to sail): navigate, _____, _____, _____

14. *pel, puls* (to drive, to push): propel, pulsate, _____, _____,

_____

15. *port* (to carry): portable, _____, _____, _____

16. *sequ, sec* (to follow): sequel, persecute, _____, _____,

_____

17. *son* (sound): supersonic, _____, _____, _____

18. *spir(e)* (to breathe, to blow): spirit, inspire, _____, _____,

_____

19. *the(o)* (God): atheist, _____, _____, _____

20. *vinc, vict* (to conquer): invincible, victorious, _____, _____,

_____

Supplementary Roots and Derivatives Exercise (3)

1. *art* (art, craft, skill): artifact, _____, _____, _____

2. *avi* (bird): aviation, _____, _____, _____

3. *cap, cept, ceive* (to take): capable, intercept, deceive, _____,

   _____, _____

4. *chrom(o)* (color): chromium, _____, _____, _____

5. *derm* (skin): dermatologist, _____, _____, _____

6. *duc(e), duct* (to lead): conduct, conducive, _____, _____,

   _____

7. *dyn(am)* (power): dynamic, _____, _____, _____

8. *grat, grac* (pleasing): gratitude, graceful, _____, _____,

   _____

9. *iatr* (healing): psychiatrist, _____, _____, _____

10. *junct, join* (to join): junction, adjoining, _____, _____,

    _____

11. *leg* (law): illegal, _____, _____, _____

12. *mon(it)* (to warn, to remind): monument, monitor, _____,

    _____, _____

13. *nomen, nomin* (name): nomination, _____, _____,

    _____

14. *physi* (nature, natural): physician, _____, _____,

    _____

15. *pot, poss* (to be able): potent, possible, _____, _____,

    _____

16. *rupt* (to break): rupture, _____, _____, _____

17. *sci* (to know): scientific, _____, _____, _____

18. *sed, sid(e), sess* (to sit): sediment, reside, obsession, _____,

_____, _____

19. *test* (to bear witness): testify, _____, _____, _____

20. *therm(o)* (heat): thermostat, _____, _____, _____

Chapter

3

Words from Roots II

This chapter continues where the last one left off—that is, with sequences of exercises featuring derivatives of two roots with the same meaning. Then, sequences 23 through 26 present derivatives of three roots with the same meaning. Finally, the last ten sequences present a wider variety of connections between the featured roots and their derivatives. Sometimes one root has many meanings; other times several roots have one or similar meanings. In some sequences, the featured roots are logically or topically related. In all instances, the connections are explained in the introductory paragraph. Thus, you should read that paragraph carefully.

As in the previous chapter, each sequence includes a bonus root with one or two derivatives. Similarly, at the conclusion of the chapter there are two supplementary roots and derivatives exercises. Because these supplementary exercises are a little more advanced than those at the end of the previous chapter, you will need a college-level dictionary to complete them with confidence. For example, without a dictionary, you might confuse derivatives of the root *mor,* meaning "custom," with derivatives of such roots as *mor,* meaning "stupid," *mor,* meaning "to delay," *morb,* meaning "disease," *mord,* meaning "to bite," *morph,* meaning "form," or *mort/mori,* meaning "death."

Words from Roots (21)

Most of us are at least a little familiar with the Greek root *psych(o)*, meaning "mind." There is also a Latin root meaning "mind." It is *ment*. *Mental* work is mind work. To *mention* something is to bring it to mind. A person who suffers from *amentia* (ay-MEN-shə) is feeble-minded, and has been so since birth. The insane are often said to be *demented*. Similarly, a *psychiatrist* is a physician who specializes in disorders of the mind. A *psychosis* (siy-KOW-sis) is a major mental disorder in which the personality has lost touch with reality. The Alfred Hitchcock movie *Psycho* dealt with a character dangerously out of his mind.

WORD LIST

1. com*ment*ary (KAHM-ən-*ter*-ee), *n*: literally, the exercise of using the mind to remember and then to talk or write about an event remembered; notes or remarks presented in connection with an event and offered as a brief analysis

2. de*ment*ia (di-MEN-shə), *n*: progressive and permanent deterioration of the mental powers caused by an organic brain disorder; insanity; madness

3. *ment*ality (men-TAL-ə-tee), *n*: the total of a person's intellectual capacity; the particular cast of an individual's mind

4. *ment*ation (men-TAY-shən), *n*: the act or process of thinking; use of the mind; mental activity

5. *psyche* (SIY-kee), *n*: the mind, viewed as the functioning center of virtually all human behavior; the soul or spirit, as distinct from the body

6. *psyche*delic (siy-kə-DEL-ik), *a*: causing dramatic changes in the conscious mind; producing hallucinations or delusions

7. *psych*ic (SIY-kik), *a*: pertaining to the human mind, especially in the sense of the mind's power to perform extrasensory perception or mental telepathy; *n*, a person who can do such things

---

a (*fat*); ay (*fate*); ah (*far*); au (*doubt*); ch (*church*); e (*elf*, b*e*d, c*a*re); ee (*equal*); ə (*about*); hw (*while*); i (*fit*); iy (k*i*te); ŋ (li*n*k, si*ng*); o (*audio*, c*or*n); ow (*ocean*); oo (b*oo*k); oi (*oil*); sh (*shoe*, ambi*ti*on); th (*think*); u (*up*, det*er*); uw (*ooze*); y (*yes*, on*i*on); yu (b*u*reau, c*u*re); yuw (*youth*, *u*nity); zh (*pleasure*)

8. *psycho*somatic (*siy*-kow-sə-MAT-ik), *a*: related to physical problems and illnesses that arise from the mind or the emotions

*9. *soph*isticated (sə-FIS-tə-*kay*-tid), *a*: wise in the ways of the world; complex, as a piece of machinery; cultured

*10. *soph*omoric (*sahf*-ə-MOR-ik), *a*: literally, like a wise fool; characteristic of the immature arrogance arising from a little learning; overconfident with knowledge, yet poorly informed

TRUE-FALSE

_____ 1. The human *psyche* is not actually a physical organ.

_____ 2. One usually lifts weights to increase *psychic* powers.

_____ 3. The *commentary* on a book is seldom longer than the book itself.

_____ 4. A *sophomoric* point of view is a very *sophisticated* point of view.

_____ 5. The *mentality* of a child is different from that of an adult.

_____ 6. A person suffering from some type of *dementia* is normally expected to be clear-headed.

_____ 7. A characteristic of *psychedelic* drugs is that they produce hallucinations.

_____ 8. *Psychosomatic* illnesses are never very serious.

_____ 9. To engage in *mentation* is to think.

_____ 10. The *sophisticated mentality* is incapable of *mentation*.

DEFINITION REPLACEMENT

_____ 1. As a people, Americans are accused of preferring action to [*mental activity*].

_____ 2. Agnes demonstrated her [*pertaining to supernormal mind powers*] powers by reading everyone's thoughts.

100

_____ 3. Whoever wrote this [*remarks analyzing something*] did not understand the purpose of the concert.

_____ 4. If you kill the body, does the [*mind and spirit*] also die?

_____ 5. Pretending [*madness or insanity*], Steadman ate the hulls and carefully placed the peanuts in the dish.

_____ 6. These third-generation computers are [*technologically complex*] pieces of machinery, not toys for the simple-minded.

_____ 7. The warrior [*a particular cast of mind*] sees reality in terms of battles.

_____ 8. Your [*overconfident from a little knowledge*] arguments betray the shallowness of your wisdom.

_____ 9. My doctor said that some apparent allergies are really [*related to physical problems arising in the mind*].

_____ 10. If you stand in the sun long enough, the heat and light can have a [*producing hallucinations*] effect.

FILL-IN AND PART-OF-SPEECH IDENTIFICATION

_____ 1. The business _____, or mind set, thinks of everything in terms of its dollar value.

_____ 2. If a man dies of a _____ illness, is he really dead? Or does he just think he is?

_____ 3. What many psychotherapists call the _____ has historically been known as the soul.

_____ 4. Marge and her twin sister have _____ powers. They talk to each other long-distance every day without benefit of the telephone.

_____ 5. I am not a very _____ person; I do not know much, and I have never been anywhere except Denver.

_____ 6. Lindsey's _____ has progressed to the point that he thinks he is the reincarnation of Elvis Presley.

_____ 7. We were surprised to see such _____ strutting about by a scholar with a reputation for wisdom.

_____ 8. We now know that taking _____ drugs can permanently damage the mind, producing hallucinations years later.

_____ 9. A hard knock on the head can severely reduce _____; the brain simply shuts down.

_____ 10. Day after day, the evening news presents a pop _____ on the American way of life.

MATCHING

_____ 1. psychedelic

_____ 2. mentation

_____ 3. dementia

_____ 4. sophisticated

_____ 5. commentary

_____ 6. psychic

_____ 7. mentality

_____ 8. psychosomatic

_____ 9. sophomoric

_____ 10. psyche

a. the particular cast of an individual's mind

b. the soul or spirit

c. a person who can perform mental telepathy

d. producing hallucinations or delusions

e. overconfident with knowledge yet poorly informed

f. related to physical problems arising in the mind

g. loss of mental powers resulting from an organic brain disorder; insanity

h. wise in the ways of the world

i. the process of thinking

j. notes or remarks presented in connection with an event

BONUS ROOT

soph(o) (wise, wisdom): pansophism, philosopher, philosophic, philosophical, philosophize, philosophy, Sophia, sophist, sophisticate, sophistication, sophistry, Sophocles, unsophisticated

Words from Roots (22)

The roots *ben(e)* and *bon*, or *boun*, mean "well" or "good." Although both roots are Latin, the second comes to English usage by way of French. A *benefit* is something good and helpful rather than bad and harmful. Similarly, a *bonus* is something good, often money, received for doing good work. To wish travelers *bon voyage* (*bahn* voi-AHZH) is to wish them a good journey. A *bountiful* (BAUN-ti-fəl) harvest is a good one because it is abundant.

WORD LIST

1. *bene*diction (*ben-ə-DIK-shən*), *n*: the invocation of a divine blessing, as at the close of a religious service; a state of blessedness, or a blessing

2. *bene*factor (*BEN-ə-fak-tər*), *n*: one who does something good, as giving another (financial) help

3. *bene*ficiary (*ben-ə-FISH-ee-er-ee*), *n*: one who receives a benefit (or payment), as from an insurance policy or will

4. *bene*volence (*bə-NEV-ə-ləns*), *n*: an inclination to do good things; an act of kindness or charity

5. *ben*ign (*bi-NIYN*), *a*: not malignant; gracious and kindly; good-natured; showing mildness and gentleness

6. *bon*a fide (*BOW-nə fiyd, BAHN-ə fiyd*), *a*: in good faith; genuine; without deceit

7. *bon*anza (*bə-NAN-zə*), *n*: a sudden and unexpected source of good things, such as money or riches; a windfall

8. *bon*homie (*bahn-ə-MEE*), *n*: an amiable, easygoing disposition; a good nature; affable manner; friendliness

---

a (fat); ay (fate); ah (far); au (doubt); ch (church); e (elf, bed, care); ee (equal); ə (about); hw (while); i (fit); iy (kite); ŋ (link, sing); o (audio, corn); ow (ocean); oo (book); oi (oil); sh (shoe, ambition); th (think); u (up, deter); uw (ooze); y (yes, onion); yu (bureau, cure); yuw (youth, unity); zh (pleasure)

9. *bounteous* (BAUN-tee-əs), *a*: yielding good things freely and generously; plentiful and abundant

*10. in*equity* (in-EK-wət-ee), *n*: an instance or situation wherein things are not equal, in the sense of being unfair or unjust

TRUE-FALSE

_____ 1. A tax collector is usually thought of as a *beneficiary*.

_____ 2. Winning the New York lottery would indeed be a *bonanza*.

_____ 3. One is likely to hear a *benediction* in church.

_____ 4. *Bonhomie* is a feeling of deep, dark depression.

_____ 5. A person with a *benign* disposition will likely be good-natured and easygoing.

_____ 6. When nature is *bounteous*, it is most harsh.

_____ 7. Life is filled with *inequities*.

_____ 8. A *benefactor* is someone who is good at building factories.

_____ 9. A *bona fide* hero is a real hero.

_____ 10. *Benevolence* is one of the dominant characteristics of a tyrant.

DEFINITION REPLACEMENT

_____ 1. [*An act of charity*] is not the usual business of business.

_____ 2. A [*plentiful and abundant*] harvest left the village with more grain than it could store.

_____ 3. Of the four seasons, summer is usually the most [*showing mildness and gentleness*].

_____ 4. A veritable [*a windfall*] of donations poured in after the television show about the family's misfortune.

_____ 5. If we are happy, life itself seems like a [*a divine blessing*].

_____ 6. A terrible [*a situation wherein things are not equal*] exists between my sister's abilities and my own.

_____ 7. Some people view the government as an institutional [*one who gives another financial help*].

_____ 8. Maggie displays such a pleasant [*an amiable, easygoing disposition*] that it is impossible not to like her.

_____ 9. For most people, a [*genuine*] effort is required to do well in college.

_____ 10. Alas, I am the [*one who receives a benefit*] of my father's nose and my mother's ears.

FILL-IN AND PART-OF-SPEECH IDENTIFICATION

_____ 1. Everyone was relieved to learn that Mother's tumor was _____, not malignant.

_____ 2. I was surprised to discover that I was a _____ of my uncle's will.

_____ 3. Laura presented statistical evidence of salary _____ between men and women in the company.

_____ 4. My sister has become a _____ real estate agent; she passed her exam last week.

_____ 5. A spirit of _____ pervaded the conference; everyone was quite friendly.

_____ 6. After a month-long drought, the drenching rain was a _____, a blessing from the elements.

_____ 7. A _____ supply of game made it possible for us to survive the winter in the wilderness.

_____ 8. The principal _____ of the shelter for battered women and children is also the president of the local bank.

_____ 9. A _____ of orders for the Christmas season saved our little company.

_____ 10. The fraternity's _____ in supporting the local youth clubs refutes the charge that the members care nothing about the community.

MATCHING

_____ 1. bona fide   a. a state of blessedness

_____ 2. benediction   b. an act of kindness or charity

_____ 3. bonanza   c. showing mildness or gentleness

_____ 4. bounteous   d. an affable manner; friendliness

_____ 5. beneficiary   e. one who does something good for another

_____ 6. bonhomie   f. a situation in which things are not equal or fair

_____ 7. benevolence   g. a sudden source of good things; a windfall

_____ 8. inequity   h. in good faith; genuine

_____ 9. benefactor   i. plentiful and abundant

_____ 10. benign   j. one who receives payment from an insurance policy

BONUS ROOT

equ (equal): adequate, equalize, equanimity, equation, equator, equilateral, equilibrium, equinox, equitable, equity, equivocal, equivocate, inadequate

Words from Roots (23)

Surprisingly, three and sometimes more classical roots may have the same meaning or closely related meanings. For example, there are three Latin roots meaning "to wander": *migr, vag,* and *err. Migratory* birds and *migrant* workers wander from place to place with the changing seasons. Likewise, a *vagabond* is a person who wanders from place to place and has no permanent home. To make an *error* is to wander from the truth or accuracy.

WORD LIST

1. ab*err*ation (*ab-ə-RAY-*shən), *n*: a departure (wandering) from that which is normal, typical, right, proper, expected, and so on; a mental lapse

*2. con*cise* (kən-SIYS), *a*: cut short, and thus brief and to the point; covering much in few words

3. e*migr*ant (EM-ə-grənt), *a*: emigrating, or leaving one country or area to settle somewhere else; *n*, a person who emigrates

4. *err*atic (i-RAT-ik), *a*: wandering; having no fixed or regular course; inconstant or unconventional; deviating from the norm

5. *err*oneous (i-ROW-nee-əs), *a*: in error, which is a wandering from the truth or accuracy; wrong, false, or mistaken

6. extra*vag*ant (ik-STRAV-ə-gənt), *a*: literally, wandering beyond reasonable bounds; exceeding usual limits; excessive and unrestrained

*7. geno*cide* (JEN-ə-siyd), *n*: the systematic extermination (killing) of an entire ethnic group

8. im*migr*ant (IM-ə-grənt), *a*: immigrating, or moving into a region or country for the first time; *n*, a person who immigrates

---

a (fat); ay (fate); ah (far); au (doubt); ch (church); e (elf, bed, care); ee (equal); ə (about); hw (while); i (fit); iy (kite); ŋ (link, sing); o (audio, corn); ow (ocean); oo (book); oi (oil); sh (shoe, ambition); th (think); u (up, deter); uw (ooze); y (yes, onion); yu (bureau, cure); yuw (youth, unity); zh (pleasure)

9. *vagary* (VAY-gə-ree), *n*: an unexpected wandering, as of the mind; a whimsical or weird notion; an eccentric action; an oddity

10. *vagrant* (VAY-grənt), *n*: a person with no home or intention of employment who wanders from place to place; a vagabond; *a*, aimlessly roaming or wandering about

TRUE-FALSE

_____ 1. An *immigrant* is a person who moves out of a country intending to become a *vagrant.*

_____ 2. *Extravagant* precautions tend to be excessive.

_____ 3. The intent of *genocide* is the improvement of minority rights.

_____ 4. A *vagary* of the mind is usually unpredictable.

_____ 5. *Concise* explanations include an *extravagant* number of examples and instances.

_____ 6. An *erroneous* conclusion is a wrong one.

_____ 7. An *emigrant* is a person who remains in his or her country of birth.

_____ 8. An *aberration* in a person's behavior is not typical of the individual's personality.

_____ 9. Generally speaking, *erratic* behavior is very conventional.

_____ 10. For a lifelong *vagrant* to suddenly enroll in a school of business would be something of an *aberration.*

DEFINITION REPLACEMENT

_____ 1. The first galactic [*a person leaving one country for another*] has not yet left Earth to live on another planet.

_____ 2. [*The systematic killing of an ethnic group*] has occurred more often in human history than many people realize.

_____ 3. It was a sudden [*a whimsical or weird notion*] of the mind that made me buy this ugly painting.

_____ 4. The stock market's sudden rise of three hundred points was only an [*a departure from that which is normal*].

_____ 5. My great-grandmother was an [*a person moving into a country*], coming to America when she was only nine.

_____ 6. Much of what I thought I knew when I was young has now been proven [*wrong or false*].

_____ 7. To be [*covering much in few words*], my answer is no.

_____ 8. We were surprised to discover the [*a person with no home*] sleeping in the basement.

_____ 9. Edward's [*deviating from the norm*] actions were caused by a chemical imbalance in the brain.

_____ 10. You should be less [*excessive and unrestrained*] in your praise of scoundrels.

FILL-IN AND PART-OF-SPEECH IDENTIFICATION

_____ 1. Thousands of _____ from all over Europe arrived in the United States during the early years of the twentieth century.

_____ 2. Because of some _____ in the mechanism, my garage door started going up and down by itself.

_____ 3. Yes, I would call the gown _____; after all, it cost more than two thousand dollars.

_____ 4. Tom's heartbeat became _____ after he took the allergy medicine, but it became more regular after a few days.

_____ 5. My cat, a whimsical creature, seems motivated by one _____ after another.

_____ 6. In the 1950s, Jewish _____ were flocking out of the Soviet Union.

_____ 7. I would say that prejudice led to your _____ opinions about these people. You were simply wrong.

_____ 8. My brother has always led a _____ life, aimlessly roaming about and never holding a steady job.

_____ 9. During World War II, Adolf Hitler practiced _____ on the Jews in Germany.

_____ 10. If Jane had been any more _____, she would have said nothing at all.

MATCHING

_____ 1. emigrant

_____ 2. genocide

_____ 3. erratic

_____ 4. vagary

_____ 5. extravagant

_____ 6. aberration

_____ 7. vagrant

_____ 8. erroneous

_____ 9. immigrant

_____ 10. concise

a. in error, false, or mistaken

b. a whimsical wandering of the mind

c. a departure from that which is normal, typical, or right

d. a person who moves into a country for the first time

e. the systematic killing of a group of people

f. short and to the point

g. inconstant or unconventional; with no fixed course

h. a person with no home or employment

i. exceeding usual limits; excessive and unrestrained

j. a person who moves out of a country

BONUS ROOT

cid(e), cis(e) (to cut, to kill): circumcise, decide, decisive, fratricide, germicide, herbicide, homicide, incision, incisive, incisor, insecticide, matricide, patricide, precise, precision, scissors, suicide

Words from Roots (24)

The Latin roots *ali* and *alter* mean "another" or "other." Similarly, the Greek root *all(o)* means "other." An *alibi* places a person somewhere other than at the scene of the crime. An *alias* is another name. An *alternative* is the other choice. As we have already seen, the *alter ego* is literally one's other self. An *allergy* is the result of some other force affecting the body. And an *allograph* (AL-ə-*graf*) is any of several ways of writing the same alphabetic character, as *A* or *a*.

WORD LIST

1. *alien* (AY-lee-ən, AYL-yən), *a*: from another place; foreign and thus strange; *n*, a foreigner or outsider; an extraterrestrial

2. *alienate* (AY-lee-ə-*nayt*, AYL-yə-*nayt*), *v*: to make someone unfriendly, withdrawn, or indifferent

3. *allegory* (AL-ə-*gor*-ee), *n*: a symbolic story in which characters and events carry a secondary, or other, set of meanings

4. *allergen* (AL-ər-jən), *n*: any substance that induces an allergic reaction

5. *altercation* (ol-tər-KAY-shən), *n*: a heated or angry argument with another person; a noisy quarrel

6. *altruistic* (*al*-truw-IS-tik), *a*: having an unselfish regard for the welfare of other people; selfless

*7. *armada* (ahr-MAH-də), *n*: a fleet of warships

8. in*ali*enable (in-AYL-yə-nə-bəl), *a*: that cannot be taken away by someone else or transferred to another person

9. in*alter*able (in-OL-tər-ə-bəl), *a*: that cannot be changed to something other than what it is

10. sub*alter*n (səb-OL-tərn), *a*: literally, below another, and thus of lower, secondary, or subservient rank; *n*, a subordinate

---

a (f*a*t); ay (f*a*te); ah (f*a*r); au (d*ou*bt); ch (*ch*urch); e (*e*lf, b*e*d, c*a*re); ee (*e*qual); ə (*a*bout); hw (*wh*ile); i (f*i*t); iy (k*i*te); ŋ (li*n*k, si*ng*); o (*au*dio, c*o*rn); ow (*o*cean); oo (b*oo*k); oi (*oi*l); sh (*sh*oe, ambi*ti*on); th (*th*ink); u (*u*p, de*te*r); uw (*oo*ze); y (*y*es, on*i*on); yu (b*u*reau, c*u*re); yuw (*you*th, *u*nity); zh (plea*s*ure)

TRUE-FALSE

_____ 1. To some people, flower pollen is an *allergen*.

_____ 2. A *subaltern* is expected to take orders.

_____ 3. When you *alienate* people, they become your friends for life.

_____ 4. An *armada* is a giant squidlike sea creature with dozens of arms and hands.

_____ 5. An *alien* is from somewhere else.

_____ 6. *Altruistic* individuals are usually very self-centered.

_____ 7. That which is *inalienable* cannot be taken away.

_____ 8. An *allegory* is a type of crocodile that often appears in symbolic stories for children.

_____ 9. An *inalterable* situation cannot be changed.

_____ 10. An *altercation* is a major change in the structure of something.

DEFINITION REPLACEMENT

_____ 1. Today, we usually call an [*a nation's warships*] a fleet.

_____ 2. My opposition to the proposal is [*that cannot be changed to something else*].

_____ 3. For a percentage of the population, the iodine in shrimp is an [*any substance that induces an allergic reaction*].

_____ 4. E.T. was a friendly [*an extraterrestrial*], but the Thing was not.

_____ 5. I was awakened by an [*a heated or angry argument*] between my two roommates.

_____ 6. In a dictatorship, ordinary people have no [*that cannot be taken away*] rights.

_____ 7. Unfortunately, Emmett can [*to make someone unfriendly*] some people with a single glance.

_____ 8. It was the job of the [*a person of subordinate rank*] to come in early and light the fires.

_____ 9. The instructor read an [*a symbolic story*] in which a single blemish on a woman's cheek drove her husband mad.

_____ 10. Regardless of what happened, her motives were [*having an unselfish regard for others*].

FILL-IN AND PART-OF-SPEECH IDENTIFICATION

_____ 1. Nathan maintains that because we tend to see ordinary things as symbols anyway, all of life may be thought of as an _____.

_____ 2. The vice president is _____ to the president.

_____ 3. The continuing disagreement between the president of the company and the representative of the electrical union culminated in an _____ at the contract negotiations.

_____ 4. I was something completely _____ to the members of the primitive tribe. I may as well have come from outer space.

_____ 5. In a democracy, your right to speak your mind is _____; no one can take it away from you.

_____ 6. If we _____ our allies, we are likely to find the world a more hostile place.

_____ 7. Gravity is _____; we cannot change it.

_____ 8. An _____ of Tall Ships sailed past the island where we spend the summer.

_____ 9. I find hard work to be a powerful _____; it makes me break out in a blue funk.

_____ 10. In this age of people being wrapped up in themselves, it is unusual to come across such an _____ individual as Benedict.

MATCHING

_____ 1. allegory   a. a substance that causes an allergic reaction

_____ 2. inalterable   b. having an unselfish regard for others

_____ 3. armada   c. a foreigner or outsider

_____ 4. alienate   d. that cannot be changed

_____ 5. altruistic   e. a story with symbolic elements

_____ 6. inalienable   f. a noisy quarrel

_____ 7. allergen   g. a fleet of warships

_____ 8. altercation   h. a subordinate person

_____ 9. alien   i. that cannot be taken away

_____ 10. subaltern   j. to make withdrawn or indifferent

BONUS ROOT

arm (arm, weapon): alarm, armaments, armature, armipotent, armistice, armor, armory, army, disarm

Words from Roots (25)

Latin includes three distinct roots meaning "strong." They are *fort, firm,* and *rob.* A *fortress* is a place that has been strengthened against attack. To make an *effort* is to employ one's strength to get something done. An *infirmary* is a place where people who are not strong or healthy go for medical attention. To *confirm* a reservation is to make sure of it, to make it strong. A person in *robust* health is strong and vital.

WORD LIST

1. af*firm*ative (ə-FUR-mə-tiv), *a*: showing strength, confidence, optimism, and hope; giving assent or agreeing; *n,* a word or expression indicating agreement

*2. con*tempor*ary (kən-TEM-pə-*rer*-ee), *a*: alive or occurring at the same time; modern; *n,* a person living in the same time period as another; a modern person

3. cor*rob*orate (kə-RAHB-ə-*rayt*), *v*: to make the validity of something stronger; to confirm, as a story, by giving evidence or proof; to support or bolster

*4. ex*tempor*aneous (ek-*stem*-pə-RAY-nee-əs), *a*: done without time to prepare; without preparation; impromptu

5. *firm*ament (FUR-mə-mənt), *n*: the sky or heavens viewed as a strong, solid vault or arch above the earth; by extension, any protective cover

6. *forte* (FORT, FOR-tay), *n*: one's special area of accomplishment; *a,* loud or strong, as playing music; *adv,* loudly or forcefully

7. *fort*ify (FOR-tə-*fiy*), *v*: to make stronger; to establish defenses

8. *fort*itude (FOR-tə-*tuwd*), *n*: strength of character allowing one to endure adversity with quiet courage

a (fat); ay (fate); ah (far); au (doubt); ch (church); e (elf, bed, care); ee (equal); ə (about); hw (while); i (fit); iy (kite); ŋ (link, sing); o (audio, corn); ow (ocean); oo (book); oi (oil); sh (shoe, ambition); th (think); u (up, deter); uw (ooze); y (yes, onion); yu (bureau, cure); yuw (youth, unity); zh (pleasure)

9. infirmity (in-FUR-mə-tee), *n*: some specific absence of normal physical strength; a frailty or defect; feebleness

10. *robust* (row-BUST, ROW-*bust*), *a*: strong, healthy, vigorous, and hardy; powerfully built; requiring strength or endurance; full-bodied or boisterous

TRUE-FALSE

_____ 1. To *fortify* a building is to make it your *forte*.

_____ 2. A *firmament* should protect rather than expose.

_____ 3. *Fortitude* is the foremost attribute of a coward.

_____ 4. An *extemporaneous* performance is done with little or no preparation.

_____ 5. Often, a variety of *infirmities* accompany old age.

_____ 6. To *corroborate* a story is to prove it false.

_____ 7. Gymnasts generally look quite *robust*.

_____ 8. The people who grew up with you are your *contemporaries*.

_____ 9. You would normally expect a lion tamer's *forte* to be tightrope walking.

_____ 10. For the most part, pessimists are very *affirmative* fellows.

DEFINITION REPLACEMENT

_____ 1. Benjamin Franklin was a famous [*a person living in the same time period as another*] of George Washington.

_____ 2. Liquor does not really [*to make stronger*] the body against cold weather.

_____ 3. No one will [*to confirm*] the fact that I attended every class session for the entire quarter.

_____ 4. The Star Wars defense system is supposed to provide a huge [*any protective cover*] to save the country from nuclear attack.

_____ 5. Everyone answered in the [*a word indicating agreement*].

_____ 6. Douglas suffers from a mysterious [*a frailty or defect*] of unknown origin.

_____ 7. More than [*strength of character*] will be required to face that mob.

_____ 8. We made an [*without preparation*] effort, but not much came of it.

_____ 9. Max does everything [*loudly or forcefully*], full-speed and stereo-phonic.

_____ 10. Our middle linebacker is as [*powerfully built*] as a gorilla.

FILL-IN AND PART-OF-SPEECH IDENTIFICATION

____ 1. We were all surprised when someone in such apparent _____ health was suddenly struck down by a virus.

____ 2. I do not really have a _____ of any kind; I am what you might call a generalist at life.

____ 3. Life itself is _____; we do not get a chance to practice or rehearse before living it.

____ 4. A considerable amount of _____ is required to stick it out for four years in college.

____ 5. Shirley has an _____ attitude; she is always confident, optimistic, and upbeat.

____ 6. The televangelist said that we should _____ our souls against the devil through constant prayer.

____ 7. I cannot _____ your story until you explain what lies I must tell.

____ 8. An arthritic foot was the _____ that put the tennis star out of action.

_____ 9. A few thousand years ago, many humans believed that a _____ shielded the flat earth like a dome or vault.

_____ 10. Although I like _____ furniture, my sister prefers traditional.

MATCHING

_____ 1. extemporaneous
_____ 2. fortitude
_____ 3. affirmative
_____ 4. robust
_____ 5. firmament
_____ 6. forte
_____ 7. contemporary
_____ 8. infirmity
_____ 9. corroborate
_____ 10. fortify

a. alive at the same time; modern

b. one's strong point

c. strength of character

d. to confirm or make stronger

e. a defect or frailty

f. to establish a defense and make stronger

g. showing strength, confidence, and optimism

h. without time for preparation; impromptu

i. strong, healthy, and vigorous

j. a protective cover

BONUS ROOT

tempor (time): contemporaneous, contretemps, extemporize, pro tem, tempo, temporal, temporary, temporize

Words from Roots (26)

The Greek roots *lex* and *log(ue)* and the Latin root *verb* all mean "word." *Lex(i)* also means "phrase" or "saying." A *lexicon* (LEK-sə-kahn) is a word list or dictionary. A *dialogue* includes an exchange of spoken words. *Logic* is the science or art of speech and reason. To quote *verbatim* is to quote word for word. A *neologism,* as we have already learned, is a new word or an old word used in a new way.

WORD LIST

1. ana*logy* (ə-NAL-ə-jee), *n*: a reasoned comparison indicating similarities between two things not usually considered alike, as between the passing of a single year and the entire life of a person—often expressed with "like" or "as"

2. dys*lexia* (dis-LEK-see-ə), *n*: a brain dysfunction causing an individual to see written words as scrambled letters

3. eu*logize* (YUW-lə-*jiyz*), *v*: to speak or write words of approval, as about a person; to praise

4. *lexi*cographer (*lek*-sə-KAHG-rə-fər), *n*: a person who compiles or writes dictionaries

5. *logo*rrhea (*lo*-gə-REE-ə), *n*: an excessive flow of words; talkativeness—often used humorously

*6. *mari*time (MAR-ə-*tiym*), *a*: on, near, or living close to the sea; related to navigation or shipping; characteristic of sailors; nautical

7. pro*logue* (PROW-*log*), *n*: introductory portion of a written work or an oral presentation; something that comes before and leads to something else

8. pro*verb* (PRAH-*vurb*), *n*: a brief saying expressing some commonly held truth, as "Haste makes waste."

---

a (fat); ay (fate); ah (far); au (doubt); ch (church); e (elf, bed, care); ee (equal); ə (about); hw (while); i (fit); iy (kite); ŋ (link, sing); o (audio, corn); ow (ocean); oo (book); oi (oil); sh (shoe, ambition); th (think); u (up, deter); uw (ooze); y (yes, onion); yu (bureau, cure); yuw (youth, unity); zh (pleasure)

9. *verbalize* (VUR-bə-*liyz*), *v*: to express in spoken words, sometimes to excess; to use a word that is not a verb as if it were one, as "We must *sequence* our activities."

10. *verbose* (vər-BOWS), *a*: using or containing more words than are necessary; long-winded

TRUE-FALSE

_____ 1. A *prologue* is the same thing as a postscript.

_____ 2. To *eulogize* is to criticize harshly.

_____ 3. A person who is chronically *verbose* may be developing a case of *logorrhea*.

_____ 4. A *lexicographer* should know a great deal about words.

_____ 5. To *verbalize* is to express in spoken words.

_____ 6. The purpose of an *analogy* is to point out previously unnoticed differences between two things.

_____ 7. "Hope deferred makes the heart sick" is a *proverb*.

_____ 8. *Maritime* is synonymous with daylight savings time.

_____ 9. A person with *dyslexia* has trouble hearing clearly.

_____ 10. The main symptom of *logorrhea* is running off at the mouth.

DEFINITION REPLACEMENT

_____ 1. A [*one who compiles dictionaries*] who has dyslexia is a glutton for punishment.

_____ 2. The [*introductory portion of a work*] to this book is almost fifty pages long.

_____ 3. The mind takes to [*a reasoned comparison indicating similarities*] like a duck to water.

_____ 4. Did you understand the point of that [*a brief saying expressing a commonly held truth*]?

_____ 5. Apparently there is no effective vaccine against [*an excessive flow of words*].

_____ 6. If we [*to express in spoken words*] our fears, will they go away?

_____ 7. [*A brain dysfunction causing written words to appear scrambled*] is more common among left-handed people than among right-handed people.

_____ 8. I am articulate, but you are [*using more words than necessary*].

_____ 9. The [*related to navigation or shipping*] union failed to ratify the new contract.

_____ 10. I cannot [*to praise with good words*] someone I have never heard of.

FILL-IN AND PART-OF-SPEECH IDENTIFICATION

_____ 1. _____ seems to be a malady of television sportscasters, who insist on overexplaining everything that happens on the field.

_____ 2. Whether he is dead or not, how can you _____ such a bona fide scoundrel?

_____ 3. Noah Webster was America's first great _____.

_____ 4. Pirates are a part of _____ folklore.

_____ 5. Some people _____ too much, especially those suffering from logorrhea.

_____ 6. "Not studying at college is like buying a round-the-world plane ticket and then staying home" is an example of an _____, not a proverb.

_____ 7. Hidden among the unnecessary words of the _____ response was a fairly decent answer.

_____ 8. "A penny saved is a penny earned" is a _____ rendered meaningless by inflation and the federal tax system.

_____ 9. A student in my history class, as a result of having _____, reads very slowly.

_____ 10. In a way, youth is the _____ to life.

MATCHING

_____ 1. lexicographer   a. to praise someone in speech or writing

_____ 2. proverb   b. characteristic of sailors

_____ 3. analogy   c. running off at the mouth

_____ 4. verbalize   d. a person who writes dictionaries

_____ 5. logorrhea   e. an introduction to a written work

_____ 6. dyslexia   f. a reasoned comparison, often using "like" or "as"

_____ 7. verbose   g. to express in words

_____ 8. eulogize   h. long-winded

_____ 9. prologue   i. a brief saying expressing a commonly held truth

_____ 10. maritime   j. a brain dysfunction causing words to appear scrambled

BONUS ROOT

mar (sea, pool): aquamarine, mal de mer, marina, marinade, marinate, marine, mariner, marsh, marshy, mere, mermaid, merman, submarine, ultramarine

Words from Roots (27)

In classical times, ordinary people were not so highly regarded as they are today. The masses were often viewed as a rabble and of less innate worth than the ruling class or aristocracy. The Greek root *dem(o)*, meaning "people," comes to us in such words as *democrat, democracy,* and *pandemic* (pan-DEM-ik). Similarly, the Latin root *popul* means "people" and comes to us in such words as *popular* and *population.* Greek democracy, however, included only official citizens, not the masses, who were slaves. In Roman times, and even today, that which is popular may be defined as "of the common people." A popular entertainment is one enjoyed by ordinary people. Two additional Latin roots that specifically mean "common people" are *pleb* and *vulg*. Today a *plebe* is a freshman at the U.S. Naval Academy or Military Academy, and that which is *vulgar* is so called because it is without taste, refinement, or culture—that is, characteristic of the common people viewed as low or base.

WORD LIST

1. *dem*agogue (DEM-ə-*gahg*), *n*: in ancient times, a leader of the common people; today, a leader who will resort to virtually any tactic to maintain power over people

2. *dem*ographic (*dem*-ə-GRAF-ik), *a*: related to the (statistical) study of human populations, their density, distribution, and so on

3. di*vulg*e (di-VULJ), *v*: to make known, as to the common people

4. en*dem*ic (en-DEM-ik), *a*: native to a particular region or people; constantly present

*5. in*anim*ate (in-AN-ə-mit), *a*: possessing neither life nor spirit; not alive

6. *pleb*eian (pli-BEE-ən), *n*: one of the common people; a coarse or vulgar person; *a*, of the common people; coarse or common

7. *pleb*iscite (PLEB-ə-*siyt*), *n*: a direct vote by the common people, as on an important political issue, to approve or disapprove government action

a (fat); ay (fate); ah (far); au (doubt); ch (church); e (elf, bed, care); ee (equal); ə (about); hw (while); i (fit); iy (kite); ŋ (link, sing); o (audio, corn); ow (ocean); oo (book); oi (oil); sh (shoe, ambition); th (think); u (up, deter); uw (ooze); y (yes, onion); yu (bureau, cure); yuw (youth, unity); zh (pleasure)

123

8. *popul*ace (PAHP-yə-lis), *n*: the masses; the common people; the population

9. *Popul*ist, *popul*ist (PAHP-yə-list), *n*: a member of the Populist Party; one who advocates equitable treatment for the common people; *a*, of the Populist Party; favoring the common people

10. *vulg*arism (VUL-gə-*riz*-əm), *n*: a nonstandard, coarse, or obscene expression or act

TRUE-FALSE

_____ 1. *Plebeian* tastes are common, even coarse.

_____ 2. Above all things, a *demagogue* craves power.

_____ 3. Today the *Populist* Party is one of the two major political parties in the United States.

_____ 4. An *endemic* characteristic is one that comes and goes.

_____ 5. In the United States, we do not normally conduct *plebiscites* at the national level.

_____ 6. The purpose of a *demographic* survey would likely be to learn the causes of acid rain.

_____ 7. All *vulgarisms* are verbal.

_____ 8. To *divulge* the truth is to hide it.

_____ 9. The *populace* of this country comprises a great mixture of peoples.

_____ 10. Rocks are *inanimate* objects, even pet rocks.

DEFINITION REPLACEMENT

_____ 1. The government will never [*to make known to the people*] the contents of this top secret document.

_____ 2. The candidate who goes against fundamental [*favoring the common people*] opinion risks rejection at the polls.

_____ 3. During the day, vampires are [*not alive*] creatures.

_____ 4. Sooner or later, the [*the masses or common people*] will rise up against a demagogue.

_____ 5. A [*one who wants to lead the people at any cost*] would not hesitate to try to fix an election.

_____ 6. When my brother uttered a [*a coarse expression*] at the dinner table, Mother scolded him sharply.

_____ 7. Bluegrass music is [*native to*] to the people of the Appalachian Mountains.

_____ 8. In their heart of hearts, would-be demagogues view the masses as [*coarse and common*] sheep.

_____ 9. Our system of electing a president is not really a national [*a direct vote by the common people*].

_____ 10. [*Related to the statistical study of population*] experts predict that by the twenty-first century white Anglo-Saxon males will be a minority in the United States.

FILL-IN AND PART-OF-SPEECH IDENTIFICATION

_____ 1. Hostility between Democrats and Republicans seems _____ to our political process.

_____ 2. I am such a populist that I favor a nationwide _____, a vote, for a national health system—no matter what the cost.

_____ 3. _____ studies show that our population is increasing more rapidly in the South and Southwest.

_____ 4. Quite naturally, _____ sentiments usually appeal to the populace.

_____ 5. Even though computers may be _____ pieces of machinery, some of them seem to have humanlike quirks.

_____ 6. I would call a Styrofoam headstone a _____ of the worst kind, obscene and offensive.

_____ 7. Adolf Hitler was probably the most sinister _____ of this century.

_____ 8. We are all members of the nation's _____, no matter what our occupation or ancestry might be.

_____ 9. If a passion for tacos is _____, then call me coarse and common at the dinner table.

_____ 10. If you _____ your encounter with an extraterrestrial, people will think you are crazy.

MATCHING

_____ 1. inanimate

_____ 2. divulge

_____ 3. populist

_____ 4. endemic

_____ 5. plebeian

_____ 6. populace

_____ 7. demagogue

_____ 8. plebiscite

_____ 9. vulgarism

_____ 10. demographic

a. related to the distribution of human population

b. coarse, common, or ordinary

c. a person who will do anything to maintain power over other people

d. one who advocates fair treatment for the common people

e. not alive

f. a popular vote of the people

g. a coarse or obscene expression

h. native to a particular people or region

i. the masses; the population

j. to make known to the populace in general

BONUS ROOT

anim (life, spirit, soul): animadversion, animal, animate, animated, animation, animosity, animus, equanimity, magnanimous, pusillanimous, unanimity, unanimous

Words from Roots (28)

Some roots, even though they do not have the same or perhaps even similar meanings, are so compatible that they almost beg to be considered together. The Greek roots *chron* and *meter* are two such roots. The first, *chron(o)*, means "time." A *chronic* complainer is someone who complains all the time. A *chronicle* is a record of events arranged in order of time. The second root, *meter, metr(o),* or *metry,* means "measure." An *altimeter* (al-TIM-ə-tər) measures altitude, and a *barometer* measures atmospheric pressure. The *metric* system is a decimal system of weights and measures, and *geometry* employs lines and shapes to measure space and distance relationships. These two roots are so compatible that they can be combined to produce the word *chronometer* (krə-NAHM-ə-tər), which is an instrument for measuring very precise periods of time.

WORD LIST

1. ana*chron*ism (ə-NAK-rə-*niz*-əm), *n*: (the representation of) anything out of its proper place in time or history

2. asym*metr*ical (*ay*-sə-ME-tri-kəl), *a*: without a measured balance; lacking balance of form or proportion

3. *chrono*graph (KRAHN-ə-*graf*), *n*: an instrument for measuring (and recording) brief periods of time; a digital clock or watch

4. *chrono*logical (*krahn*-ə-LAHJ-i-kəl), *a*: arranged in a time sequence, as by order of occurrence

5. *chrono*logy (krə-NAHL-ə-jee), *n*: the arrangement of events in chronological order of occurrence, or the events themselves

*6. *cryptic* (KRIP-tik), *a*: having a hidden or unclear meaning; baffling or mysterious

7. *metro*nome (ME-trə-*nowm*), *n*: a pendulum device that beats out (musical) tempo

a (fat); ay (fate); ah (far); au (doubt); ch (church); e (elf, bed, care); ee (equal); ə (about); hw (while); i (fit); iy (kite); ŋ (link, sing); o (audio, corn); ow (ocean); oo (book); oi (oil); sh (shoe, ambition); th (think); u (up, deter); uw (ooze); y (yes, onion); yu (bureau, cure); yuw (youth, unity); zh (pleasure)

8. para*meter* (pə-RAM-ə-tər), *n*: a constant factor or characteristic element, as in the statement, "Rapidly developing technology is one of the *parameters* of modern life."

9. syn*chron*ize (SIN-krə-*niyz*), *v*: to (cause to) occur at the same time; to make simultaneous

10. tele*metry* (tə-LEM-ə-tree), *n*: the science or technology of automatic measurement and transmission of data from remote sources, as from outer space to earth

TRUE-FALSE

_____ 1. Any *chronological* arrangement is based on time.

_____ 2. *Metronomes* are tiny little creatures who compose classical music.

_____ 3. An *asymmetrical* pattern displays absolute balance and proportion.

_____ 4. To *synchronize* our watches is to set them together.

_____ 5. *Chronographs* measure the intensity of earthquakes.

_____ 6. A *cryptic* remark may well include a hidden meaning.

_____ 7. Modern systems of *telemetry* make extensive use of computers.

_____ 8. Mispronounced names are usually called *anachronisms*.

_____ 9. A *parameter* is the same thing as a perimeter.

_____ 10. A *chronology* records items in historical order.

DEFINITION REPLACEMENT

_____ 1. [*Digital watches*] were very popular a few years ago, but not so much now.

_____ 2. One [*a constant factor or element*] of a college student's life is uneasiness about classroom performance.

_____ 3. Whether we want to or not, we live our lives in [*arranged in a time sequence*] order.

_____ 4. Because of the many time zones on earth, you can never [*to make simultaneous*] all the clocks in the world.

_____ 5. The [*events arranged in order of occurrence*] of human civilization is only about four or five thousand years long.

_____ 6. At one time or another, every student of the piano has used a [*a pendulum device that beats out musical tempo*].

_____ 7. Today, a woman who stays at home to take care of the house and rear six or eight children is an [*anything out of its time in history*].

_____ 8. Without a sophisticated system of [*the technology of the transmission of data from remote sources*], space flight would not be possible.

_____ 9. It is not a good idea to be [*having a hidden or unclear meaning*] when you write for a general audience.

_____ 10. Such an [*lacking balance or proportion*] placement of the furniture left the room looking lopsided.

FILL-IN AND PART-OF-SPEECH IDENTIFICATION

_____ 1. Instead of being written in _____ order, some novels move back and forth in time.

_____ 2. In a way, the sun is the earth's _____; it measures out the tempo of the passing days and seasons.

_____ 3. The Becksons are living _____; their house has neither electricity nor plumbing.

_____ 4. Because of a faulty system of _____, communications were cut off, and the spaceship was lost.

_____ 5. At the back of my history text is a basic _____ of American history, a chronological listing of major events.

_____ 6. Change is one of the _____ of a high-tech society; it is always present, day by day.

_____ 7. I can never _____ my study habits with the instructor's test schedule.

_____ 8. I know the bowl is _____; I am still inexperienced at the potter's wheel.

_____ 9. The remark was so _____ that no one in the audience understood it.

_____ 10. Our cross-country coach does not need a _____ to check the times of the runners; a sundial will do.

MATCHING

_____ 1. chronograph   a. a list of events arranged in chronological order

_____ 2. telemetry   b. to make happen at the same time

_____ 3. asymmetrical   c. a digital clock or watch

_____ 4. chronology   d. baffling or mysterious; hidden

_____ 5. parameter   e. a device for measuring musical tempo

_____ 6. cryptic   f. arranged in a time sequence

_____ 7. anachronism   g. lacking balance of form or proportion

_____ 8. metronome   h. a system of the measurement and transmission of data from a distant source

_____ 9. synchronize

_____ 10. chronological   i. a constant factor or element

j. anything out of its usual place in time

BONUS ROOT

crypt(o) (hidden): Apocrypha, apocryphal, crypt, cryptogram, cryptographer, cryptography, decryption, encryption, krypton

Words from Roots (29)

Three Latin roots of similar construction denote family relationships. The first is *frater(n)* or *fratr,* which means "brother." The second is *mater(n)* or *matr,* which means "mother." And the third is *pater(n)* or *patr,* which means "father." Thus, a *fraternity* is literally a group of brothers. *Maternity* is the state of being a mother. And *paternity* is the state of being a father. You may notice that modern usage has dissolved the gender limitations on some words formerly used to refer only to men.

WORD LIST

1. alma *mater* (AL-mə MAHT-ər), *n:* literally, one's fostering mother; the school, college, or university that one has attended or from which one has graduated; the school anthem

2. con*fratern*ity (*kahn*-frə-TUR-nə-tee), *n:* a group of people joined together for some common purpose, or the bond itself that joins them

3. *frater*nize (FRAT-ər-*niyz*), *v:* to associate or socialize with, as in a brotherly fashion; to be friendly with

4. *fratr*icide (FRA-trə-*siyd*), *n:* the killing of one's own brother; someone who commits such an act

5. *matr*iarch (MAY-tree-*ahrk*), *n:* a woman who rules, as in a family, tribe, clan, or other group

6. *matr*iculate (mə-TRIK-yə-*layt*), *v:* to enroll, as in a college or university—which then becomes one's alma mater

7. *patern*alism (pə-TUR-nə-*liz*-əm), *n:* a policy or practice of treating people or controlling situations with a strong and stereotypically fatherly hand

8. *patr*ician (pə-TRISH-ən), *n:* a person of the higher or ruling class; *a,* noble, cultured, or aristocratic

---

a (f*a*t); ay (f*a*te); ah (f*a*r); au (d*ou*bt); ch (*ch*urch); e (*e*lf, b*e*d, c*a*re); ee (*e*qual); ə (*a*bout); hw (*wh*ile); i (f*i*t); iy (k*i*te); ŋ (li*n*k, si*ng*); o (*au*dio, c*or*n); ow (*o*cean); oo (b*oo*k); oi (*oi*l); sh (*sh*oe, ambi*ti*on); th (*th*ink); u (*u*p, de*te*r); uw (*oo*ze); y (*y*es, on*i*on); yu (b*u*reau, c*u*re); yuw (*y*outh, *u*nity); zh (plea*s*ure)

9. *patron* (PAY·trən), *n*: one who supports, protects, or encourages another or others—often with money; a regular customer

*10. *veracity* (və·RAS·ə·tee), *n*: precision in sticking to the truth; truthfulness; absolute accuracy

TRUE-FALSE

_____ 1. A *patrician* is a landless Roman peasant.

_____ 2. Only mothers can sing an *alma mater*.

_____ 3. To question one's *veracity* is to question one's truthfulness.

_____ 4. A *matriarch* is an ancient sailing vessel.

_____ 5. A *confraternity* of people may include women as well as men.

_____ 6. Corporate *paternalism* has often opposed organized labor.

_____ 7. In a sense, the murder of any human being is *fratricide*.

_____ 8. To *matriculate* at college is to withdraw from school and join the navy.

_____ 9. A *patron* of the arts supports the arts.

_____ 10. To *fraternize* is to try to cause trouble in the family.

DEFINITION REPLACEMENT

_____ 1. We expected a person with royal blood to have a more [*noble or aristocratic*] view of life.

_____ 2. In college we [*to associate with*] with a greater variety of people than we did at home.

_____ 3. A local [*a group of people joined for a common purpose*] of attorneys defended the migrant workers.

_____ 4. With absolute [*precision in sticking to the truth*], Brenda repeated what she had witnessed.

_____ 5. This [*a person who kills a brother*] did not even bother to answer the charges.

_____ 6. Until I ran out of hair, I was a longtime [*a regular customer*] of the Bonzo Barbershop.

_____ 7. Only a few people actually knew the words to the [*a school anthem*].

_____ 8. From 1558 to 1603, Queen Elizabeth I was the [*a woman who rules a country*] of England.

_____ 9. Your inclination toward [*a practice of controlling people with a firm hand*] is not much appreciated by your employees.

_____ 10. If you [*to enroll in a college*] too late in the summer, your choice of classes may be limited.

FILL-IN AND PART-OF-SPEECH IDENTIFICATION

_____ 1. _____ on a grand scale can become genocide.

_____ 2. Almost anyone can _____ at a state university, now that colleges are competing for students.

_____ 3. Choose your college carefully because it will be your _____ forever.

_____ 4. Your _____ tastes are too expensive for your middle-class income.

_____ 5. Although I do not question your motives, I do question your _____; you are misinformed.

_____ 6. A _____ of Christian athletes dedicated to improving the quality of student life on campus conducted the program.

_____ 7. _____ has gone out of style when it comes to anything as complex as running a large university; the job is simply too big for one person to make all the decisions.

133

_____ 8. My great-grandmother, the _____ who ruled both sides of the family, never learned to read.

_____ 9. Although only moderately wealthy, Mrs. Forster is a _____ of both the little theater and the children's hospital.

_____ 10. My friends have suggested that I not _____ with such shady characters.

MATCHING

_____ 1. fraternize

_____ 2. veracity

_____ 3. alma mater

_____ 4. matriarch

_____ 5. patron

_____ 6. confraternity

_____ 7. paternalism

_____ 8. fratricide

_____ 9. patrician

_____ 10. matriculate

a. a group of people joined together for some common purpose

b. to enroll, as at a college

c. to associate with in a friendly manner

d. noble, cultured, or aristocratic

e. the practice of controlling people with a strong, fatherly hand

f. a woman who rules a family

g. absolute truthfulness

h. a regular customer

i. the school from which one has graduated

j. someone who kills a brother

BONUS ROOT

ver(i) (true): aver, veracious, verdict, verifiable, verification, verify, verily, verisimilar, verisimilitude, veritable, veritas, very

Words from Roots (30)

Three similar physical motions are indicated by the Latin roots *flect, tort,* and *vert.* The first, *flect* or *flex,* means "to bend." That which is *flexible* can be bent. To *deflect* a blow is to bend it to one side. To *genuflect* (JEN·yə·*flekt*) is to bend the knee. The second root, *tort,* means "to twist." Originally, *torture* featured a twisting of the victim's arms and legs. To *distort* a statement is to twist its meaning. *Contortionists* are able to twist their bodies and limbs into strange positions. The third root, *vert* or *vers,* means "to turn." If you *reverse* yourself, you turn back. To *divert* attention from yourself is to turn it away. An *adversary* is someone who has turned against you.

WORD LIST

1. ad*vers*ity (ad·VUR·sə·tee), *n:* a situation wherein things have turned bad; a condition of trouble, poverty, misfortune, and the like

2. a*vert* (ə·VURT), *v:* to turn away, to keep from taking place; to prevent or ward off

*3. *clam*orous (KLAM·ər·əs), *a:* characterized by continuous loud and complaining voices; noisy complaining; insistent

4. dis*tort*ion (dis·TOR·shən), *n:* a twisting out of normal shape, form, or appearance; a misrepresentation, as of the facts

5. ex*tort*ion (ik·STOR·shən), *n:* literally, twisting money out of someone, as by threats, violence, or trickery

6. in*flect*ion (in·FLEK·shən), *n:* a slight change (bending) in tone or modulation of the voice, as in a point of emphasis

7. in*flex*ible (in·FLEK·sə·bəl), *a:* difficult to bend or be bent; firm to the point of being stubborn or unyielding

8. per*vert*ed (pər·VUR·tid), *a:* turned away from that which is considered sensible, good, right, or proper

---

a (*fat*); ay (*fate*); ah (*far*); au (*doubt*); ch (*church*); e (*elf, bed, care*); ee (*equal*); ə (*about*); hw (*while*); i (*fit*); iy (k*i*te); ŋ (li*nk*, si*ng*); o (*audio, corn*); ow (*ocean*); oo (b*ook*); oi (*oil*); sh (*shoe,* ambi*tion*); th (*think*); u (*up,* de*ter*); uw (*ooze*); y (*yes,* on*i*on); yu (b*u*reau, c*u*re); yuw (*youth, unity*); zh (*pleasure*)

135

9. sub*ver*sive (səb-VUR-siv), *a*: intending to overturn or destroy established institutions or beliefs; *n*, a person regarded as subversive

10. *tortu*ous (TOR-chə-wəs), *a*: characterized by much twisting; crooked; indirect, and thus devious, deceitful, or tricky; highly involved

TRUE-FALSE

_____ 1. A *clamorous* complaint is a long and loud one.

_____ 2. Interest paid on money in the bank, especially if it is quite high, is called *extortion*.

_____ 3. To a demagogue, the truth can seem *subversive*.

_____ 4. *Adversity* is something almost everyone enjoys.

_____ 5. *Inflections* of the voice may be thought of as verbal punctuation marks.

_____ 6. Diplomats should always be *inflexible*.

_____ 7. To *avert* danger is to seek it out or to train for it.

_____ 8. *Tortuous* logic is always straightforward, direct, and to the point.

_____ 9. A *distortion* of the truth is a misrepresentation of it.

_____ 10. *Perverted* thinking can turn logic on its ear.

DEFINITION REPLACEMENT

_____ 1. The college is guilty of [*twisting money out of someone by trickery*] when it charges students a matriculation fee to be used to renovate the fieldhouse.

_____ 2. The [*characterized by continuous loud complaining*] protests by the students were ignored by the city council.

_____ 3. Only [*turned away from that which is right*] justice would allow a convicted murderer to go free on a technicality of courtroom procedure.

_____ 4. Surely we can think of a less [*devious, deceitful, or tricky*] way to accomplish our goal.

_____ 5. So far, the greatest [*a situation wherein things have turned bad*] of my life occurred when my parents divorced.

_____ 6. Are college teachers being [*intending to destroy established beliefs*] when they challenge ideas held by students?

_____ 7. Your [*a twisting of the facts*] of the situation fooled no one.

_____ 8. The witness spoke without noticeable [*a change in the modulation of the voice*] and without emotion.

_____ 9. The company will never [*to keep from taking place*] a strike now.

_____ 10. Such an [*unable to be bent*] material is likely to snap under pressure.

FILL-IN AND PART-OF-SPEECH IDENTIFICATION

_____ 1. Such _____ developed in the sound system that the music became unrecognizable.

_____ 2. The convicted child abuser, who said he felt no remorse, displayed a _____ attitude about the rearing of children.

_____ 3. Especially for the young, the death of a sibling is always an _____, a very great misfortune.

_____ 4. Both sides promised not to be _____ in the negotiations, but to bend to compromise.

_____ 5. We cannot _____ all the adversities of life; some of them will not be turned aside.

_____ 6. The directions for putting this thing together are intentionally _____ _____; they are devious and tricky beyond belief.

_____ 7. Convicted on a dozen counts of _____, the accused admitted tricking retired people out of their savings.

_____ 8. I would call a secret organization that wants to overthrow the government

_____. Wouldn't you?

_____ 9. After a while, such _____ complaining becomes tiring; the insistent noise is just too much.

_____ 10. Just from the _____ of your voice, I can tell that you are keeping something from me.

MATCHING

_____ 1. clamorous   a. a condition of trouble or misfortune

_____ 2. perverted   b. stubborn and unyielding

_____ 3. inflexible   c. intending to overthrow established order

_____ 4. avert   d. a modulation of the voice

_____ 5. tortuous   e. characterized by loud and complaining voices

_____ 6. extortion   f. turned away from what is good, right, or proper

_____ 7. subversive   g. a twisting out of normal shape or form

_____ 8. adversity   h. the twisting of money out of someone, as by threats

_____ 9. inflection   i. devious, deceitful, or tricky

_____ 10. distortion   j. to turn away or prevent

BONUS ROOT

clam, claim (to cry out): acclaim, acclamation, claim, claimant, clamor, declamatory, disclaim, disclaimer, exclaim, exclamation, exclamatory, proclaim, proclamation, reclaim

Words from Roots (31)

The root *gen* comes to us from both Latin and Greek and has several related meanings: "cause" or "origin," "birth" or "breeding," "kind" or "species," and "race." To *generate* is to cause to come into being. Our *genes* are the blueprint for our physical makeup. The *gentry* are people of good or high breeding. *Nitrogen* is a gas so called because it is a component of all living things. *Genetics* is the science of heredity. *Genocide*, as we have already learned, is the systematic extermination of an entire ethnic group.

WORD LIST

1. congenital (kən·JEN·ə·təl), *a*: existing at or present from birth; inherent

2. eugenics (yuw·JEN·iks), *n*: the study of improving the heredity of the human (or other) species through genetic control

3. *generic* (jə·NER·ik), *a*: of a general kind, class, or group; not protected by a trademark

4. *genesis* (JEN·ə·sis), *n*: the beginning, birth, or origin of anything; the cause of the beginning of something

5. *genial* (JEE·nyəl, JEE·nee·əl), *a*: promoting life and growth, and thus warm, friendly, and sympathetic; amiable

6. *genre* (ZHAHN·rə), *n*: a specific type or kind, as a literary work or work of art

7. homogenize (hə·MAHJ·ə·niyz), *v*: to make all of the same kind; to make uniform and consistent throughout

*8. incorporate (in·KOR·pə·rayt), *v*: to make into one body; to combine with something already existing; to form a corporation; to merge or unite

9. ingenuous (in·JEN·yə·wəs), *a*: literally, freeborn, and thus frank and honest; open and candid, but in a simple or childlike way; naive or gullible

10. progeny (PRAHJ·ə·nee), *n*: the collective offspring of anything, and thus the children, descendants, or followers of; the result

---

a (fat); ay (fate); ah (far); au (doubt); ch (church); e (elf, bed, care); ee (equal); ə (about); hw (while); i (fit); iy (kite); ŋ (link, sing); o (audio, corn); ow (ocean); oo (book); oi (oil); sh (shoe, ambition); th (think); u (up, deter); uw (ooze); y (yes, onion); yu (bureau, cure); yuw (youth, unity); zh (pleasure)

TRUE-FALSE

_____ 1. *Generic* drugs are not protected by a trademark.

_____ 2. To *homogenize* milk is to freeze it, so all the bacteria will die.

_____ 3. To *incorporate* ideas is to distinguish between them.

_____ 4. *Ingenuous* persons are easily taken advantage of.

_____ 5. A *genial* disposition is warm, friendly, and amiable.

_____ 6. *Congenital* traits are always peculiar in nature.

_____ 7. The *progeny* of apes will be more apes.

_____ 8. The purpose of *eugenics* is to reduce the cost of rearing children in urban areas.

_____ 9. A *genre* is a French policeman.

_____ 10. The *genesis* of anything is its conclusion.

DEFINITION REPLACEMENT

_____ 1. In such a [*promoting life and growth*] climate, it is impossible not to have a nice garden.

_____ 2. The village will never [*to form a corporation*] itself and become a legal city.

_____ 3. The [*the beginning, birth, or origin*] of the Arab-Israeli conflict occurred thousands of years ago.

_____ 4. Shopping malls [*to make all the same*] climatic conditions throughout the year.

_____ 5. The movie was just another horror flick, typical of its [*a specific type or kind*].

_____ 6. My beard is not [*present at birth*]; I grew it in high school.

_____ 7. Four years of college often change the [*frank and honest, but childlike*] expression on a student's face.

_____ 8. Those dedicated to [*the study of improving heredity*] always seem to want to make what is good even better.

_____ 9. Yuppies are the [*the collective offspring*] of the post–World War II baby boom.

_____ 10. The [*of a general kind, class, or group*] soups contain less sodium than the brand-name ones we used to buy.

FILL-IN AND PART-OF-SPEECH IDENTIFICATION

_____ 1. With the development of bioengineering and cloning, _____ will likely become an important field in the future.

_____ 2. Such an _____ reply could come only from a person with the mind of a child.

_____ 3. The _____ of each day is sunrise.

_____ 4. We are the _____ of our ancestors, the offspring and descendants.

_____ 5. We should _____ as much traditional Americana into our new sales campaign as possible.

_____ 6. If in the future, through eugenics, we _____ society, everyone will be just alike. How boring!

_____ 7. What a _____ chap Osgood is—warm, friendly, and amiable. I wonder what is wrong with him.

_____ 8. Freedom of speech was a _____ right in this country, present almost from the birth of the nation.

_____ 9. The novella is a different literary _____ from the short story, a completely different type of work.

_____ 10. I have found that _____ shredded wheat tastes more like the box than it does brand-name shredded wheat. But, then, I save a nickel.

MATCHING

_____ 1. genesis   a. the science of improving heredity

_____ 2. progeny   b. to make all of the same kind

_____ 3. incorporate   c. the beginning, birth, or origin or something

_____ 4. genial   d. of a general kind, class, or group

_____ 5. homogenize   e. a specific type or kind

_____ 6. congenital   f. the collective offspring of anything

_____ 7. genre   g. to make into one body

_____ 8. eugenics   h. naive and gullible

_____ 9. ingenuous   i. promoting life and growth; friendly

_____ 10. generic   j. existing or present from birth

BONUS ROOT

corp(or) (body): corporal, corporation, corporeal, corps, corpse, corpulent, corpus, corpuscle, corsage, corset

Words from Roots (32)

Because the root *gen* is so widely used in modern English, this sequence includes nine additional derivatives. Keep in mind the many related meanings of the root. A *genus* is a classification of plants or animals having common distinguishing characteristics. *Biogenesis* (*biy*-ow-JEN-ə-sis), as we learned, involves the *generation* of living organisms from other similar organisms. A *gentleman* is a man of good or high birth. *Genealogy* (*jee*-nee-AHL-ə-jee) is the study of family descent from one generation to the next.

WORD LIST

1. carcino*gen* (kahr-SIN-ə-jen), *n*: any substance that causes cancer, the first part of the term coming from the Greek word for crab or cancer

2. de*gen*erate (di-JEN-ər-it), *a*: characteristic of a lower type or kind; having declined from a former or normal state or condition; degraded; *n*, a morally corrupt person; (di-JEN-ə-*rayt*), *v*: to decline or lose former good qualities

3. disin*gen*uous (*dis*-ən-JEN-yə-wəs), *a*: presenting a false appearance of simple frankness and sincerity while actually being devious and insincere; lacking candor

4. en*gen*der (in-JEN-dər), *v*: to bring into being; to cause to exist; to give rise to

5. *gen*eralization (*jen*-ər-ə-lə-ZAY-shən), *n*: an inclusive statement that originates from an observation of specific details; the statement of a broad principle

6. *gen*teel (jen-TEEL), *a*: displaying qualities of good breeding, politeness, manners, and taste—sometimes used humorously

7. indi*gen*ous (in-DIJ-ə-nəs), *a*: native to a particular region; existing naturally; inborn

*8. mis*anthrop*ic (*mis*-ən-THRAHP-ik), *a*: like a misanthrope, a person who hates or distrusts everyone; always showing contempt for humankind

---

a (f*a*t); ay (f*a*te); ah (f*a*r); au (d*ou*bt); ch (*ch*ur*ch*); e (*e*lf, b*e*d, c*a*re); ee (*e*qual); ə (*a*bout); hw (*wh*ile); i (f*i*t); iy (k*i*te); ŋ (li*n*k, si*ng*); o (*au*dio, c*o*rn); ow (*o*cean); oo (b*oo*k); oi (*oi*l); sh (*sh*oe, ambi*ti*on); th (*th*ink); u (*u*p, de*te*r); uw (*oo*ze); y (*y*es, on*i*on); yu (b*u*reau, c*u*re); yuw (*you*th, *u*nity); zh (plea*s*ure)

9. primo*geni*ture (*priy*-mə-JEN-ə-chər), *n*: the state of being the firstborn child of the same parents; the practice of most or all of the inheritance going to the firstborn son

10. pro*geni*tor (prow-JEN-ə-tər), *n*: a direct ancestor of a line of descent; the ultimate source or origin of something; the originator

TRUE-FALSE

_____ 1. To *engender* anger is to avert it.

_____ 2. *Indigenous* art is native to a particular part of the country.

_____ 3. Caring for the needy is a *misanthropic* activity.

_____ 4. *Genteel* people would never pick their teeth at the dinner table.

_____ 5. A *progenitor* produces progeny.

_____ 6. To *degenerate* is to improve dramatically.

_____ 7. *Primogeniture* involves an equal distribution of an estate among its heirs.

_____ 8. A *disingenuous* smile is the opposite of an ingenuous one.

_____ 9. The presentation of a specific example is called a *generalization*.

_____ 10. *Carcinogens* are used by physicians to prevent cancer.

DEFINITION REPLACEMENT

_____ 1. No one wants a [*a morally corrupt person*] as mayor of the village.

_____ 2. You cannot pretend to be [*displaying qualities of politeness and refinement*] and at the same time use double negatives.

_____ 3. It would appear that almost everything consumed in excess is a [*any substance that causes cancer*] these days.

144

_____ 4. The news media are sometimes [*lacking candor*] when they say that the public has a right to know.

_____ 5. Some would disagree with the [*an inclusive statement that originates from specific details*] "The greatest good is one that benefits the greatest number."

_____ 6. Elephants are [*native to a particular region*] to parts of Africa.

_____ 7. [*The practice of all the inheritance going to the firstborn son*] is not the law of the land in the United States.

_____ 8. Johnny Carson was not the [*the originator*] of the television talk show.

_____ 9. You [*to give rise to*] hostility by being hostile.

_____ 10. Air-lifting hundreds of tons of food to famine-stricken Ethiopia was hardly a [*showing contempt for humankind*] enterprise.

FILL-IN AND PART-OF-SPEECH IDENTIFICATION

_____ 1. Some social critics argue that the _____ state of the traditional American family, greatly declined from a generation or two ago, is the genesis of many of our current social problems.

_____ 2. Traditional Christianity teaches that God is the _____ of the human race, indeed of all creatures great and small.

_____ 3. Such _____ sentiments suggest that you have never met a person you either like or trust.

_____ 4. A _____ has little weight unless it is supported by specific evidence.

_____ 5. Life seems less _____ than it once was; so few people are polite or mannerly.

_____ 6. The little duchy's tradition of _____ gives all the family's wealth to the oldest son upon the death of his father.

_____ 7. Mountain music is _____ to West Virginia. It has long been native to the region.

_____ 8. Some people think a welfare state cannot possibly _____ a work ethic in its people.

_____ 9. Several of the substances in cigarette smoke are proven _____.

_____ 10. I see hypocrisy in your _____ pretense of supporting women's rights; you really want women to go quietly to work at minimum-wage jobs.

MATCHING

_____ 1. disingenuous

_____ 2. indigenous

_____ 3. primogeniture

_____ 4. degenerate

_____ 5. engender

_____ 6. genteel

_____ 7. misanthropic

_____ 8. generalization

_____ 9. progenitor

_____ 10. carcinogen

a. to bring into being

b. a substance that causes cancer

c. hating or distrusting all people

d. native to a particular region

e. an inclusive statement of an abstract principle

f. the direct ancestor or originator

g. lacking candor; insincere

h. the practice of all inheritance going to the firstborn son

i. displaying qualities of good breeding

j. a morally corrupt person; to decline

BONUS ROOT

anthrop(o) (man, human being): anthropocentric, anthropogenesis, anthropoid, anthropologist, anthropology, anthropomorphic, anthropomorphism, anthropopathy, anthropophagy, misanthrope, misanthropy, philanthropic, philanthropist, philanthropy

Words from Roots (33)

Light is something special, mandatory for life. According to the Biblical account of the Creation in the book of Genesis, God had to summon the light to make possible the creation of living things. The Greek root meaning "light" is *phot(o)* or *phos*. Such modern words as *phosphorus, phosphate, photograph,* and *photon* are obvious derivatives. Latin roots meaning "light" include *luc, lumin,* and *lus*. The last one actually means "to light." A *lucid* statement is a clear one. To *illuminate* a room is to turn the light on. And that which possesses *luster* glitters or shines.

WORD LIST

1. *elu*cidate (i-LUW-sə-*dayt*), *v*: to shed some light on a subject, as through clear explanation; to make clear

2. il*lus*trative (i-LUS-trə-tiv), *a*: illuminating by providing or serving as an example

3. *lumin*ary (LUW-mə-*ner*-ee), *n*: something that gives off light, as an object or star; a brilliant person, or one who enlightens others; any famous person; a celebrity

4. *lus*trous (LUS-trəs), *a*: radiant, either in fact or in character; bright, but without glitter; having a sheen; brilliant; splendid

5. pel*luc*id (pə-LUW-sid), *a*: admitting the maximum passage of light; extremely clear and easy to understand; transparent

6. *phos*phorescent (*fahs*-fə-RES-ənt), *a*: giving off a continuous glowing light but little heat; displaying lingering or declining *lumin*escence (*luw*-mə-NES-əns), or cold light

7. *photo*genic (*fow*-tə-JEN-ik), *a*: that photographs well, usually said of a person; suitable for photographing

8. *photo*mural (*fow*-tə-MYUR-əl), *n*: an enlarged photograph attached directly to the surface of a wall

---

a (fat); ay (fate); ah (far); au (doubt); ch (church); e (elf, bed, care); ee (equal); ə (about); hw (while); i (fit); iy (kite); ŋ (link, sing); o (audio, corn); ow (ocean); oo (book); oi (oil); sh (shoe, ambition); th (think); u (up, deter); uw (ooze); y (yes, onion); yu (bureau, cure); yuw (youth, unity); zh (pleasure)

9. trans*lucent* (trans-LUW-sənt), *a*: allowing light, but not a clear image, to pass through; partially transparent; indistinct

*10. veri*simil*itude (*ver-ə-si-MIL-ə-tuwd*), *n*: literally, a true likeness, and thus the quality of appearing to be true or real; something that appears authentic; plausibility

TRUE-FALSE

_____ 1. A *luminary* is a person who glows in the dark because of exposure to radioactivity.

_____ 2. *Photomurals* are found on walls.

_____ 3. People afraid of being *photographed* are said to be *photogenic*.

_____ 4. To *elucidate* is to explain clearly and precisely.

_____ 5. The flames of a fire are *phosphorescent*.

_____ 6. A *lustrous* performance is a splendid one.

_____ 7. The lenses in eyeglasses are usually *translucent*.

_____ 8. The achievement of *verisimilitude* is the usual goal of prayer.

_____ 9. That which is *illustrative* serves as an example.

_____ 10. A *pellucid* statement is almost impossible not to understand.

DEFINITION REPLACEMENT

_____ 1. The newly waxed floors look better than good; they look [*radiant or splendid*].

_____ 2. In the mountains we camped beside a [*extremely clear or transparent*] stream.

_____ 3. Nothing will give [*plausibility*] to this silly tale you have told.

_____ 4. Please [*to make clear*] the situation so that I will know what to do.

_____ 5. We are putting [*partially transparent*] glass in the solarium.

_____ 6. On summer nights, fireflies display a [*giving off a lingering light*] glow.

_____ 7. This situation is really [*serving as an example*] of nothing.

_____ 8. I am not [*that photographs well*]; the camera always adds twenty pounds to my delicate frame.

_____ 9. The distant [*something that gives off light*] turned out to be a campfire.

_____ 10. The wallpaper in the family room is actually a [*an enlarged photograph attached to a wall*] of Niagara Falls.

FILL-IN AND PART-OF-SPEECH IDENTIFICATION

_____ 1. I think you could call Barbra Streisand a _____ of the motion picture business.

_____ 2. After the spaceship landed, a _____ glow came out of the ground, producing an eerie light.

_____ 3. The frosted shower stall is _____; you cannot quite see through it.

_____ 4. Made of _____ satin, the blouse had a soft sheen.

_____ 5. The _____ at the public library is an aerial picture of the town taken just after World War II.

_____ 6. We must _____ our position in such a way that the average person will understand it.

_____ 7. The characters in the play possessed little _____; they were nothing at all like real people.

_____ 8. Such a _____ statement of the situation seemed to clear up half the problems we thought we were facing.

_____ 9. Most movie stars are _____; they look good on film.

_____ 10. The grammatical errors in your paper are _____ of your inexperience with language.

MATCHING

_____ 1. luminary   a. illuminating by providing an example

_____ 2. phosphorescent   b. a large photograph attached directly to a wall

_____ 3. translucent   c. a famous person; a celebrity

_____ 4. elucidate   d. that photographs well

_____ 5. pellucid   e. displaying lingering luminescence

_____ 6. verisimilitude   f. having a radiant sheen; brilliant

_____ 7. illustrative   g. to shed some light on by explaining

_____ 8. photogenic   h. plausibility

_____ 9. photomural   i. partially transparent

_____ 10. lustrous   j. extremely clear and easy to understand

BONUS ROOT

simil, simul (like, resembling): assimilate, assimilation, dissimilar, dissimilarity, facsimile, similar, similarity, simile, similitude, simulate, simulation, simulator, simultaneous, simultaneously

Words from Roots (34)

This sequence and the next consider four Latin roots, all beginning with the letter *t*, all having verb meanings, and all but one having multiple spellings. Each also has a good distribution of modern English derivatives. The first is *tang, tact, tig,* or *tag,* meaning "to touch." *Tangible* evidence is evidence that can be touched. To *contact* friends is to get in touch with them. You catch a *contagious* disease by touching someone who has it. The second *t*-root is *ten, tin,* or *tain,* which means "to hold." A *tenant* is one who holds a lease, as on an apartment. To *continue* means literally "to hold together." And to *detain* is to hold back or away.

WORD LIST

1. abs*tin*ence (AB·stə·nəns), *n*: a holding back, as from doing something or indulging oneself

2. con*tag*ion (kən·TAY·jən), *n*: the spreading of a disease among people who are in direct contact; such a disease; the spreading of anything, as an idea or emotion

3. con*tig*uous (kən·TIG·yə·wəs), *a*: touching on one side or at one point; adjacent or nearby

4. in*tang*ible (in·TAN·jə·bəl), *a*: that cannot be touched or held in the hand; without specific or definable value; *n,* anything with a value that cannot be specifically calculated

*5. *lite*rati (*lit-ə-RAH*-tee), *n*: collectively, the educated, or well-lettered, members of society; scholarly people

*6. ob*lite*rate (ə·BLIT·ə·*rayt*), *v*: literally, away from letters, and thus to strike out or erase words; to blot out, efface, or destroy altogether

7. *tact*ful (TAKT·fəl), *a*: possessing the right touch in handling difficult or complex situations; skillful in dealing with people

8. *ten*acious (tə·NAY·shəs), *a*: holding firmly; clinging or persistent

---

a (*fat*); ay (*fate*); ah (*far*); au (*doubt*); ch (*church*); e (*elf, bed, care*); ee (*equal*); ə (*about*); hw (*while*); i (*fit*); iy (*kite*); ŋ (*link, sing*); o (*audio, corn*); ow (*ocean*); oo (*book*); oi (*oil*); sh (*shoe, ambition*); th (*think*); u (*up, deter*); uw (*ooze*); y (*yes, onion*); yu (*bureau, cure*); yuw (*youth, unity*); zh (*pleasure*)

9. *tenure* (TEN-yər), *n*: the period of time that one holds a position; the status of holding a position on a permanent basis

10. un*ten*able (un-TEN-ə-bəl), *a*: that cannot be (logically) held, defended, or maintained

TRUE-FALSE

_____ 1. Hard cash is one of life's great *intangibles.*

_____ 2. To *obliterate* is to transcribe carefully on blank paper.

_____ 3. *Contagions* are likely to be infectious.

_____ 4. An *untenable* idea is one that no one is willing to challenge.

_____ 5. Nations *contiguous* to each other must always be at war.

_____ 6. *Tactful* individuals are skillful in dealing with others.

_____ 7. *Literati* are tiny letters too small to read.

_____ 8. My *tenure* as a teacher is the length of time I have been teaching.

_____ 9. *Abstinence* of any type requires a certain amount of self-control.

_____ 10. A *tenacious* fighter never gives up.

DEFINITION REPLACEMENT

_____ 1. People who produce music deal in an [*that cannot be touched or held in the hand*] product.

_____ 2. An athlete's [*the period of time that one holds a position*] in the major leagues is limited by age.

_____ 3. It was as if an angry [*the spreading of anything*] swept through the crowd.

_____ 4. We could never [*to remove altogether*] the scratches on the face of the monument.

_____ 5. A row of [*touching on one side*] houses was built where the old stadium used to be.

_____ 6. How [*skillful in handling difficult situations*] of you not to mention the unfortunate incident.

_____ 7. To be one of the [*educated or scholarly people*], you must read widely.

_____ 8. This bill is politically [*that cannot be defended*] because anyone who supports it will be voted out of office.

_____ 9. In this age of self-indulgence, [*a holding back from doing something*] of any type has gone out of style.

_____ 10. Margaret has a [*clinging or persistent*] memory, seldom forgetting anything.

FILL-IN AND PART-OF-SPEECH IDENTIFICATION

_____ 1. Each of the forty-eight _____ states of the United States touches one or more other states.

_____ 2. Simply stated, your position is _____; it cannot be supported, at least not by specific evidence.

_____ 3. Ida has an _____ quality about her, one that I cannot precisely define, but it makes her valuable to the company.

_____ 4. Franklin Roosevelt had a longer _____ in office than any other American president.

_____ 5. _____ is one hundred percent effective as a method of birth control; if you do not have sex, you will not produce babies.

_____ 6. Muriel is _____ on this point; she will never give it up.

_____ 7. Mostly members of the local _____ patronize this bookstore.

_____ 8. The _____ did not finally die out until everyone in the village had experienced a bout with the flu.

9. Please be _____ when dealing with your instructors; you want to avoid hurting their feelings or bruising their egos.

10. The passage of time will eventually _____ the unpleasant memory from your mind.

MATCHING

_____ 1. literati   a. a spreading disease

_____ 2. abstinence   b. touching, adjacent, or nearby

_____ 3. tactful   c. clinging or persistent

_____ 4. tenure   d. to blot out altogether

_____ 5. contiguous   e. a holding back, as from indulging oneself

_____ 6. tenacious   f. that cannot be held, defended, or maintained

_____ 7. intangible   g. the period of time one holds a position

_____ 8. untenable   h. well-lettered or scholarly people

_____ 9. contagion   i. skillful in dealing with people

_____ 10. obliterate   j. that cannot be touched

BONUS ROOT

liter(a) (letter): alliteration, alliterative, illiteracy, literacy, literal, literature, littérateur, semiliterate

Words from Roots (35)

The third *t*-root is *tend, tens,* or *tent,* meaning "to stretch." If you *contend* with a problem, you literally stretch yourself to it. *Tension* includes a stretching or straining, as of the mind and emotions. The canvas of a *tent* is stretched over the poles and ropes. To *extend* something is to stretch it out. The final *t*-root is *tract,* meaning "to drag" or "to draw." A *tractor* has big tires for better *traction,* so it can drag other pieces of machinery. To *extract* a tooth is to draw it out, and a *contract* occurs when two people draw up a bargain together.

WORD LIST

1. con*tent*ious (kən-TEN-shəs), *a*: literally, stretched out together, and thus always ready to argue, dispute, quarrel; including controversy or quarrelsomeness

2. dé*tente* (day-TAHNT), *n*: a movement away from tension; a relaxation of strained relations, as between nations

3. dis*tend*ed (dis-TEN-did), *a*: literally, stretched apart; enlarged or expanded, as from internal pressure

4. dis*tract*ion (dis-TRAK-shən), *n*: anything that draws the mind apart or away from what it is trying to concentrate on

*5. in*cred*ulous (in-KREJ-ə-ləs), *a*: not believing or unwilling to believe; showing doubt; skeptical

6. in*tract*able (in-TRAK-tə-bəl), *a*: not able to be drawn, and thus difficult to manage or keep in line; unruly

7. os*tens*ible (ah-STEN-sə-bəl), *a*: literally, stretched out before one, and thus seeming or apparent; professed; plausible

8. pre*tent*ious (pri-TEN-shəs), *a*: stretching out before, in the sense of making an elaborate or extravagant show; affecting distinction, excellence, grandness, dignity, importance, and so on

---

a (*fat*); ay (*fate*); ah (*far*); au (*doubt*); ch (*church*); e (*elf, bed, care*); ee (*equal*); ə (*about*); hw (*while*); i (*fit*); iy (*kite*); ŋ (*link, sing*); o (*audio, corn*); ow (*ocean*); oo (*book*); oi (*oil*); sh (*shoe, ambition*); th (*think*); u (*up, deter*); uw (*ooze*); y (*yes, onion*); yu (*bureau, cure*); yuw (*youth, unity*); zh (*pleasure*)

9. pro*tract*ed (prow-TRAK-tid), *a*: drawn out over a period of time, usually unnecessarily so

10. re*tract* (ri-TRAKT), *v*: to draw back or withdraw; to take back, as a previous statement or promise

TRUE-FALSE

_____ 1. To *retract* a statement is to deny you ever made it.

_____ 2. The primary purpose of *détente* is to prepare for war.

_____ 3. *Distractions* usually help one to concentrate.

_____ 4. A *pretentious* act is likely to be one intended for show.

_____ 5. *Contentious* people are contented individuals who never want to argue or quarrel.

_____ 6. An *ostensible* motive is an apparent motive.

_____ 7. An *incredulous* smile is likely to show skepticism.

_____ 8. *Intractable* children can be difficult to manage.

_____ 9. That which is *distended* is stretched or expanded.

_____ 10. A *protracted* discussion is one that is cut short.

DEFINITION REPLACEMENT

_____ 1. Many in the audience remained [*unwilling to believe*] of the promises made by the candidates.

_____ 2. Karl's [*seeming or apparent*] reason for going to church is to find tranquillity, but I think he is really looking for a suitable wife.

_____ 3. Silence can be a [*anything that draws the mind away*] if you are used to noise.

_____ 4. My cat is as [*affecting distinction or importance*] as a full professor.

_____ 5. What this family needs is a little marital [*a relaxation of strained relations*].

_____ 6. We had a [*drawn out over a period of time*] fall, with no frost | iuntil Thanksgiving.

_____ 7. The [*unruly*] protesters refused to do what the officers told them to do.

_____ 8. I do not like to associate with [*inclined to argue or dispute*] people.

_____ 9. I will [*to take back*] my accusations if you will do the same.

_____ 10. Your [*enlarged or expanded*] midsection suggests that you had a good dinner.

FILL-IN AND PART-OF-SPEECH IDENTIFICATION

_____ 1. Your _____ manner does not convince anyone that you are a grand, important person.

_____ 2. The swollen and _____ joint was quite painful.

_____ 3. My _____ uncle is always looking for a controversy or something to argue about.

_____ 4. I prefer not to have the _____ of loud music when I am trying to study.

_____ 5. My _____ purpose in going to the library was to study, but I really wanted to meet some friends from high school.

_____ 6. From your _____ expression, I can tell that you do not believe me.

_____ 7. I will not _____ my statements, and I will never apologize.

_____ 8. _____ students simply refuse to be instructed; they would prefer to be difficult.

_____ 9. Because of fundamental differences, _____ between communist and capitalist countries is very difficult to bring about.

_____ 10. The _____ meeting dragged on late into the night.

MATCHING

_____ 1. contentious   a. unable to believe; skeptical

_____ 2. ostensible   b. a relaxation of strained relations

_____ 3. distraction   c. stretched apart; enlarged or expanded

_____ 4. incredulous   d. seeming or apparent; plausible

_____ 5. pretentious   e. hard to manage; unruly

_____ 6. retract   f. extended over a period of time

_____ 7. distended   g. always ready to argue, dispute, or quarrel

_____ 8. protracted   h. to take back

_____ 9. intractable   i. affecting distinction, excellence, or importance

_____ 10. détente   j. anything that draws the mind away from concentration

BONUS ROOT

cred (to believe): accreditation, credence, credentials, credibility, credible, credit, creditor, credo, credulity, credulous, creed, discredit, incredible, miscreant

Words from Roots (36)

The three-part prescription for a bland and uninvolved life—"*See* no evil, *hear* no evil, *speak* no evil"—calls to mind an interesting cluster of Latin roots with many modern derivatives. First, the root *vid* or *vis* means "to see." On MTV we see rock *videos.* That which is *invisible* cannot be seen. Sequence 7 considered the root *spec(t)* or *spic,* which means "to look" as well as "to see." Remember that anything *specious* looks reasonable or logical at first glance but later proves otherwise. Second, the root meaning "to hear" is *aud(it).* An *audiovisual* presentation is both heard and seen. That which is *audible* can be heard. Third, there are two roots meaning "to speak": *dict* and *loqu* or *locut.* Your *diction* is your manner of speaking words, and to *contradict* is to speak against. Similarly, your *elocution* (*el-ə-KYUW-shən*) is your style or manner of speaking, and that which is *eloquent* is fluently or persuasively spoken.

WORD LIST

1. *audio*phile (O-dee-ə-*fiyl*), *n*: a person devoted to or expert in sound reproduction, as on high-fidelity records, tapes, or compact discs

2. *audi*tion (o-DISH-ən), *n*: a hearing to test whether an actor or musician is good enough for a particular part or performance; *v*, to perform in such a hearing

3. circum*locut*ion (*sur*-kəm-low-KYUW-shən), *n*: literally, speaking around or in a circle, and thus a roundabout way of saying something; talk that is unnecessarily wordy and slow getting to the point

4. col*loqu*ial (kə-LOW-kwee-əl), *a*: literally, to speak together, and thus characteristic of language used by people speaking in informal situations; conversational or informal

*5. *fid*elity (fə-DEL-ə-tee), *n*: steadfast faithfulness to one's promises or obligations; technological faithfulness

6. in*aud*ible (in-O-də-bəl), *a*: not loud enough to be heard

---

a (fat); ay (fate); ah (far); au (doubt); ch (church); e (elf, bed, care); ee (equal); ə (about); hw (while); i (fit); iy (kite); ŋ (link, sing); o (audio, corn); ow (ocean); oo (book); oi (oil); sh (shoe, ambition); th (think); u (up, deter); uw (ooze); y (yes, onion); yu (bureau, cure); yuw (youth, unity); zh (pleasure)

159

7. in*vid*ious (in-VID-ee-əs), *a*: characteristic of that which when seen will produce envy, animosity, or ill will; causing offense

8. *loqu*acious (low-KWAY-shəs), *a*: too talkative; excessively wordy; overfond of speaking

9. *vi*sionary (VIZH-ə-*ner*-ee), *a*: seen only in the mind's eye, and thus not real; impractical and idealistic; *n*, a person whose head is filled with fantastic plans and schemes

10. *vi*sta (VIS-tə), *n*: a distant, extensive, or comprehensive view of something; a mental view, as over a stretch of time

TRUE-FALSE

_____ 1. *Colloquial* language is informal but not illiterate.

_____ 2. *Loquacious* people usually make the best listeners.

_____ 3. An *audiophile* is a person who renovates antique automobiles.

_____ 4. *Visionaries* are sometimes impractical people.

_____ 5. Personal *fidelity* must include trustworthiness.

_____ 6. *Invidious* behavior is intended to provoke genial responses in others.

_____ 7. When performing an *audition,* a person expects to be listened to.

_____ 8. *Inaudible* sounds can be heard only by dogs.

_____ 9. A view that is obscured is called a *vista.*

_____ 10. *Circumlocution* may be the forte of a person suffering from logorrhea.

DEFINITION REPLACEMENT

_____ 1. "Laidback" is a well-known [*informal*] expression.

_____ 2. This [*producing envy, animosity, or ill will*] display of wealth will please no one.

160

_____ 3. I enjoy good music decently recorded, but I am not an [*a person devoted to sound reproduction on high-fidelity recordings*].

_____ 4. The usually beautiful [*a distant and full view*] was obscured by fog.

_____ 5. No one questions your [*steadfast faithfulness*] to the cause.

_____ 6. The [*a test for a part in a play*] was a disaster; I forgot my lines.

_____ 7. This view of the future is not [*idealistic and fantastic*] enough; it has no room for the imagination.

_____ 8. Skip the [*a roundabout way of saying something*] and come to the point of what you want to say.

_____ 9. To a deaf person, all sounds are [*not loud enough to be heard*].

_____ 10. Everyone thought the [*excessively wordy*] senator would prattle on forever.

FILL-IN AND PART-OF-SPEECH IDENTIFICATION

_____ 1. Because I was the only person to show up for the _____, I got the part.

_____ 2. Marian is quite _____; she must have been vaccinated with a phonograph needle.

_____ 3. _____ language is often inappropriate for a formal written monograph.

_____ 4. The full _____ of the valley can be seen only from the south promontory.

_____ 5. This whistle produces a sound _____ to the human ear, or so I have been told.

_____ 6. James is such a fanatical _____ that he can never find a recording that pleases him completely.

_____ 7. Why are you surprised that your _____ behavior provoked animosity?

_____ 8. These plans are _____, even a little futuristic, but not very practical.

_____ 9. If _____ means talking in circles, we should all be a little dizzy by now.

_____ 10. An audiophile demands precise phonic _____ in recorded music.

MATCHING

_____ 1. colloquial   a. to perform as a test for a part in a play

_____ 2. invidious   b. an expert at high-fidelity recording

_____ 3. fidelity   c. producing ill will or offense

_____ 4. visionary   d. not loud enough to be heard

_____ 5. audiophile   e. talk that is slow getting to the point

_____ 6. loquacious   f. a comprehensive view of something

_____ 7. inaudible   g. one addicted to fantastic schemes

_____ 8. audition   h. characteristic of informal language

_____ 9. vista   i. overfond of speaking

_____ 10. circumlocution   j. faithfulness to one's obligations

BONUS ROOT

fid(e) (faith): affidavit, bona fide, confidant, confide, confidence, confident, confidential, confidentiality, diffidence, diffident, fiduciary, infidel, infidelity, perfidious, perfidy

Supplementary Roots and Derivatives Exercise (4)

1. *agr(o)* (field): agriculture, _____, _____, _____

2. *andr(o)* (man, male): android, _____, _____,
   _____

3. *ced(e), ceed, cess* (to go, to yield): proceed, recede, process, _____,
   _____, _____

4. *cord, card* (heart): cordial, cardiac, _____, _____,
   _____

5. *cruc* (cross): crucifix, _____, _____, _____

6. *dorm* (to sleep): dormitory, _____, _____, _____

7. *fac(t), fic, fect* (to make, to do): factory, efficient, effective, _____,
   _____, _____

8. *gnos, cogn* (to know): prognosis, recognize, _____, _____,
   _____

9. *hema, hemo, em* (blood): hemorrhage, _____, _____,
   _____

10. *jud(ic)* (judge): prejudice, _____, _____, _____

11. *liber, liver* (free): liberty, deliver, _____, _____,
    _____

12. *mor* (custom): morality, _____, _____, _____

13. *neg* (to deny): negative, _____, _____, _____

14. *pend, pens* (to hang, to weigh): pendant, dispense, _____,
    _____, _____

15. *pon, pos(e)* (to place, to put): opponent, impose, _____, _____,

   _____

16. *rat* (to reckon, to reason): rational, _____, _____,

17. *sanct* (holy): sanctuary, _____, _____, _____

18. *stru(ct)* (to build): instrument, instruction, _____, _____,

   _____

19. *umbr* (shade): umbrella, _____, _____, _____

20. *vest* (to dress, to clothe): vestments, _____, _____,

   _____

Supplementary Roots and Derivatives Exercise (5)

1. *ac, acer, acid, acri* (bitter, sour, sharp): acute, acerbic, acidity, acrid, _____,

   _____, _____

2. *alb* (white): albino, _____, _____, _____

3. *clar* (clear): clarity, _____, _____, _____

4. *clud(e), clus, claus, clos* (to shut, to close): seclude, exclusive, closet, _____,

   _____, _____

5. *dign* (worthy): dignify, _____, _____, _____

6. *dur* (hard, lasting): durable, _____, _____, _____

7. *erg, urg* (work, power): energetic, _____, _____,

   _____

8. *fus, fund, found* (to pour, to melt): transfusion, refund, foundry, _____,

   _____, _____

9. *heli(o)* (sun): heliotrope, _____, _____, _____

10. *lev* (light in weight, to raise): elevator, _____, _____,

    _____

11. *mut(e)* (to change): mutation, _____, _____, _____

12. *neur(o)* (nerve): neurotic, _____, _____, _____

13. *op(t)* (eye, sight): optometrist, _____, _____, _____

14. *plas(t)* (to form): plastic, _____, _____, _____

15. *prob, prove* (to test, good): probation, approve, _____, _____,

    _____

16. *reg, rect* (to rule, straight, right): regulate, rectify, _____,

    _____, _____

17. *sat(is)* (enough): satisfaction, _____, _____, _____

18. *solv, solu* (to free, to loosen): solvent, solution, _____, _____,

    _____

19. *tom* (to cut): anatomy, _____, _____, _____

20. *trib* (to assign, to allot, to pay): contribution, _____, _____,

    _____

Chapter

Words with Prefixes

A*prefix* is a letter or cluster of letters—with a dictionary meaning of its own—that comes at the beginning of a word. Quite often, a prefix is actually an old Latin or Greek preposition that now joins with a root, and subsequently with a suffix, to form a word. For example, the Latin prefix *ad-*, joined with the Latin root *mitt* and the suffix *-ance*, produces the English word *admittance*.

This chapter contains twenty sequences of exercises, which present three categories of prefixes: (1) time and position, (2) quality and condition, and (3) number and amount. Begin each sequence by familiarizing yourself with the featured prefix or prefixes. Each prefix is defined and followed by a word or words containing the prefix. A blank space is provided after the sample words so that you may add a few samples of your own. Next, study the word list. Then complete the two exercises: (1) fill-in and part-of-speech identification and (2) matching. Following every fourth sequence there is a completion exercise in which you can finish sentences containing words from the word lists.

As you work through this chapter, you will note that the spelling of a few prefixes changes when they are attached to words or roots beginning with certain sounds. This process is called *assimilation* (ə-sim-ə-LAY-shən), and such prefixes are called *assimilating prefixes*. The following list demonstrates two things about the assimilating prefix *sub-*, which means "under," "beneath," or "below." First, it shows the many sounds that *sub-*

can precede to help form words. Second, it shows the seven assimilations of the prefix, which are marked with asterisks.

prefix		root		suffix		word
sub-	+	arct	+	-ic	=	subarctic
sub-	+	base	+	-ment	=	subbasement
sub-	+	cult	+	-ure	=	subculture
sub-	+	duct	+	-ion	=	subduction
sub-	+	ject	+	-ive	=	subjective
sub-	+	limin	+	-al	=	subliminal
sub-	+	mar	+	-ine	=	submarine
sub-	+	norm	+	-al	=	subnormal
sub-	+	ordin	+	-ate	=	subordinate
sub-	+	popul	+	-ation	=	subpopulation
sub-	+	reg	+	-ion	=	subregion
sub-	+	script	+	-ion	=	subscription
sub-	+	tract	+	-ion	=	subtraction
sub-	+	urb	+	-an	=	suburban
sub-	+	vers	+	-ive	=	subversive
*suc-	+	cess	+	-ful	=	successful
*suf-	+	fer	+	-able	=	sufferable
*sug-	+	gest	+	-ible	=	suggestible
*sum-	+	mon			=	summon
*sup-	+	press	+	-ion	=	suppression
*sur-	+	rog	+	-ate	=	surrogate
*sus-	+	cept	+	-ible	=	susceptible
*sus-	+	pens	+	-ion	=	suspension
*sus-	+	ten	+	-ance	=	sustenance

The other assimilating prefixes included in the chapter are *ad-*, *com-*, *ex-*, *in-*, *ob-*, and *syn-*. Each is marked by an asterisk.

Words with Prefixes (1)

Time and Position

PREFIXES

*1. *ad-, ac-, af-, ag-, al-, an-, ap-, ar-, as-, at-* (to, toward): admit, accurate, affirm, aggravate,

allot _____

_____

_____

WORD LIST

1. *ac*cede (ak-SEED), *v*: to arrive at or enter upon, as a new position or office; to agree to or give in to

2. *ac*climate (AK-lə-*mayt*), *v*: to adjust to a different climate, environment, or set of circumstances

3. *ad*mixture (ad-MIKS-chər), *n*: the action of mixing or mingling, or the state of being mingled or mixed; anything that is to be mixed in

4. *ad*monish (ad-MAHN-ish), *v*: to caution mildly; to urge or warn; to remind

5. *af*fable (AF-ə-bəl), *a*: of a pleasant and easy nature; easy to approach or to talk to

6. *af*fluent (AF-*luw*-ənt), *a*: flowing freely, as with wealth and riches; prosperous

7. *ag*grandize (ə-GRAN-*diyz*), *v*: to make (appear) greater, as in power, stature, or sphere of influence

8. *ag*gregation (*ag*-rə-GAY-shən), *n*: a group, body, or mass, as of people or distinct things

9. *al*leviate (ə-LEE-vee-*ayt*), *v*: literally, to make lighter, and thus to make less severe or burdensome

10. *al*ly (AL-iy), *n*: any person, group, or country joined with another or others in a common purpose; a supporter; (ə-LIY), *v*: to become an ally

---

a (fat); ay (fate); ah (far); au (doubt); ch (church); e (elf, bed, care); ee (equal); ə (about); hw (while); i (fit); iy (kite); ŋ (link, sing); o (audio, corn); ow (ocean); oo (book); oi (oil); sh (shoe, ambition); th (think); u (up, deter); uw (ooze); y (yes, onion); yu (bureau, cure); yuw (youth, unity); zh (pleasure)

FILL-IN AND PART-OF-SPEECH IDENTIFICATION

_____ 1. The recipe included a strange _____ of spices.

_____ 2. We do not _____ our popularity internationally by shooting down airliners of Third World countries.

_____ 3. Great Britain is an _____, a friend, of the United States.

_____ 4. I will _____ to your wishes because I think they are reasonable.

_____ 5. I take aspirin to _____ my headaches.

_____ 6. My history instructor is _____ enough in social situations, but she is all business in class.

_____ 7. _____ people look prosperous even when they dress down.

_____ 8. Only gradually did I _____ myself to living in such a cold climate.

_____ 9. An _____ of angry property owners gathered outside the assessor's office.

_____ 10. Speaking as a friend, I _____ you to spend more time on your studies.

MATCHING

_____ 1. aggrandize   a. to adjust to a different climate

_____ 2. accede   b. to caution mildly; to warn

_____ 3. affluent   c. a supporter in a common cause

_____ 4. alleviate   d. to arrive at or enter upon; to agree

_____ 5. acclimate   e. a group or mass, as of people

_____ 6. affable   f. to make less severe

_____ 7. ally   g. to make (appear) greater

_____ 8. admixture   h. easy to approach or talk to

_____ 9. aggregation   i. prosperous

_____ 10. admonish   j. anything that is mixed in

Words with Prefixes (2)

Time and Position

PREFIXES

*1. *ad-, ac-, af-, ag-, al-, an-, ap-, ar-, as-, at-* (to, toward): annex, appoint, arrest, asset, attend

_____

_____

WORD LIST

1. *an*nihilate (ə-NIY-ə-*layt*), *v*: to reduce to nothing; to destroy totally; to conquer or crush

2. *an*notation (*an*-ə-TAY-shən), *n*: a critical or explanatory note, as to a manuscript; commentary

3. *ap*parition (*ap*-ə-RISH-ən), *n*: the appearance of something strange or unusual, as a ghost or vision; an unexpected sight

4. *ap*plicable (AP-li-kə-bəl, ə-PLIK-ə-bəl), *a*: that can be sensibly applied; appropriate or relevant

5. *ar*ray (ə-RAY), *v*: to arrange items in some specific order; to dress up in showy attire; *n*, a systematic grouping; any impressive display; fine clothing; an arrangement of numbers

6. *ar*rears (ə-RIRZ), *n*: the condition of having not met a (financial) responsibility on time; the state of being behind

7. *as*pire (ə-SPIYR), *v*: literally, to breathe toward, and thus to seek, yearn, or wish for something

8. *as*signation (*as*-ig-NAY-shən), *n*: a secret meeting, as between lovers; a rendezvous

9. *at*tenuated (ə-TEN-yə-*way*-tid), *a*: having become diluted, weak, feeble, or slender; less severe than before

10. *at*trition (ə-TRISH-ən), *n*: the action or process of becoming less, as in strength, numbers, or authority

---

a (fat); ay (fate); ah (far); au (doubt); ch (church); e (elf, bed, care); ee (equal); ə (about); hw (while); i (fit); iy (kite); ŋ (link, sing); o (audio, corn); ow (ocean); oo (book); oi (oil); sh (shoe, ambition); th (think); u (up, deter); uw (ooze); y (yes, onion); yu (bureau, cure); yuw (youth, unity); zh (pleasure)

FILL-IN AND PART-OF-SPEECH IDENTIFICATION

_____ 1. Your suggestion simply is not _____; it has no relevance to the problem.

_____ 2. As usual, I am in _____ with my homework; I will never catch up.

_____ 3. The rate of _____ among freshman students is almost fifty percent. They just keep dropping out of school.

_____ 4. A substantial increase in ultraviolet radiation may _____ the human race. We will be wiped out.

_____ 5. For years, the lovers had a weekly _____ in a small hotel by the sea.

_____ 6. A colorful _____ of hot-air balloons drifted across the afternoon sky as if in formation.

_____ 7. You should not _____ to a position in life beyond your ability.

_____ 8. The _____ in the margins of a used textbook can make it more valuable than a new one.

_____ 9. _____ from lack of food, the once strong fellow could hardly stand upright.

_____ 10. Is there a difference between an _____ and a ghost?

MATCHING

_____ 1. arrears   a. to destroy totally

_____ 2. assignation   b. an impressive display

_____ 3. annihilate   c. a critical or explanatory note

_____ 4. attenuated   d. the process of becoming less, as in number

_____ 5. applicable   e. the state of being behind

_____ 6. aspire   f. diluted, weak, or feeble

_____ 7. annotation   g. to wish or yearn for something

_____ 8. attrition   h. a ghost or vision

_____ 9. array   i. a secret meeting of lovers

_____ 10. apparition   j. appropriate or relevant

Words with Prefixes (3)

Time and Position

PREFIXES

1. *ab(s)-* (away, from): abduct, abstract _____

2. *ambi-, amphi-* (both, around): ambidextrous, amphibious _____
_____

3. *ante-* (before): antedate, antecedent _____

4. *cata-* (down): catastrophe, catapult _____

WORD LIST

1. *ab*dicate (AB-də-*kayt*), *v*: to give up in a formal way, as a high office or position of authority; to renounce or deny

2. *ab*original (*ab*-ə-RIJ-ə-nəl), *n*: a person, plant, or animal native to a specific area from earliest times; *a*, indigenous

3. *abs*truse (ab-STRUWS), *a*: deep and complex, and thus difficult to understand

4. *amb*iance (AM-bee-əns), *n*: the general surrounding atmosphere or environment

5. *amb*iguous (am-BIG-yə-wəs), *a*: literally, to wander around, and thus having more than one possible meaning; not clear; indefinite, uncertain, or vague

6. *amphi*theater (AM-fə-*thee*-ə-tər), *n*: a large circular building or open space with rising rows of seats all around; a big lecture hall

7. *ante*bellum (*an*-ti-BEL-əm), *a*: before the war, especially the American Civil War; typical of how things were before any war

8. *ante*diluvian (*an*-ti-də-LUW-vee-ən), *a*: literally, from before the Biblical Flood, and thus out-of-date or old-fashioned; *n*, an old-fashioned or primitive person or thing

9. *cata*clysm (KAT-ə-*kliz*-əm), *n*: any great upheaval, such as a flood, deluge, or earthquake, causing sudden and violent changes; a disaster

10. *cata*tonic (*kat*-ə-TAHN-ik), *a*: characteristic of catatonia, a condition in which the body loses the ability to move, the limbs remaining frozen in whatever position they are placed

a (f*a*t); ay (f*a*te); ah (f*a*r); au (d*ou*bt); ch (*ch*urch); e (*e*lf, b*e*d, c*a*re); ee (*e*qual); ə (*a*bout); hw (*wh*ile); i (f*i*t); iy (k*i*te); ŋ (li*n*k, si*ng*); o (*au*dio, c*or*n); ow (*o*cean); oo (b*oo*k); oi (*oi*l); sh (*sh*oe, ambi*ti*on); th (*th*ink); u (*u*p, det*er*); uw (*oo*ze); y (*y*es, on*i*on); yu (b*u*reau, c*u*re); yuw (*you*th, *u*nity); zh (plea*s*ure)

FILL-IN AND PART-OF-SPEECH IDENTIFICATION

_____ 1. The new convention center has a nice _____; it is very pleasant to be in.

_____ 2. Absolutely _____, the boy remained as motionless as a statue for hours.

_____ 3. Our _____ impulses have come down to us from the earliest times of human history.

_____ 4. The earthquake was a _____ of major proportions.

_____ 5. The government's new tax laws are so _____ that not even the IRS experts understand them.

_____ 6. Alas, the _____ homes in many Southern cities have been broken up into small apartments.

_____ 7. The performance took place in the second-floor _____.

_____ 8. Your ideas are not just out-of-date; they are _____—from before the Flood.

_____ 9. Your statement was so fuzzy and _____ that it was impossible to figure out what you meant.

_____ 10. If you _____ your parental responsibilities, your children will have little guidance.

MATCHING

_____ 1. abstruse   a. a big lecture hall

_____ 2. antebellum   b. the general surrounding environment

_____ 3. cataclysm   c. deep and complex

_____ 4. aboriginal   d. frozen in position

_____ 5. antediluvian   e. to give up formally

_____ 6. ambiance   f. having more than one possible meaning

_____ 7. catatonic   g. old-fashioned or out-of-date

_____ 8. amphitheater   h. one native to a region from earliest times

_____ 9. ambiguous   i. a violent upheaval or disaster

_____ 10. abdicate   j. before the war

174

Words with Prefixes (4)

Time and Position

PREFIXES

1. *circum-* (around): circumlocution, circumstance _____

   _____

2. *de-* (down, from, negative): degenerate, definitive _____

   _____

3. *dia-* (through, across, between): diameter _____

   _____

4. *epi-* (on, upon, outside): epidemic, epilepsy _____

   _____

WORD LIST

1. *circum*spect (SUR-kəm-*spekt*), *a*: very careful in considering all matters before acting; always cautious and careful
2. *circum*vent (*sur*-kəm-VENT), *v*: to get the better of, as by crafty diversion; to go around rather than confront directly
3. *de*celerate (dee-SEL-ə-*rayt*), *v*: to slow down
4. *de*ficient (di-FISH-ənt), *a*: lacking some important or essential quality; inadequate, defective, or incomplete
5. *de*fray (di-FRAY), *v*: either to pay money or to provide for the payment of money; to cover costs or expenses
6. *dia*logue (DIY-ə-*log*), *n*: a conversation between two or more parties; an exchange of ideas, usually suggesting harmony
7. *dia*phanous (diy-AF-ə-nəs), *a*: literally, to show through, and thus of so fine a texture as to be partially transparent; vague or indistinct; translucent
8. *epi*phany (i-PIF-ə-nee), *n*: an appearance or manifestation of a divine being; a sudden revelation of some essential truth; an intuitive grasp of a specific reality
9. *epi*sodic (*ep*-ə-SAHD-ik), *a*: characterized by unimportant details and vaguely related incidents; broken down into small narrative parts

---

a (*f*a*t*); ay (*f*a*te*); ah (*f*a*r*); au (*d*ou*bt*); ch (*ch*ur*ch*); e (*e*lf, b*e*d, c*a*re); ee (*e*qu*a*l); ə (*a*bout); hw (*wh*ile); i (*f*i*t*); iy (k*i*te); ŋ (li*nk*, si*ng*); o (*a*udio, c*o*rn); ow (*o*cean); oo (b*oo*k); oi (*o*il); sh (*sh*oe, ambi*ti*on); th (*th*ink); u (*u*p, det*e*r); uw (*oo*ze); y (*y*es, oni*o*n); yu (b*u*reau, c*u*re); yuw (*y*outh, *u*nity); zh (plea*s*ure)

10. *epi*tome (i-PIT-ə-mee), *n*: a highly typical, almost perfect, example of something; a perfect representation of

FILL-IN AND PART-OF-SPEECH IDENTIFICATION

_____ 1. In comparison with European systems of education, American public education is greatly _____ in teaching foreign languages.

_____ 2. We can _____ the cost of the trip by taking jobs along the way.

_____ 3. The search committee must be very _____ in reviewing the credentials of all candidates for the position.

_____ 4. You are the _____ of the confused student; you have no idea what you want to do with your life.

_____ 5. The _____ in the novel was too clever to be realistic.

_____ 6. This narrative is _____ at best, totally disconnected in many places.

_____ 7. Can we _____ all this government red tape without breaking the law?

_____ 8. This _____ gown is made of sheer nylon.

_____ 9. In a brief _____, the misguided soul realized the truth about himself.

_____ 10. You must _____ quickly as you approach the south turn on the track.

MATCHING

_____ 1. circumspect   a. to slow down

_____ 2. epiphany   b. careful in considering all matters before acting

_____ 3. dialogue   c. having many brief narrative parts

_____ 4. circumvent   d. almost transparent

_____ 5. episodic   e. a sudden revelation of truth

_____ 6. decelerate   f. lacking some important quality

_____ 7. diaphanous   g. a perfect representation of something

_____ 8. defray   h. to get around, as by being crafty

_____ 9. epitome   i. an exchange of ideas

_____ 10. deficient   j. to provide for payment

Completion Exercise for Prefixes 1 through 4

1. To *accede* to another's wishes is to _____.

2. To *acclimate* oneself is to _____.

3. An *admixture* includes more than _____.

4. To *admonish* is to _____.

5. *Affable* people are usually easy to _____.

6. *Affluent* individuals are generally _____.

7. To *aggrandize* authority is to _____.

8. An *aggregation* will include _____.

9. To *alleviate* suffering is to _____.

10. A true *ally* will usually _____.

11. To *annihilate* poverty would be to _____.

12. *Annotations* are often found in _____.

13. An *apparition* might _____.

14. That which is *applicable* is _____.

15. To *array* oneself elaborately is to _____.

16. To be in *arrears* is to be _____.

17. To *aspire* to greatness is to _____.

18. The purpose of an *assignation* is to _____.

19. An *attenuated* appearance suggests _____.

20. *Attrition* occurs as _____.

21. To *abdicate* a position is to _____.

22. Plants *aboriginal* to a region are _____.

23. *Abstruse* logic will likely be _____.

24. The *ambiance* of a situation includes _____.

25. An *ambiguous* statement is not _____.

26. An *amphitheater* is designed for _____.

27. *Antebellum* conditions existed before _____.

28. An *antediluvian* opinion is one that is _____.

29. A *cataclysm* will likely cause _____.

30. A *catatonic* individual remains _____.

31. To be *circumspect* is to be very _____.

32. To *circumvent* authority is to _____.

33. To *decelerate* is to _____.

34. If one's skills are *deficient,* they are _____.

35. To *defray* expenses is to _____.

36. A *dialogue* always includes _____.

37. A *diaphanous* curtain would be _____.

38. During an *epiphany,* one experiences _____.

39. An *episodic* tale includes _____.

40. The *epitome* of honesty is a(n) _____.

Words with Prefixes (5)

Time and Position

PREFIXES

*1. *com-, co-, col-, con-, cor-* (with, together, intensive): commentary, cooperate, colloquial, congenital, corroborate _____

_____

_____

WORD LIST

1. *co*eval (kow-EE-vəl), *a*: existing at the same time or during the same age; contemporary; *n*, a person or thing of the same time or age; a contemporary

2. *co*gent (KOW-jənt), *a*: forcefully convincing, as in making a point or an argument; compelling, often because of relevance

3. *col*league (KAHL-*eeg*), *n*: a (fellow) worker in the same occupation; an associate

4. *col*lusion (kə-LUW-zhən), *n*: a working together (secretly) for illicit purposes; an agreement to do something illegal

5. *com*mensurate (kə-MEN-sə-rit), *a*: having equal or corresponding measure, size, value, worth, or importance

6. *com*modious (kə-MOW-dee-əs), *a*: with due or ample measure, and thus comfortable, spacious, suitable, or well-appointed

7. *con*sensus (kən-SEN-səs), *n*: a general feeling of agreement; an opinion held by all or almost all

8. *con*vivial (kən-VIV-ee-əl), *a*: lively together, in the sense of including feasting, drinking, and good company; sociable and festive

9. *cor*relate (KOR-ə-*layt*), *v*: to bring two or more things into a mutual, complementary, parallel, or reciprocal relationship; to coordinate

10. *cor*respondence (*kor*-ə-SPAHN-dəns), *n*: communication, as by the exchange of letters; the letters themselves; a similarity, likeness, or agreement between two things or situations

a (*f*at); ay (*f*ate); ah (*f*ar); au (*d*oubt); ch (*ch*urch); e (*e*lf, b*e*d, c*a*re); ee (*e*qual); ə (*a*bout); hw (*wh*ile); i (*f*it); iy (*k*ite); ŋ (li*n*k, si*ng*); o (*a*udio, c*o*rn); ow (*o*cean); oo (b*oo*k); oi (*oi*l); sh (*sh*oe, ambi*ti*on); th (*th*ink); u (*u*p, de*te*r); uw (*oo*ze); y (*y*es, on*i*on); yu (b*u*reau, c*u*re); yuw (*you*th, *u*nity); zh (plea*s*ure)

FILL-IN AND PART-OF-SPEECH IDENTIFICATION

_____ 1. My new apartment is quite _____; it includes all the creature comforts most people want.

_____ 2. A friend and _____ for many years, Professor Fogarty is my office partner.

_____ 3. We must _____ the two versions of the story in order to determine what really happened.

_____ 4. The prosecutor was accused of _____ with the defense attorney.

_____ 5. There is a close _____ between the human eye and a camera.

_____ 6. _____ elements of the drought are extreme heat and lack of rain.

_____ 7. I had thought the class reunion would be a _____ affair, but the years had made strangers of everyone.

_____ 8. As yet, there is no national _____ about whether President Kennedy was the victim of a conspiracy; people still disagree.

_____ 9. _____ arguments, because they are convincing, are difficult to ignore.

_____ 10. Your salary is not _____ with your value to the company; you are underpaid.

MATCHING

_____ 1. commodious   a. existing at the same time

_____ 2. collusion   b. having a corresponding measure

_____ 3. correlate   c. comfortable, spacious, or well-appointed

_____ 4. cogent   d. festive and sociable

_____ 5. consensus   e. to coordinate

_____ 6. commensurate   f. a working associate

_____ 7. convivial   g. an agreement to do something illegal

_____ 8. coeval   h. a general feeling of agreement

_____ 9. correspondence   i. forcefully convincing

180 _____ 10. colleague   j. communication, as by an exchange of letters

Words with Prefixes (6)

Time and Position

PREFIXES

1. *en-, em-* (in, into, intensive): endemic, empathy _____

_____

2. *extra-, extro-* (outside, beyond): extravagant _____

_____

3. *inter-* (between, among): intermittent _____

4. *intro-, intra-* (inside, within, inward): introspection, intrastate _____

_____

WORD LIST

1. *em*bellish (im-BEL-ish), *v*: to add to; to decorate or ornament; to improve by the addition of detail; to enhance
2. *en*croachment (in-KROWCH-mənt), *n*: the act or instance of intruding upon another's land, domain, possessions, or rights; a trespass
3. *extra*neous (ek-STRAY-nee-əs), *a*: coming from without or existing on the outside; not an essential part of; not pertinent or relevant
4. *extra*terrestrial (*ek*-strə-tə-RES-tree-əl), *a*: from, or originating from, outside the limits of the earth; *n*, an extraterrestrial being or item
5. *extro*vert (EKS-trə-*vurt*), *n*: a person outgoing and much interested in the external world; *a*, outgoing
6. *inter*face (IN-tər-*fays*), *n*: a surface forming a common boundary between two things; the place at which two systems come together and operate with each other; *v*, to connect two things to work together, as a computer and any kind of machine
7. *inter*lude (IN-tər-*luwd*), *n*: a brief period between events of greater significance, as a minor entertainment between halves of an athletic contest; a time in between
8. *inter*necine (*in*-tər-NEE-sin), *a*: equally harmful, destructive, or deadly to all sides or parties involved; mutually harmful
9. *intra*mural (*in*-trə-MYUR-əl), *a*: literally, within the walls; existing within the confines of an institution, especially a school

a (fat); ay (fate); ah (far); au (doubt); ch (church); e (elf, bed, care); ee (equal); ə (about); hw (while); i (fit); iy (kite); ŋ (link, sing); o (audio, corn); ow (ocean); oo (book); oi (oil); sh (shoe, ambition); th (think); u (up, deter); uw (ooze); y (yes, onion); yu (bureau, cure); yuw (youth, unity); zh (pleasure)

181

10. *introvert* (IN·trə-*vurt*), *n*: a person greatly occupied with inner thoughts and feelings; *a*, introspective; occupied with inner thoughts and feelings

FILL-IN AND PART-OF-SPEECH IDENTIFICATION

_____ 1. There was only one _____ in the spaceship.

_____ 2. An _____ could not be devised to connect the two incompatible systems.

_____ 3. The college operates several _____ athletic leagues for both men and women.

_____ 4. Must you always _____ the truth with your fantasies?

_____ 5. A chronic _____, Robin does not like to be alone.

_____ 6. Between halves of the championship game, we were provided an _____ _____ featuring Chinese jugglers.

_____ 7. I did not appreciate the _____ upon my land. After all, it is private property.

_____ 8. A major nuclear war would be an _____ confrontation of the worst kind, leaving few if any survivors.

_____ 9. Typically, an _____ prefers solitude to mingling with large groups of people.

_____ 10. There was so much _____ material in the excavation that it took a long time to analyze the site.

MATCHING

_____ 1. extraneous   a. to connect two things so they will work together

_____ 2. interlude   b. to enhance

_____ 3. interface   c. not pertinent or relevant

_____ 4. intramural   d. an intrusion upon another's land

_____ 5. embellish   e. introspective

_____ 6. internecine   f. an outgoing person

_____ 7. encroachment   g. a brief entertainment

_____ 8. extraterrestrial   h. within the walls, as of a college

_____ 9. introvert   i. equally harmful to all concerned

182 _____ 10. extrovert   j. an alien

Words with Prefixes (7)

Time and Position

PREFIXES

*1. *ex-, e-, ec-, ef-, es-* (out, away, from): expedite, emit, eject, eclectic, effective, efface, essay

WORD LIST

1. *ec*centric (ik-SEN-trik), *a*: out of the center, and thus off-center, odd, unusual, or strange; *n*, a person who consistently exhibits unconventional behavior

2. *ec*static (ik-STAT-ik), *a*: characterized by an emotional extreme, as of joy, delight, rapture, passion, grief, horror, and so on

3. *ef*fervescent (ef-ər-VES-ənt), *a*: bubbling over, as with liveliness or optimism; high-spirited

4. *ef*fete (e-FEET), *a*: incapable of producing; without vigor; sterile; having little moral stamina; too refined

5. *ef*ficacious (ef-ə-KAY-shəs), *a*: producing or resulting in the desired effect; effective

6. *e*radicate (i-RAD-ə-*kayt*), *v*: to root out; to get rid of, uproot, or destroy completely; to obliterate

7. *es*capade (ES-kə-*payd*), *n*: a reckless, carefree adventure; an episode during which one is free from worry

8. *es*capist (ə-SKAYP-ist), *a*: wanting to avoid or run away from the realities, routines, and responsibilities of real life; *n*, a person who seeks to avoid reality

9. *ex*hume (ig-ZYUWM, iks-HYUWM), *v*: to take out of the ground; to disinter; to remove from the grave; to bring to light, reveal, or uncover

10. *ex*onerate (ig-ZAHN-ə-*rayt*), *v*: to take away a burden, and thus to free from a charge of guilt; to establish as innocent or blameless

---

a (fat); ay (fate); ah (far); au (doubt); ch (church); e (elf, bed, care); ee (equal); ə (about); hw (while); i (fit); iy (kite); ŋ (link, sing); o (audio, corn); ow (ocean); oo (book); oi (oil); sh (shoe, ambition); th (think); u (up, deter); uw (ooze); y (yes, onion); yu (bureau, cure); yuw (youth, unity); zh (pleasure)

FILL-IN AND PART-OF-SPEECH IDENTIFICATION

_____ 1. A steady diet of _____ literature can cause one to lose touch with reality.

_____ 2. Sandy always has the bubbly, _____ smile of a happy child.

_____ 3. The press will _____ every old scandal in the lives of the candidates.

_____ 4. I would say that my psychology instructor is _____; he wears earrings that play electronic music.

_____ 5. The plan proved _____; it accomplished exactly what we wanted it to accomplish.

_____ 6. Nothing will _____ me of the charges because I am guilty.

_____ 7. The entire village became _____ when its Little League team won the state championship.

_____ 8. If you _____ all of my flaws, there will be little left of me.

_____ 9. Even today, the man with an _____ manner risks being labeled a wimp.

_____ 10. The actor's autobiography detailed one reckless _____ after another.

MATCHING

_____ 1. effervescent   a. odd or unconventional

_____ 2. escapist   b. to bring to light or uncover

_____ 3. eradicate   c. without vigor; sterile

_____ 4. ecstatic   d. bubbling over, as with optimism

_____ 5. exhume   e. a carefree adventure

_____ 6. efficacious   f. avoiding reality

_____ 7. escapade   g. characterized by intense emotions, high or low

_____ 8. eccentric   h. to free from blame

_____ 9. exonerate   i. to root out completely

184 _____ 10. effete   j. producing the desired results

Words with Prefixes (8)

Time and Position

PREFIXES

1. *para-* (beside, alongside): parameter _____

*2. *in-, il-, im-, ir-* (into, within, on, toward): inhale, incision, illustrative, immigrant, impediment, irradiate _____

WORD LIST

1. *ill*uminate (i·LUW·mə·*nayt*), *v:* to give light, light up, or brighten; to explain, instruct, or inform

2. *ill*uminati (i·*luw*·mə·NAHT·ee), *n:* individuals who (collectively) possess or claim to possess special knowledge in some area—often used humorously

3. *im*bibe (im·BIYB), *v:* to drink, especially liquor; to "drink in" with any of the senses; to absorb or inhale

4. *im*pale (im·PAYL), *v:* to torture, as by fixing on a stake; to pierce with something pointed; to punish or render helpless

5. *in*carnate (in·KAHR·nit), *a:* literally, in the flesh, and thus in bodily form; personified; flesh-colored

6. *in*gest (in·JEST), *v:* to take into the body, as food; to take into the mind, as information or material from books

7. *ir*ritant (IR·ə·tənt), *n:* something causing anger, impatience, or inflammation; *a,* causing irritation

8. *para*phrase (PAR·ə·*frayz*), *n:* a reworded statement expressing essentially the same meaning as the original statement; the process of writing or speaking such a statement; *v,* to write or speak a paraphrase

9. *para*professional (*par*·ə·prə·FESH·ə·nəl), *n:* a worker who is not a member of a specific profession but who works alongside others who are

10. *para*psychology (*par*·ə·siy·KAHL·ə·jee), *n:* the branch of psychology dealing with psychic phenomena, such as clairvoyance and telepathy

---

a (f*a*t); ay (f*a*te); ah (f*a*r); au (d*ou*bt); ch (*ch*urch); e (*e*lf, b*e*d, c*a*re); ee (*e*qual); ə (*a*bout); hw (*wh*ile); i (f*i*t); iy (k*i*te); ŋ (li*n*k, si*ng*); o (*au*dio, c*o*rn); ow (*o*cean); oo (b*oo*k); oi (*oi*l); sh (*sh*oe, ambi*ti*on); th (*th*ink); u (*u*p, det*e*r); uw (*oo*ze); y (*y*es, on*i*on); yu (b*u*reau, c*u*re); yuw (*you*th, *u*nity); zh (plea*s*ure)

FILL-IN AND PART-OF-SPEECH IDENTIFICATION

____ 1. The butcherbird, or shrike, can _____ its victims on thorns or other sharp objects.

____ 2. Not all psychologists consider _____ a serious scientific discipline.

____ 3. Most Americans _____ more food than is necessary to maintain good health.

____ 4. The scientific _____ gathered at the conference to discuss extra-terrestrial life.

____ 5. It is the role of a _____ to work closely with professional colleagues.

____ 6. If you _____ too much, you are likely to feel ill the following morning.

____ 7. Constant loud noise is an _____ that I cannot tolerate for very long.

____ 8. If you will _____ me on the topic, I will then be better informed.

____ 9. The statement was a _____, not an exact quotation.

____ 10. Devlin is the devil _____; I am surprised he does not have horns and a tail.

MATCHING

____ 1. impale   a. in the flesh or bodily form

____ 2. paraphrase   b. one who works alongside a professional

____ 3. illuminati   c. to consume, as food

____ 4. paraprofessional d. to enlighten or inform

____ 5. imbibe   e. to fix on a stake

____ 6. irritant   f. people possessing great knowledge

____ 7. illuminate   g. to restate in one's own words

____ 8. parapsychology   h. to drink

____ 9. incarnate   i. something causing anger

____ 10. ingest   j. branch of psychology dealing with psychic phenomena

Completion Exercise for Prefixes 5 through 8

1. *Coeval* forces exist at _____.

2. A *cogent* remark will likely be _____.

3. A *colleague* is someone who _____.

4. To be in *collusion* with is to _____.

5. "Brains *commensurate* with beauty" means _____.

6. A *commodious* apartment will likely be _____.

7. In a *consensus* there is _____.

8. *Convivial* people usually enjoy _____.

9. To *correlate* activities is to _____.

10. A *correspondence* between two events suggests _____.

11. To *embellish* the truth is to _____.

12. An *encroachment* involves _____.

13. *Extraneous* items are items not _____.

14. *Extraterrestrial* matter would come from _____.

15. *Extroverts* usually like to _____.

16. An *interface* is a place where _____.

17. An *interlude* is a(n) _____.

18. An *internecine* struggle results in _____.

19. An *intramural* activity is one occurring _____.

20. Generally, *introverts* do not _____. **187**

21. *Eccentric* people can sometimes be _____.

22. When we are *ecstatic,* we are _____.

23. An *effervescent* liquid will _____.

24. An *effete* effort is one showing _____.

25. *Efficacious* results are those _____.

26. To *eradicate* one's enemies is to _____.

27. During an *escapade,* one does not _____.

28. An *escapist* mentality refuses to _____.

29. To *exhume* an old idea is to _____.

30. To *exonerate* of wrongdoing is to _____.

31. To *illuminate* the mind is to _____.

32. The *illuminati* are people who _____.

33. To *imbibe* to excess is to _____.

34. To *impale* someone with the truth is to _____.

35. An angel *incarnate* is an angel in _____.

36. To *ingest* information is to _____.

37. An *irritant* will likely cause _____.

38. To *paraphrase* a statement is to _____.

39. *Paraprofessionals* work closely with _____.

40. *Parapsychology* includes _____.

Words with Prefixes (9)

Time and Position

PREFIXES

1. *hyper-* (over, above): hypersensitive _____

2. *hypo-* (under): hypodermic _____

*3. *ob-, oc-, op-* (to, toward, against): obliterate, occasion, oppression _____

_____

_____

WORD LIST

1. *hyper*bole (hiy-PUR-bə-lee), *n*: literally, a throwing over or beyond, and thus an overstatement or exaggeration of the truth

2. *hyper*tension (*hiy*-pər-TEN-shən), *n*: high blood pressure

3. *hypo*critical (*hip*-ə-KRIT-i-kəl), *a*: pretending to be more virtuous than one really is; pretending to have qualities that one does not possess

4. *hypo*thetical (*hiy*-pə-THET-i-kəl), *a*: based upon, having the qualities of, or connected with a hypothesis; theoretical, suppositional, or conjectural rather than matter-of-fact

5. *ob*lique (ow-BLEEK, ə-BLEEK), *a*: not straightforward or to the point; indirect (slanting) and evasive

6. *ob*livion (ə-BLIV-ee-ən), *n*: a condition in which the mind forgets everything; forgetfulness; the state of having been forgotten (by others)

7. *oc*cluded (ə-KLUWD-id), *a*: closed shut, stopped up, or blocked

8. *oc*cupant (AHK-yə-pənt), *n*: a person who lives at a specific residence, place, or location

9. *op*portune (*ahp*-ər-TUWN), *a*: right for the purpose; the most suitable, appropriate, or accommodating

10. *op*probrious (ə-PROW-bree-əs), *a*: expressing scorn, reproach, or abuse; disrespectful or abusive; less often—shameful, disgraceful, or infamous

---

a (f*a*t); ay (f*a*te); ah (f*a*r); au (d*ou*bt); ch (*ch*urch); e (*e*lf, b*e*d, c*a*re); ee (*e*qual); ə (*a*bout); hw (*wh*ile); i (f*i*t); iy (k*i*te); ŋ (li*n*k, si*ng*); o (*au*dio, c*o*rn); ow (*o*cean); oo (b*oo*k); oi (*oi*l); sh (*sh*oe, ambi*ti*on); th (*th*ink); u (*u*p, det*e*r); uw (*oo*ze); y (*y*es, on*i*on); yu (b*u*reau, c*u*re); yuw (*you*th, *u*nity); zh (plea*s*ure)

FILL-IN AND PART-OF-SPEECH IDENTIFICATION

_____ 1. _____ examples are not real-life examples; they are mental creations.

_____ 2. There has been no permanent _____ of the vacant estate for several years.

_____ 3. The sound of a revolving helicopter blade can be an _____ reminder of war for the Vietnam veteran.

_____ 4. _____, or high blood pressure, can be caused by many things.

_____ 5. The drains, _____ by debris, would allow no water to pass through.

_____ 6. Such _____ remarks do not suggest much respect for the people you are abusing.

_____ 7. We are all _____ when we pretend unwavering virtue.

_____ 8. The _____ of sleep is interrupted by dreams.

_____ 9. You must choose the most _____ moment to announce your candidacy; timing is everything.

_____ 10. At what point does _____ become an ordinary untruth?

MATCHING

_____ 1. hyperbole   a. theoretical or suppositional

_____ 2. occupant   b. high blood pressure

_____ 3. hypocritical   c. expressing scorn or abuse

_____ 4. oblique   d. a mindless state

_____ 5. opprobrious   e. blocked off or stopped up

_____ 6. hypertension   f. indirect or evasive

_____ 7. occluded   g. right for the purpose; appropriate

_____ 8. hypothetical   h. pretending to be what one is not

_____ 9. opportune   i. one who lives at a specific residence

_____ 10. oblivion   j. an overstatement or exaggeration

Words with Prefixes (10)

Time and Position

PREFIXES

1. *peri-* (around, near): perigee, perimeter _____

2. *post-* (after, behind): postscript _____

3. *pre-* (before, in front of): precursor, premise _____

_____

4. *re-* (back, again): retract, recurrent _____

WORD LIST

1. *peri*patetic (*per-ə-pə*-TET-ik), *n*: a person who cannot stay in one place; *a,* walking or moving from place to place; unsettled

2. *peri*pheral (pə-RIF-ər-əl), *a*: away from the center (of activity); of minor or secondary importance; on the edges

3. *post*humous (PAHS-chə-məs), *a*: (taking place) after death

4. *post*lude (POWST-*luwd*), *n*: organ music played at (after) the conclusion of a church service; any concluding piece of music or a final chapter or phase of something

5. *post*partum (*powst*-PAHR-təm), *a*: related to the time just after childbirth

6. *pre*cocious (pri-KOW-shəs), *a*: developed or matured ahead of time

7. *pre*monition (*prem-ə*-NISH-ən), *n*: an advance feeling or forewarning, usually that something bad is going to happen; presentiment

8. *pre*posterous (pri-PAHS-tər-əs), *a*: literally, with the first last and the last first, and thus contrary to the usual order of things; ridiculous or absurd

9. *re*ciprocal (ri-SIP-rə-kəl), *a*: affecting both sides mutually, and usually to the benefit of both

10. *re*surgence (ri-SUR-jəns), *n*: the condition or instance of coming again to life, popularity, or forcefulness

---

a (f*a*t); ay (f*a*te); ah (f*a*r); au (d*ou*bt); ch (*ch*urch); e (*e*lf, b*e*d, c*a*re); ee (*e*qual); ə (*a*bout); hw (*wh*ile); i (f*i*t); iy (k*i*te); ŋ (li*n*k, si*ng*); o (*au*dio, c*o*rn); ow (*o*cean); oo (b*oo*k); oi (*oi*l); sh (*sh*oe, ambi*ti*on); th (*th*ink); u (*u*p, det*e*r); uw (*oo*ze); y (*y*es, on*i*on); yu (b*u*reau, c*u*re); yuw (*you*th, *u*nity); zh (plea*s*ure)

191

FILL-IN AND PART-OF-SPEECH IDENTIFICATION

_____ 1. This is a _____ issue, an item of only secondary importance.

_____ 2. A _____ trade agreement between the United States and Japan would likely result in an increase in trade.

_____ 3. A _____ child, my sister learned to read when she was only four.

_____ 4. Retirement may be viewed as the _____ to life.

_____ 5. _____ infection was once a dreaded killer of young mothers.

_____ 6. Your scheme is so _____ that no one would invest money in it.

_____ 7. In recent years there has been a _____ of interest in religious fundamentalism.

_____ 8. Americans are a _____ people, constantly moving from place to place.

_____ 9. I had a _____ of the flood a week before the rain began to fall.

_____ 10. _____ praise is of small comfort to the hero in the ground.

MATCHING

_____ 1. posthumous   a. an advance warning, as of something bad

_____ 2. premonition   b. moving about from place to place

_____ 3. peripheral   c. ridiculous or absurd

_____ 4. resurgence   d. music at the end of a church service

_____ 5. precocious   e. the condition of coming to life again

_____ 6. peripatetic   f. following death

_____ 7. reciprocal   g. related to the time just after childbirth

_____ 8. postlude   h. around the edges

_____ 9. preposterous   i. affecting both sides mutually

_____ 10. postpartum   j. developed ahead of time

Words with Prefixes (11)

Time and Position

PREFIXES

1. *pro-* (forward, ahead of, forth): prologue _____

2. *retro-* (backward): retrospect _____

3. *se-* (apart, away from): secure _____

4. *tele-* (far): telepathy _____

5. *trans-* (across, beyond, over): translucent _____

WORD LIST

1. *profuse* (prə-FYUWS), *a*: pouring forth in great quantity; generous, sometimes to excess; abundant

2. *prospectus* (prə-SPEK-təs), *n*: an advance printed program or outline, as of a commercial, artistic, literary, or other venture

3. *retroactive* (*re*-trow-AK-tiv), *a*: applying to or influencing an earlier period; becoming effective at a specific time in the past

4. *retrofit* (RE-trow-*fit*), *v*: to install newly developed parts or improvements on a piece of machinery or a system originally made when such parts did not exist or were not available; *n*, such an installed item

5. *seduce* (si-DUWS), *v*: literally, to lead aside; to lead astray; to persuade to do something less than upright

6. *sedulous* (SEJ-ə-ləs), *a*: literally, apart from trickery, and thus diligent and hardworking; persistent; accomplished only through perseverance

7. *telegenic* (*tel*-ə-JEN-ik), *a*: having physical traits that project well on television

8. *telekinesis* (*tel*-ə-kə-NEE-sis), *n*: the supposed ability to move objects by mental or mystical powers, and without the help of traditional mechanical means

9. *transcend* (tran-SEND), *v*: to go beyond normal limits; to rise above (the ordinary); to exceed

10. *transpose* (trans-POWZ), *v*: to reverse the normal order or position of, as words or numbers; to interchange

a (*fat*); ay (*fate*); ah (*far*); au (*doubt*); ch (*church*); e (*elf*, b*e*d, c*a*re); ee (*equal*); ə (*about*); hw (*while*); i (*fit*); iy (k*i*te); ŋ (li*n*k, si*ng*); o (*audio*, c*o*rn); ow (*ocean*); oo (b*oo*k); oi (*oil*); sh (*shoe*, ambi*ti*on); th (*think*); u (*up*, de*ter*); uw (*ooze*); y (*yes*, on*i*on); yu (b*u*reau, c*u*re); yuw (*youth*, *u*nity); zh (plea*s*ure) **193**

FILL-IN AND PART-OF-SPEECH IDENTIFICATION

_____ 1. You can _____ this classic car with a catalytic converter and then burn lead-free gas.

_____ 2. Years of _____ training, play, and practice are required to make it to the major leagues.

_____ 3. Your behavior _____ ordinary meanness; you are a devil in disguise.

_____ 4. From a detailed _____, I learned about the company's new profit-sharing plan.

_____ 5. When my eyes are tired, I sometimes _____ words as I read.

_____ 6. Madame LaFarge is so good at _____ that she moved our house without so much as a crowbar.

_____ 7. My pay raise is _____; it goes back to last January.

_____ 8. Only the most _____ models are used in television commercials for cosmetics.

_____ 9. You cannot _____ me with praise; I prefer money.

_____ 10. A _____ display of wildflowers grew in the highland meadow, extending as far as the eye could see.

MATCHING

_____ 1. retroactive   a. projecting well on television

_____ 2. seduce   b. a program printed in advance

_____ 3. telekinesis   c. to go beyond normal limits

_____ 4. profuse   d. to install new items on something old

_____ 5. telegenic   e. to reverse or interchange

_____ 6. transpose   f. becoming active at a time in the past

_____ 7. prospectus   g. the ability to move objects with the mind

_____ 8. sedulous   h. generous or abundant

_____ 9. transcend   i. to lead astray

194 _____ 10. retrofit   j. diligent, hard-working, or persistent

Words with Prefixes (12)

Time and Position

PREFIXES

1. *super-* (over, above): supersonic _____

   _____

*2. *syn-*, *syl-*, *sym-* (with, together, at the same time): synchronize, syllable, symbiotic _____

   _____

   _____

WORD LIST

1. *super*cilious (*suw*-pər-SIL-ee-əs), *a*: haughty and scornful, especially as revealed by a facial expression including raised eyebrows

2. *super*numerary (*suw*-pər-NUW-mə-*rer*-ee), *a*: above or beyond the necessary, required, or usual number; *n*, a person hired but not really needed; a person with no real function; an extra

3. *super*sede (*suw*-pər-SEED), *v*: to go beyond or take the place of, usually because of superiority; to replace

4. *super*structure (SUW-pər-*struk*-chər), *n*: that part of a structure or system that is built on top of an underlying foundation; the visible part of a building above the foundation

5. *syl*logism (SIL-ə-*jiz*-əm), *n*: a form of deductive reasoning consisting of a major premise, a minor premise, and a conclusion; for example, "All dogs bark (*major premise*); a Doberman barks (*minor premise*); therefore, a Doberman is a dog (*conclusion*)."

6. *sym*biosis (*sim*-bi-OW-sis), *n*: the relationship whereby two or more things (organisms) live in close association, usually to the benefit of both

7. *sym*posium (sim-POW-zee-əm), *n*: a meeting or conference organized for the discussion of intellectual topics; a collection of articles published on a single topic

8. *syn*drome (SIN-*drowm*), *n*: a group of characteristics indicating a condition; a describable condition

---

a (f*a*t); ay (f*a*te); ah (f*a*r); au (d*ou*bt); ch (*ch*ur*ch*); e (*e*lf, b*e*d, c*a*re); ee (*e*qual); ə (*a*bout); hw (*wh*ile); i (f*i*t); iy (k*i*te); ŋ (li*n*k, si*ng*); o (*au*dio, c*o*rn); ow (*o*cean); oo (b*oo*k); oi (*oi*l); sh (*sh*oe, ambi*ti*on); th (*th*ink); u (*u*p, de*te*r); uw (*oo*ze); y (*y*es, on*i*on); yu (b*u*reau, c*u*re); yuw (*you*th, *u*nity); zh (plea*s*ure)

9. *synopsis* (si-NAHP-sis), *n*: a brief summary, as of a novel or play; a recap, as of events

10. *synthesis* (SIN-thə-sis), *n*: a combining of diverse elements into an entity; the whole of something, being made up of diverse parts

FILL-IN AND PART-OF-SPEECH IDENTIFICATION

_____ 1. The international _____ on AIDS was attended by researchers from all around the globe.

_____ 2. The evening news offers a _____, or summary, of the day's events.

_____ 3. Do you think Japan will _____ the United States as the strongest economic power in the world?

_____ 4. The _____ of any economic system can be no stronger than its foundation.

_____ 5. True friendship is a kind of _____ from which both parties receive benefits.

_____ 6. The burnout _____, now almost an epidemic, seems to be affecting people in all kinds of high-pressure jobs.

_____ 7. An expert at the _____ gesture, my aunt can put most people down with one raised eyebrow.

_____ 8. A _____ with a false premise will probably have a false conclusion.

_____ 9. This book is really a _____ of all the author's earlier works.

_____ 10. By eliminating many of the _____ branches, the company could save a bundle of money at no harm to itself.

MATCHING

_____ 1. supersede   a. haughty and scornful

_____ 2. synopsis   b. a tripartite form of deductive reasoning

_____ 3. supernumerary   c. a meeting or conference

_____ 4. syllogism   d. a combining of elements into something new

_____ 5. syndrome   e. to go beyond or replace

_____ 6. superstructure   f. a summary or recap

_____ 7. symposium   g. a relationship of mutual benefit

_____ 8. supercilious   h. a condition made up of several symptoms

_____ 9. synthesis   i. the visible part of a structure

_____ 10. symbiosis   j. beyond that which is necessary; extra

Completion Exercise for Prefixes 9 through 12

1. *Hyperbole* always includes _____.

2. *Hypertension* is also called _____.

3. *Hypocritical* people sometimes _____.

4. *Hypothetical* examples are not _____.

5. An *oblique* reference will likely be _____.

6. In a state of *oblivion,* one _____.

7. An *occluded* weather front is one that _____.

8. *Occupants* are people who _____.

9. The *opportune* moment is just the _____.

10. An *opprobrious* attitude suggests _____.

11. *Peripatetic* individuals have difficulty _____.

12. A *peripheral* area is one _____.

13. *Posthumous* honors are given _____.

14. A *postlude* is played at _____.

15. *Postpartum* depression occurs _____.

16. *Precocious* students tend to _____.

17. A *premonition* usually _____.

18. *Preposterous* lies are lies that _____.

19. *Reciprocal* praise is praise given _____.

20. A *resurgence* of interest involves _____. **197**

21. *Profuse* profits are profits on _____.

22. From a *prospectus*, one might _____.

23. A *retroactive* agreement _____.

24. A *retrofit* is an item that _____.

25. To *seduce* the mind is to _____.

26. A *sedulous* effort is one including _____.

27. A *telegenic* nose is one that _____.

28. The power of *telekinesis* can be used to _____.

29. To *transcend* mortality is to _____.

30. To *transpose* thoughts is to _____.

31. *Supercilious* individuals tend to be _____.

32. *Supernumerary* personnel can easily be _____.

33. To *supersede* one's idols is to _____.

34. A *superstructure* must have a(n) _____.

35. *Syllogisms* always end with a(n) _____.

36. From a *symbiosis*, both parties _____.

37. *Symposiums* are organized for the purpose of _____.

38. A *syndrome* will likely include _____.

39. The purpose of a *synopsis* is to _____.

40. Any *synthesis* includes _____.

Words with Prefixes (13)

Quality and Condition

PREFIXES

1. *a-, an-* (not, without): apathy, anemic _____

2. *ant(i)-* (in opposition to): antarctic, antipathy _____

_____

3. *contra-, contre-, contro-, counter-* (opposed to, opposite): contradiction, controversy,

counterpart _____

_____

WORD LIST

1. *a*moral (ay-MOR-əl), *a*: without the ordinary ability to distinguish right from wrong; neither moral nor immoral

2. *an*ecdote (AN-ik-*dowt*), *n*: a brief, amusing, and usually biographical narrative—originally unpublished and thus not generally known

3. *an*omaly (ə-NAHM-ə-lee), *n*: literally, not the same, and thus anything that represents a departure from the normal or usual; an exception

4. *ant*agonistic (an-*tag*-ə-NIS-tik), *a*: actively (angrily) in opposition to; mutually opposing

5. *anti*social (*an*-ti-SOW-shəl), *a*: contrary to the basic principles of society; generally harmful to the welfare of people; unfriendly

6. *a*typical (ay-TIP-i-kəl), *a*: not typical, usual, normal, or characteristic; abnormal

7. *contra*band (KAHN-trə-*band*), *n*: anything that is against the law to buy and sell, especially something imported or exported

8. *contre*temps (KAHN-trə-*tahn*), *n*: an unfortunate or inopportune happening; an awkward or embarrassing mishap

9. *contro*vert (KAHN-trə-*vurt*), *v*: to argue against; to dispute, contradict, or deny; to debate

10. *counter*mand (KAUN-tər-*mand*), *v*: to cancel or revoke, as a previous order; *n*, a command reversing an earlier one

---

a (*fat*); ay (*fate*); ah (*far*); au (*doubt*); ch (*church*); e (*elf*, b*e*d, c*a*re); ee (*equal*); ə (*about*); hw (*while*); i (*fit*); iy (*kite*); ŋ (*link*, *sing*); o (*audio*, c*o*rn); ow (*ocean*); oo (*book*); oi (*oil*); sh (*shoe*, ambi*ti*on); th (*think*); u (*up*, det*er*); uw (*ooze*); y (*yes*, on*i*on); yu (*bureau*, c*u*re); yuw (*youth*, *u*nity); zh (*pleasure*)

199

FILL-IN AND PART-OF-SPEECH IDENTIFICATION

_____ 1. The couple had become so _____ toward each other that they could not speak without having a quarrel.

_____ 2. The second order _____, or reverses, the first one.

_____ 3. The exploding blue star proved to be an _____, an exception, rather than the rule.

_____ 4. Why _____ so strongly a point of such minor significance?

_____ 5. An anomaly is _____ rather than typical.

_____ 6. Even when they kill, wild animals are _____ in their behavior, neither immoral nor moral.

_____ 7. The first _____ of the evening occurred when the guest of honor accidentally went into the wrong toilet.

_____ 8. No one is surprised when _____ people make antagonistic remarks.

_____ 9. My history instructor often tells humorous _____ from the lives of famous people.

_____ 10. Dealing in _____ may be profitable, but it can land you in jail.

MATCHING

_____ 1. anomaly   a. a brief and amusing story

_____ 2. contraband   b. in angry opposition to; mutually opposing

_____ 3. amoral   c. an order reversing an earlier one

_____ 4. atypical   d. an event that is not normal; an exception

_____ 5. antisocial   e. an awkward or embarrassing mishap

_____ 6. controvert   f. unusual or abnormal

_____ 7. anecdote   g. neither moral nor immoral

_____ 8. countermand   h. to argue or debate

_____ 9. antagonistic   i. something bought or sold illegally

_____ 10. contretemps   j. contrary to the basic principles of society

Words with Prefixes (14)

Quality and Condition

PREFIXES

1. *dis-* (not, away, apart): distended _____

2. *dys-* (bad, badly): dysfunction _____

3. *eu-* (good, well): eugenics, eulogize _____

4. *iso-* (equal, alike): isosceles _____

WORD LIST

1. *dis*array (*dis*-ə-RAY), *n*: a condition or situation of confusion, untidiness, or disorder

2. *dis*enchanted (*dis*-in-CHANT-id), *a*: no longer under the power or influence of; disappointed with

3. *dis*passionate (dis-PASH-ən-it), *a*: not passionate, and thus without emotion; calm, distant, or impartial

4. *dys*lexia (dis-LEK-see-ə), *n*: a brain dysfunction causing an individual to see written words as scrambled letters

5. *dys*peptic (dis-PEP-tik), *a*: characteristic of one who suffers from impaired (bad) digestion, and thus grouchy or gloomy

6. *eu*phemism (YUW-fə-*miz*-əm), *n*: a mild word or expression used in place of a distasteful or unpleasant one, as "passing" for "death"

7. *eu*phoria (yuw-FOR-ee-ə), *n*: a feeling (sometimes insufficiently motivated) of extreme well-being; an emotional "high"

8. *eu*thanasia (*yuw*-thə-NAY-zhə), *n*: literally, a good death, and thus the practice of suppressing the pain of a dying person; by extension, in recent times, the painless killing of a terminally ill person; mercy killing

9. *iso*magnetic (*iy*-sow-mag-NET-ik), *a*: having the same or equal magnetic force

10. *iso*metric (*iy*-sə-ME-trik), *a*: having an equal measure, as in a method of physical exercise where one set of muscles is tensed against another set exerting equal pressure

---

a (f*a*t); ay (f*a*te); ah (f*a*r); au (d*ou*bt); ch (*ch*urch); e (*e*lf, b*e*d, c*a*re); ee (*e*qual); ə (*a*bout); hw (*wh*ile); i (f*i*t); iy (k*i*te); ŋ (li*n*k, si*ng*); o (*au*dio, c*or*n); ow (*o*cean); oo (b*oo*k); oi (*oi*l); sh (*sh*oe, ambi*ti*on); th (*th*ink); u (*u*p, det*er*); uw (*oo*ze); y (*y*es, oni*o*n); yu (b*u*reau, c*u*re); yuw (*you*th, *u*nity); zh (plea*s*ure)

201

FILL-IN AND PART-OF-SPEECH IDENTIFICATION

_____ 1. This _____ character is always grouchy and gloomy.

_____ 2. My whole life is in _____; everything is confusion.

_____ 3. The earth and the moon are not _____; thus, the moon orbits the earth.

_____ 4. The intermittent _____ of adolescence subsides as one begins to face the realities of life in college.

_____ 5. Many people have become _____ with political rhetoric and high-sounding promises; they have heard it all before.

_____ 6. The excessive use of _____ by the middle class suggests that many people do not like to call a spade a spade.

_____ 7. We do not include as _____ the painless execution of convicted murderers.

_____ 8. My cousin is as _____ as a distant star, always calm and impartial.

_____ 9. You can get an _____ workout by simply tensing the muscles of one arm against those of the other.

_____ 10. Many students with _____ can read, but they often read very slowly.

MATCHING

_____ 1. dispassionate   a. disappointed with

_____ 2. isomagnetic   b. a good word used in place of a harsh one

_____ 3. disarray   c. having equal measure

_____ 4. euphoria   d. emotionally calm and distant

_____ 5. dyspeptic   e. mercy killing

_____ 6. isometric   f. having equal magnetic force

_____ 7. disenchanted   g. a situation of confusion or disorder

_____ 8. euthanasia   h. a brain dysfunction causing reading difficulty

_____ 9. dyslexia   i. an emotional "high"

_____ 10. euphemism   j. grouchy because of poor digestion

Words with Prefixes (15)

Quality and Condition

PREFIXES

*1. *in-, ig-, il-, im-, ir-* (not): inaudible, ignorant, illegal, immortal, irreligious _____

_____

_____

_____

WORD LIST

1. *ig*noble (ig-NOW-bəl), *a*: not noble, and thus possessing a low or base character; dishonorable

2. *il*legible (i-LEJ-ə-bəl), *a*: not legible, and thus impossible to read or make out the meaning of

3. *il*licit (i-LIS-it), *a*: prohibited by law; illegal; improper

4. *im*moderate (i-MAHD-ər-it), *a*: not moderate, and thus without a reasonable measure of restraint; excessive

5. *im*mutable (i-MYUWT-ə-bəl), *a*: not changeable, and thus never changing or wavering

6. *in*clement (in-KLEM-ənt), *a*: showing no mercy; harsh, severe, or stormy

7. *in*cognito (*in*-kahg-NEE-tow), *a*: not known; disguised; *adv,* under an assumed name; *n,* a person living or traveling under a disguise or an assumed name

8. *in*credible (in-KRED-ə-bəl), *a*: not believable, and thus too strange or unusual to be believed; improbable

9. *ir*rational (i-RASH-ə-nəl), *a*: not rational, and thus lacking the power to think clearly; senseless or absurd

10. *ir*resolute (i-REZ-ə-*luwt*), *a*: not resolute, and thus wavering, indecisive, or vacillating

---

a (f*a*t); ay (f*a*te); ah (f*a*r); au (d*ou*bt); ch (*ch*ur*ch*); e (*e*lf, b*e*d, c*a*re); ee (*e*qual); ə (*a*bout); hw (*wh*ile); i (f*i*t); iy (k*i*te); ŋ (li*n*k, si*ng*); o (*au*dio, c*o*rn); ow (*o*cean); oo (b*oo*k); oi (*oi*l); sh (*sh*oe, ambi*ti*on); th (*th*ink); u (*u*p, det*er*); uw (*oo*ze); y (*y*es, oni*o*n); yu (b*u*reau, c*u*re); yuw (*you*th, *u*nity); zh (plea*s*ure)

FILL-IN AND PART-OF-SPEECH IDENTIFICATION

_____ 1. The candidate is charged with accepting _____ contributions to her campaign fund and may face prosecution.

_____ 2. People sometimes behave in _____, or senseless, ways when their feelings have been hurt.

_____ 3. Gravity seems to be an _____ law of nature; it does not change.

_____ 4. Because the letter was signed "An _____," I did not know who wrote it.

_____ 5. The duke's turning the peasants off the land was an _____ act unbefitting his rank.

_____ 6. After eight weeks of _____ weather, a little sunshine was a welcome surprise.

_____ 7. _____ consumption, even of wholesome foods, may not be good for one's health.

_____ 8. The tale was too _____ to be believed by anyone.

_____ 9. These _____ characters continue to vacillate; they cannot make up their minds about anything.

_____ 10. Your handwriting is so _____ that I did not even realize it was handwriting.

MATCHING

_____ 1. illicit   a. not believable

_____ 2. inclement   b. impossible to read

_____ 3. irrational   c. with name unknown

_____ 4. ignoble   d. without restraint; excessive

_____ 5. incredible   e. prohibited by law

_____ 6. immutable   f. indecisive or wavering

_____ 7. incognito   g. senseless or absurd

_____ 8. illegible   h. dishonorable; not noble

_____ 9. irresolute   i. without mercy; harsh or severe

_____ 10. immoderate   j. that cannot be changed

Words with Prefixes (16)

Quality and Condition

PREFIXES

1. *hetero-* (other, different): heterodox _____

2. *homo-* (same, alike): homogenize _____

3. *mega-, megalo-* (large, great, million): megaphone, megalopolis _____

_____

4. *mis-* (bad, wrong, to hate): miscarriage _____

WORD LIST

1. *hetero*chromatic (*het-ə-row-krə-MAT-ik*), *a*: having or related to several colors

2. *hetero*geneous (*het-ər-ə-JEE-nee-əs*), *a*: composed of elements or items that are unlike; dissimilar

3. *homo*chromatic (*how-mə-krow-MAT-ik*), *a*: having, consisting of, or relating to one color; monochromatic (*mahn-ə-krow-MAT-ik*)

4. *homo*geneous (*how-mə-JEE-nee-əs*), *a*: composed of elements that are similar or alike; uniform

5. *mega*lith (*MEG-ə-lith*), *n*: a huge stone, especially one like those used in prehistoric monuments

6. *megalo*mania (*meg-ə-low-MAY-nee-ə*), *n*: a mental disorder including delusions of grandeur and infantile feelings of personal importance; the desire always to do big things

7. *mega*ton (*MEG-ə-tun*), *n*: a unit of explosive force equaling one million tons of TNT, and by extension any force of great explosive or persuasive power

8. *mis*construe (*mis-kən-STRUW*), *v*: to interpret incorrectly; to confuse; to misunderstand

9. *mis*creant (*MIS-kree-ənt*), *a*: villainous and evil; *n*, an evil person; a criminal

10. *miso*gamist (*mi-SAHG-ə-mist*), *n*: a person who hates the institution of marriage

a (f*a*t); ay (f*a*te); ah (f*a*r); au (d*ou*bt); ch (*ch*ur*ch*); e (*e*lf, b*e*d, c*a*re); ee (*e*qual); ə (*a*bout); hw (*wh*ile); i (f*i*t); iy (k*i*te); ŋ (li*n*k, si*ng*); o (*au*dio, c*o*rn); ow (*o*cean); oo (b*oo*k); oi (*oi*l); sh (*sh*oe, ambi*ti*on); th (*th*ink); u (*u*p, det*e*r); uw (*oo*ze); y (*y*es, on*i*on); yu (b*u*reau, c*u*re); yuw (*you*th, *u*nity); zh (plea*s*ure)

FILL-IN AND PART-OF-SPEECH IDENTIFICATION

_____ 1. A _____ design may also be called a monochromatic design.

_____ 2. A huge _____ stood at the entrance to the Stone Age fort.

_____ 3. If you _____ directions as simple as these, what will you do when you get to the complicated ones?

_____ 4. The United States has a _____ population, which includes people whose ancestors came from all over the world.

_____ 5. You ignoble _____! You are a total villain.

_____ 6. The population of Sweden is so _____ that to an American the streets of Stockholm seem inhabited by thousands of clones.

_____ 7. Is it a form of _____ to believe that God takes a personal interest in one's daily affairs?

_____ 8. Three or four messy divorces can make a _____ of the most romantic person.

_____ 9. A _____ pattern will include several colors.

_____ 10. A bomb of only a few _____ would destroy our town.

MATCHING

_____ 1. megalith   a. monochromatic

_____ 2. heterochromatic   b. to misunderstand

_____ 3. misogamist   c. an explosive force equal to one million tons of TNT

_____ 4. homogeneous   d. having several colors

_____ 5. misconstrue   e. an evil person

_____ 6. heterogeneous   f. an irrational desire to do big things

_____ 7. miscreant   g. one who hates the institution of marriage

_____ 8. megaton   h. a huge stone

_____ 9. homochromatic   i. composed of dissimilar parts

_____ 10. megalomania   j. made up of similar elements; uniform

206

Completion Exercise for Prefixes 13 through 16

1. *Amoral* behavior is neither _____.

2. *Anecdotes* are both _____.

3. An *anomaly* should not be taken as _____.

4. Ideas *antagonistic* to freedom are _____.

5. *Antisocial* individuals do not care much for _____.

6. An *atypical* situation may catch us _____.

7. Examples of *contraband* might include _____.

8. As a result of a *contretemps,* one can be greatly _____.

9. To *controvert* an idea is to _____.

10. To *countermand* authority is to _____.

11. A plan in *disarray* is one that is _____.

12. To be *disenchanted* with romance is to be _____.

13. *Dispassionate* justice is justice that is _____.

14. *Dyslexia* results in _____.

15. *Dyspeptic* individuals will likely be _____.

16. *Euphemisms* for "fat" include _____.

17. If you are experiencing *euphoria,* you are _____.

18. The purpose of *euthanasia* is to _____.

19. *Isomagnetic* bodies have _____.

20. *Isometric* exercises require _____.

21. An *ignoble* act is evidence of _____.

22. *Illegible* graffiti is difficult to _____.

23. An *illicit* affair is one that is _____.

24. *Immoderate* exercise goes beyond _____.

25. *Immutable* circumstances are ones that _____.

26. *Inclement* weather is characterized by _____.

27. To travel *incognito* is to travel _____.

28. An *incredible* cataclysm may produce _____.

29. *Irrational* actions are not _____.

30. An *irresolute* effort will likely be _____.

31. *Heterochromatic* designs will feature _____.

32. A *heterogeneous* aggregation will include _____.

33. A *homochromatic* beam will display only _____.

34. A *homogeneous* population will be generally _____.

35. *Megalithic* monuments are composed of _____.

36. To suffer from *megalomania* is to _____.

37. A *megaton* of evidence would be _____.

38. To *misconstrue* another's intentions is to _____.

39. We are all *miscreant* when we _____.

40. If everyone were a *misogamist*, _____.

Words with Prefixes (17)

Quality and Condition

The prefix *mal-*, meaning "bad" or "evil," is featured in so many words that it merits consideration by itself. Perhaps the fact that it has only negative meanings suggests something about both the human condition and how that condition influences the creation of words. If we suffer from *malnutrition,* we have a bad diet. If we are *maladjusted,* we are badly adjusted. A physician guilty of *malpractice* is considered not only a bad doctor, but also an evil person. And a *malingerer* is a person who pretends to be ill in order to avoid work.

WORD LIST

1. *mal*adroit (*mal*-ə-DROIT), *a*: not adroit, and thus awkward, clumsy, bungling, or without skill

2. *mal*ady (MAL-ə-dee), *n*: a bad condition; a disease or disorder; any unwholesome condition

3. *mal*aise (mə-LAYZ), *n*: a vague feeling of (approaching) illness; a general "down" feeling

4. *mal*content (MAL-kən-*tent*), *a*: not content, and thus frequently complaining, dissatisfied, critical, or rebellious; *n*, a discontented, rebellious person

5. *mal*evolent (mə-LEV-ə-lənt), *a*: wishing bad (evil) things to happen to other people; showing ill will

6. *mal*feasance (mal-FEE-zəns), *n*: misconduct, especially by a person in public office; wrongdoing

7. *mal*ice (MAL-is), *n*: an active desire to harm another person; a fixed desire to do mischief

8. *mal*ign (mə-LIYN), *v*: to speak evil of; to defame or slander

9. *mal*ignant (mə-LIG-nənt), *a*: having an evil or harmful influence; likely to cause death; virulent

10. *mal*odorous (mal-OW-dər-əs), *a*: having a bad odor; stinking

---

a (fat); ay (fate); ah (far); au (doubt); ch (church); e (elf, bed, care); ee (equal); ə (about); hw (while); i (fit); iy (kite); ŋ (link, sing); o (audio, corn); ow (ocean); oo (book); oi (oil); sh (shoe, ambition); th (think); u (up, deter); uw (ooze); y (yes, onion); yu (bureau, cure); yuw (youth, unity); zh (pleasure)

FILL-IN AND PART-OF-SPEECH IDENTIFICATION

_____ 1. This complaining _____ is never satisfied with anything.

_____ 2. Some people think that the media tend to _____ public figures, whether they have committed any wrongdoing or not.

_____ 3. There is no _____ in my cat's casual slaughter of small animals; to her it is a diversion.

_____ 4. Yes, I would call it _____ to send your second wife a card on your first wife's birthday.

_____ 5. Accused of _____ in office, the mayor resigned with contrition.

_____ 6. Fortunately, the tumor was not _____; the patient is in no danger.

_____ 7. Laziness is a _____ from which I have suffered all my life, and I cannot seem to find a cure.

_____ 8. A _____ smell came from the water filtration plant on particularly hot afternoons.

_____ 9. This year, Karen counteracted her usual midwinter _____ by going on a cruise in the Caribbean.

_____ 10. In a _____ state of mind, I wished all my enemies dead.

MATCHING

_____ 1. malcontent   a. clumsy, bungling, or awkward

_____ 2. malfeasance   b. stinking

_____ 3. malignant   c. a vague feeling of approaching illness

_____ 4. malady   d. likely to cause death

_____ 5. malign   e. misconduct or wrongdoing, as in office

_____ 6. malevolent   f. a bad condition; a disease

_____ 7. malodorous   g. a desire to do mischief

_____ 8. maladroit   h. wishing bad things to happen to others

_____ 9. malice   i. to speak evil of another

_____ 10. malaise   j. a person who is never satisfied

Words with Prefixes (18)

Quality and Condition

PREFIXES

1. *macro-* (big, large, long): macroeconomics _____

2. *micro-* (small, little): microphone _____

3. *non-* (not): nondescript, nonego _____

4. *pseudo-* (false): pseudointellectual _____

5. *un-* (not): uncertain _____

WORD LIST

1. *macro*biotics (*mak*-row-biy-AHT-iks), *n*: the theory or practice of lengthening life through special diets
2. *macro*cosm (MAK-rə-*kahz*-əm), *n*: the greater world or universe; a total system
3. *micro*cosm (MIY-krə-*kahz*-əm), *n*: a little world; a miniature model, as of the universe or a system
4. *micro*fiche (MIY-krə-*feesh*), *n*: a sheet of film containing reduced pages, as from books, newspapers, or magazines
5. *non*chalant (*nahn*-shə-LAHNT), *a*: literally, not warm, and thus displaying a cool lack of interest or concern; casual; indifferent
6. *non*conformist (*nahn*-kən-FOR-mist), *n*: a person who does not follow established practices or beliefs; *a,* regularly inclined not to observe the accepted rules, practices, or beliefs of society; contrary
7. *non*entity (nahn-EN-tə-tee), *n*: the state of not existing, or something that exists only in the imagination; a person or thing of virtually no importance
8. *pseudo*nym (SUW-də-*nim*), *n*: literally, a false name, and thus a name assumed, as by a writer; a pen name
9. *pseudo*science (SUW-dow-SIY-əns), *n*: an area of study that is questionably scientific, such as astrology and perhaps macrobiotics
10. *un*daunted (un-DON-tid), *a*: not afraid, discouraged, disheartened, or intimidated; fearless or intrepid

a (fat); ay (fate); ah (far); au (doubt); ch (church); e (elf, bed, care); ee (equal); ə (about); hw (while); i (fit); iy (kite); ŋ (link, sing); o (audio, corn); ow (ocean); oo (book); oi (oil); sh (shoe, ambition); th (think); u (up, deter); uw (ooze); y (yes, onion); yu (bureau, cure); yuw (youth, unity); zh (pleasure)

FILL-IN AND PART-OF-SPEECH IDENTIFICATION

_____ 1. On a few sheets of _____, an entire book may be reproduced.

_____ 2. Most people consider astrology a _____ at best.

_____ 3. You may call this diet an exercise in _____, but I call it food for rabbits.

_____ 4. "Mark Twain" was the _____ used by Samuel Langhorne Clemens.

_____ 5. Ted is not as _____ as he pretends; he is actually very serious-minded.

_____ 6. Calling the neophyte instructor a _____, a person of no importance, was a mistake for which the dean paid dearly.

_____ 7. The universe is a _____ that seems to go on forever.

_____ 8. The resident _____ in the English department, Lucy thinks all rules are made to be broken.

_____ 9. In spite of difficulties, Marsha remains _____ in her goal of earning a Ph.D. in psychology.

_____ 10. A college campus is not society in _____; it is an intramural community protected from society.

MATCHING

_____ 1. microfiche   a. cool, casual, or indifferent

_____ 2. pseudoscience   b. the practice of lengthening life through diet

_____ 3. macrocosm   c. a false science

_____ 4. nonentity   d. the world or universe in miniature

_____ 5. nonchalant   e. a false name

_____ 6. nonconformist   f. the greater world or universe

_____ 7. pseudonym   g. a person of no importance

_____ 8. macrobiotics   h. fearless or unafraid

_____ 9. undaunted   i. film containing reduced pages of books

212 _____ 10. microcosm   j. one who refuses to go by the rules

Words with Prefixes (19)

Number and Amount

PREFIXES

1. *bi(n)-* (two, twice): biennial, binoculars _____

2. *di-, du-* (two): divorce, duplex _____

3. *demi-, hemi-, semi-* (half, partly): demigod, hemisphere, semicircle _____

_____

_____

WORD LIST

1. *bi*cameral (biy-KAM-ər-əl), *a*: having two chambers or branches
2. *bi*lateral (biy-LAT-ər-əl), *a*: involving two parties, sides, or opinions—as in an agreement or action taken
3. *bi*nary (BIY-nər-ee), *a*: made up of two things or two parts; dual; *n*, something made up of two parts or components
4. *demi*tasse (DEM-ee-tahs), *n*: a small cup of strong black coffee, or the cup itself
5. *di*lemma (di-LEM-ə), *n*: a choice between (two) equally unacceptable alternatives
6. *du*bious (DUW-bee-əs), *a*: literally, moving in two directions, and thus doubtful or causing doubt; suspicious, questionable, or shady
7. *du*plicity (duw-PLIS-ə-tee), *n*: clever and deceitful double-dealing
8. *hemi*plegia (*hem*-ə-PLEE-jee-ə), *n*: paralysis on only one side of the body, as from a stroke
9. *semi*conductor (*sem*-i-kən-DUK-tər), *n*: a substance whose electrical conductivity is greater than that of an insulator but less than that of a conductor—with temperature being a factor
10. *semi*literate (*sem*-i-LIT-ər-it), *a*: barely able to read and write; able to read but not to write; *n*, a person with poor language skills

---

a (f*a*t); ay (f*a*te); ah (f*a*r); au (d*ou*bt); ch (*ch*ur*ch*); e (*e*lf, b*e*d, c*a*re); ee (*e*qual); ə (*a*bout); hw (*wh*ile); i (f*i*t); iy (k*i*te); ŋ (li*n*k, si*ng*); o (*au*dio, c*o*rn); ow (*o*cean); oo (b*oo*k); oi (*oi*l); sh (*sh*oe, ambi*ti*on); th (*th*ink); u (*u*p, de*ter*); uw (*oo*ze); y (*y*es, on*i*on); yu (b*u*reau, c*u*re); yuw (*you*th, *u*nity); zh (plea*s*ure)

213

FILL-IN AND PART-OF-SPEECH IDENTIFICATION

_____ 1. My _____ is that I want to be a man of leisure, but I have no money.

_____ 2. A _____ legislature has two houses rather than one.

_____ 3. I am suspicious of the motives of these _____ characters; they are up to something shady.

_____ 4. My grandfather's _____ was caused by a stroke.

_____ 5. Marriage should be something more than a _____ agreement between a man and a woman, enforceable in a court of law.

_____ 6. Studies have revealed that many _____ students, hardly able to read or write, are graduating from high school.

_____ 7. Your reputation for _____ is well-known; you are a double-dealer extraordinary.

_____ 8. A _____ star is really two stars moving around each other.

_____ 9. Inexpensive _____ have helped make personal computers possible.

_____ 10. "Figuratively speaking," Megan said, "life is a _____, and a bitter brew."

MATCHING

_____ 1. dubious

_____ 2. bicameral

_____ 3. semiliterate

_____ 4. demitasse

_____ 5. hemiplegia

_____ 6. bilateral

_____ 7. duplicity

_____ 8. semiconductor

_____ 9. binary

_____ 10. dilemma

a. involving two parties, sides, or opinions

b. a choice between unacceptable alternatives

c. doubtful, suspicious, or questionable

d. a substance that conducts electricity more effectively at higher temperatures

e. something made up of two components

f. barely able to read and write

g. paralysis on one side of the body

h. a small cup of strong black coffee

i. double-dealing

j. having two chambers or houses

Words with Prefixes (20)

Number and Amount

PREFIXES

1. *kilo-, milli-* (thousand): kilometer, millennium _____

   _____

2. *mon(o)-, uni-* (one): monograph, monarch, unicorn _____

   _____

3. *multi-, poly-* (many): multistage, polygamy _____

4. *tri-* (three): tricentennial _____

WORD LIST

1. *kilo*watt (KIL-ə-*waht*), *n*: a unit of electrical power, equal to one thousand watts

2. *milli*second (MIL-ə-*sek*-ənd), *n*: a thousandth part of a second

3. *mono*logue (MAHN-ə-*log*), *n*: a long (and often boring) speech by one person

4. *mono*poly (mə-NAHP-ə-lee), *n*: a market situation in which one company is the exclusive supplier of a commodity or service—the reverse of *mon*opsony (mə-NAHP-sə-nee), wherein there is only one buyer for a commodity or service

5. *multi*lateral (*mul*-ti-LAT-ər-əl), *a*: having many sides or participants, as an agreement or action

6. *poly*glot (PAHL-i-*glaht*), *a*: involving elements from several languages; *n*, a confusion of languages; a multilingual person; something written or spoken in several languages

7. *poly*syllabic (*pahl*-i-sə-LAB-ik), *a*: having many syllables, usually four or more

8. *tri*partite (triy-PAHR-*tiyt*), *a*: including three divisions or parts

9. *uni*cameral (yuw-nə-KAM-ər-əl), *a*: consisting of a single chamber, as a legislative body

10. *uni*lateral (*yuw*-nə-LAT-ər-əl), *a*: involving only one side or party; done by one party alone, usually without considering the opinions of others who might be affected

---

a (fat); ay (fate); ah (far); au (doubt); ch (church); e (elf, bed, care); ee (equal); ə (about); hw (while); i (fit); iy (kite); ŋ (link, sing); o (audio, corn); ow (ocean); oo (book); oi (oil); sh (shoe, ambition); th (think); u (up, deter); uw (ooze); y (yes, onion); yu (bureau, cure); yuw (youth, unity); zh (pleasure)

FILL-IN AND PART-OF-SPEECH IDENTIFICATION

_____ 1. No company has a _____ on the manufacture of automobiles.

_____ 2. Johnny Carson begins his show with a humorous _____.

_____ 3. English is a _____ language, including words and other elements borrowed from many languages.

_____ 4. The new president's _____ action, taken without consulting anyone, angered the board of directors.

_____ 5. The power company could not tell me the price of a _____ of electricity.

_____ 6. _Sesquipedalian_ is a _____ word.

_____ 7. A _____ legislative body includes only one house.

_____ 8. In little more than a _____, according to the big-bang theory, the entire universe was created.

_____ 9. We have a _____ separation of power in the federal government: executive branch, legislative branch, and judicial branch.

_____ 10. NATO is a _____ organization, including several nations.

MATCHING

_____ 1. monopoly

_____ 2. polyglot

_____ 3. unilateral

_____ 4. kilowatt

_____ 5. tripartite

_____ 6. millisecond

_____ 7. polysyllabic

_____ 8. monologue

_____ 9. unicameral

_____ 10. multilateral

a. a confusion of languages

b. a speech by one person

c. including three parts or divisions

d. the situation occurring when one company is the exclusive maker of a product

e. done by one party acting alone

f. having many sides or participants

g. a unit of electrical power

h. consisting of a single chamber

i. including many syllables

j. a thousandth part of a second

Completion Exercise for Prefixes 17 through 20

1. A *maladroit* act suggests a certain _____.

2. A *malady* will likely cause some _____.

3. A *malaise* of the spirit can result in _____.

4. *Malcontents* frequently _____.

5. *Malevolent* impulses may cause one to _____.

6. A minor *malfeasance* does not mean that one _____.

7. *Malice* may provoke one to _____.

8. To *malign* a neighbor is to _____.

9. *Malignant* antagonism sometimes _____.

10. Nothing is more *malodorous* than _____.

11. The goal of *macrobiotics* is to _____.

12. Contemplating the *macrocosm* can be _____.

13. A *microcosm* is a universe in _____.

14. One might use *microfiche* when _____.

15. Few things are more *nonchalant* than _____.

16. *Nonconformist* behavior tends to be _____.

17. A *nonentity* is a person of _____.

18. The *pseudonym* I would choose is _____.

19. A *pseudoscience* does not really _____.

20. Remaining *undaunted* is difficult when _____.

21. Our *bicameral* Congress includes both _____.

22. Any *bilateral* treaty will _____.

23. A *binary* number will include _____.

24. From a *demitasse*, one expects to drink _____.

25. A *dilemma* often requires a difficult _____.

26. *Dubious* distinctions are _____.

27. *Duplicity* always involves _____.

28. *Hemiplegia* results in a person being _____.

29. *Semiconductors* are used in _____.

30. *Semiliterate* people have difficulty _____.

31. A *kilowatt* is a unit of _____.

32. A *millisecond* is even briefer than _____.

33. *Monologues* always feature _____.

34. When a *monopoly* exists, prices usually _____.

35. Any *multilateral* treaty will _____.

36. A *polyglot* is a person who _____.

37. *Polysyllabic* words include _____.

38. A *tripartite* strategy will have _____.

39. A *unicameral* legislature is one that _____.

40. *Unilateral* action involves only _____.

Chapter

Words with Suffixes

A *suffix* is a letter or cluster of letters that comes at the end of a word. An understanding of suffixes is important to vocabulary study because suffixes not only have meaning in the dictionary sense, but they can also limit or expand the way a word may sensibly be used—that is, where it may be placed in a sentence. The suffixes presented in this chapter are of three types, forming or indicating (1) nouns, (2) adjectives, or (3) verbs.

The following list demonstrates how adding a suffix to a word can change the word's meaning or part of speech:

word		suffix		new word
American	+	-ize	=	Americanize
brother	+	-ly	=	brotherly
cheer	+	-ful	=	cheerful
color	+	-less	=	colorless
depend	+	-ence	=	dependence
false	+	-ify	=	falsify
mountain	+	-eer	=	mountaineer
real	+	-ist	=	realist
tire	+	-some	=	tiresome
weak	+	-en	=	weaken

Words with Suffixes (1)

SUFFIXES

1. *-acy, -cy* (state, quality, condition), *n*: accuracy, infancy _____

_____

2. *-ar* (like, related to), *a*: muscular _____

3. *-ative* (related to, tending to), *a*: informative, talkative _____

_____

4. *-ee* (a person doing or receiving action), *n*: employee, amputee _____

_____

WORD LIST

1. absent*ee* (*ab*-sən-TEE), *n*: one who is not present, especially at an appointed time
2. celib*acy* (SEL-ə-bə-see), *n*: the state of not being married; abstinence from any sexual activity
3. demonstr*ative* (di-MAHN-strə-tiv), *a*: tending to show feelings and emotions openly; effusive; illustrative
4. design*ee* (*dez*-ig-NEE), *n*: a person who has been selected for or appointed to a particular office or position but not yet officially installed
5. dissimil*ar* (di-SIM-ə-lər), *a*: not like something else
6. fall*acy* (FAL-ə-see), *n*: a mistake in the process of logical thought; a mistaken idea
7. insul*ar* (IN-sə-lər), *a*: characteristic of people who live on an isolated island, and thus narrow-minded and provincial
8. remuner*ative* (ri-MYUW-nə-*ray*-tiv), *a*: offering the opportunity for substantial profits; profitable
9. tent*ative* (TEN-tə-tiv), *a*: tending to be indefinite, hesitant, uncertain, timid; provisional rather than final
10. titul*ar* (TICH-ə-lər), *a*: existing in name or title but having little or no real power or authority

---

a (f*a*t); ay (f*a*te); ah (f*a*r); au (d*ou*bt); ch (*ch*ur*ch*); e (*e*lf, b*e*d, c*a*re); ee (*e*qual); ə (*a*bout); hw (*wh*ile); i (f*i*t); iy (k*i*te); ŋ (li*n*k, si*ng*); o (*au*dio, c*o*rn); ow (*o*cean); oo (b*oo*k); oi (*oi*l); sh (*sh*oe, ambi*ti*on); th (*th*ink); u (*u*p, det*er*); uw (*oo*ze); y (*y*es, on*i*on); yu (b*u*reau, c*u*re); yuw (*yo*uth, *u*nity); zh (plea*s*ure)

FILL-IN AND PART-OF-SPEECH IDENTIFICATION

____ 1. Perhaps a less _____ presentation would have been better received; the audience seemed a little conservative for all your wild gestures.

____ 2. Social service is not a very _____ profession; few people go into it for the money.

____ 3. The two examples are entirely _____, not at all alike.

____ 4. The president is only the _____ head of the company; the board of directors really runs the place.

____ 5. Most of the _____ claimed that they were not at the conference because they had other engagements.

____ 6. Margaret was quite _____ in her response; she seemed unsure of what she wanted to say.

____ 7. Baxter is the unofficial _____ for the new position as head of public relations.

____ 8. The fundamental _____ in your argument is that you incorrectly assume that all women think alike.

____ 9. The world is made less _____ by modern communications.

____ 10. Historically, a vow of _____ has been taken by Roman Catholic priests. They do not marry.

MATCHING

____ 1. designee   a. one who is not present

____ 2. insular   b. a mistake in the thought process

____ 3. absentee   c. provisional rather than final

____ 4. remunerative   d. abstinence from sexual activity

____ 5. dissimilar   e. a person designated for a position

____ 6. tentative   f. in title or name only

____ 7. celibacy   g. profitable

____ 8. titular   h. showing one's emotions openly

____ 9. fallacy   i. narrow-minded and provincial

____ 10. demonstrative   j. not like something else

Words with Suffixes (2)

SUFFIXES

1. *-ary, -ory* (like, related to), *a*: temporary, regulatory _____

   _____

2. *-ation* (action, state, condition, result of), *n*: aberration, alteration _____

   _____

3. *-fy* (to make, to cause to be), *v*: magnify _____

4. *-ine* (like, related to), *a*: divine _____

WORD LIST

1. bov*ine* (BOW-*viyn*), *a*: slow or oxlike in movement or thought; dull or stupid

2. commiser*ation* (kə-*miz*-ə-RAY-shən), *n*: the act of showing or feeling sorrow, pity, or sympathy for another

3. culin*ary* (KUL-ə-*ner*-ee), *a*: related to or used in the kitchen or in cooking

4. fragment*ary* (FRAG-mən-*ter*-ee), *a*: as if broken into bits and pieces; incomplete or disconnected

5. pac*ify* (PAS-ə-*fiy*), *v*: to make peaceful, tranquil, or calm; to appease

6. prist*ine* (PRIS-*teen*), *a*: like earlier or simpler times, and thus pure, unspoiled, or uncorrupted

7. reform*ation* (*ref*-ər-MAY-shən), *n*: the act or process of reorganizing or restructuring, as an institution or business

8. savo*ry* (SAY-vər-ee), *a*: pleasing to the taste or smell; a little salty or pungent; not sweet

9. sedent*ary* (SED-ən-*ter*-ee), *a*: inclined to sit, recline, or remain in one place; inactive

10. vil*ify* (VIL-ə-*fiy*), *v*: to (try to) make someone appear mean and evil; to make a villain of

---

a (f*a*t); ay (f*a*te); ah (f*a*r); au (d*ou*bt); ch (*ch*ur*ch*); e (*e*lf, b*e*d, c*a*re); ee (*e*qual); ə (*a*bout); hw (*wh*ile); i (f*i*t); iy (k*i*te); ŋ (li*n*k, si*ng*); o (*au*dio, c*o*rn); ow (*o*cean); oo (b*oo*k); oi (*oi*l); sh (*sh*oe, ambi*ti*on); th (*th*ink); u (*u*p, de*te*r); uw (*oo*ze); y (*y*es, on*i*on); yu (b*u*reau, *cu*re); yuw (*you*th, *u*nity); zh (plea*s*ure)

FILL-IN AND PART-OF-SPEECH IDENTIFICATION

_____ 1. It is pointless to expect much _____ from people who think only of themselves.

_____ 2. You cannot _____ a hungry child with promises of food.

_____ 3. The chef used a _____ sauce to enhance the taste of the roast.

_____ 4. My knowledge of Russian history is _____, broken by many large gaps.

_____ 5. _____ individuals prefer a nap to a jog around the neighborhood.

_____ 6. A creature of _____ intelligence should not be expected to think on his feet, nor in any other posture.

_____ 7. You only _____ yourself by speaking ill of such a good person.

_____ 8. My _____ skills have greatly improved since my divorce. I can now fend for myself in the kitchen.

_____ 9. The _____ wilderness north of the lake was destroyed by the construction of an apartment complex.

_____ 10. The new president called for a complete _____ of the company, from the ground up.

MATCHING

_____ 1. fragmentary   a. sorrow, pity, or sympathy for another

_____ 2. savory   b. pure, unspoiled, or uncorrupted

_____ 3. sedentary   c. to make a villain of

_____ 4. culinary   d. a complete restructuring

_____ 5. bovine   e. inactive; remaining in one place

_____ 6. pristine   f. pleasing to the taste or smell

_____ 7. vilify   g. related to the kitchen or to cooking

_____ 8. commiseration   h. to make peaceful

_____ 9. pacify   i. incomplete or disconnected

_____ 10. reformation   j. oxlike

Words with Suffixes (3)

SUFFIXES

1. *-ile* (able to be, like, related to), *a*: senile _____

   _____

2. *-ly* (like, characteristic of), *a*: manly _____

3. *-ment* (state, quality, that which), *n*: impediment, excitement _____

   _____

4. *-ure* (state, quality, that which), *n*: tenure, departure _____

   _____

WORD LIST

1. aggrandize*ment* (ə-GRAN-dəz-mənt), *n*: anything that makes something (appear) greater, as in power, stature, or sphere of influence; the process of making something greater

2. detri*ment* (DE-trə-mənt), *n*: a damage, injury, or disadvantage; anything that causes harm or injury

3. disclos*ure* (dis-KLOW-zhər), *n*: the process of revealing or making known, usually that which has been unknown; a revelation

4. doc*ile* (DAHS-əl), *a*: able to be easily taught or managed; submissive, especially to discipline or instruction

5. habili*ments* (hə-BIL-ə-mənts), *n*: collectively, clothing, furnishings, attire, equipment, or trappings—as those that go with a position or station in life; paraphernalia

6. port*ly* (PORT-lee), *a*: carrying a lot of weight, and thus stout, corpulent, or fat

7. puer*ile* (PYUW-ər-əl), *a*: like a child, and thus immature or silly; childish or trivial

8. rapt*ure* (RAP-chər), *n*: a state of being "carried away," as by pleasure, joy, or love; ecstasy

9. sur*ly* (SUR-lee), *a*: like an overly masterful man, and thus ill-tempered and uncivil; gloomy, rude, or threatening

10. vir*ile* (VIR-əl), *a*: like a man, and thus manly, masculine, vigorous, or forceful

a (fat); ay (fate); ah (far); au (doubt); ch (church); e (elf, bed, care); ee (equal); ə (about); hw (while); i (fit); iy (kite); ŋ (link, sing); o (audio, corn); ow (ocean); oo (book); oi (oil); sh (shoe, ambition); th (think); u (up, deter); uw (ooze); y (yes, onion); yu (bureau, cure); yuw (youth, unity); zh (pleasure)

FILL-IN AND PART-OF-SPEECH IDENTIFICATION

_____ 1. This promotion is one more _____ of Heathcliff's reputation, which grows more substantial almost daily.

_____ 2. Feelings of _____ often accompany the experience of falling in love.

_____ 3. Among the _____ of a junior executive are a three-piece suit and wingtip shoes.

_____ 4. The _____ appearance of the two muscular fighters quickly dissolved in the hundred-degree heat.

_____ 5. A part-time job can become a _____ to a student's grades, doing no small amount of damage.

_____ 6. _____ behavior tends to be childish and silly rather than mature and adult.

_____ 7. Public _____ of the mayor's dealings with gangsters drove him from office.

_____ 8. Once slender and fit, Boswell is now a _____, middle-aged executive.

_____ 9. In the morning, many people are _____ until they have consumed one or two cups of coffee.

_____ 10. Although _____ enough now, the old lion was once a ferocious beast.

MATCHING

_____ 1. disclosure   a. anything that makes something (appear) greater

_____ 2. rapture   b. stout or fat

_____ 3. aggrandizement   c. uncivil, gloomy, rude, or threatening

_____ 4. surly   d. clothing, furnishings, or equipment

_____ 5. detriment   e. manly, masculine, or vigorous

_____ 6. puerile   f. a revelation

_____ 7. habiliments   g. easily taught or disciplined

_____ 8. virile   h. immature, childish, or silly

_____ 9. portly   i. a state of ecstasy

_____ 10. docile   j. anything causing harm or injury

Words with Suffixes (4)

SUFFIXES

1. *-age* (state, quality, action), *n*: bondage, hostage _____

_____

2. *-ery, -ary* (state, quality, action, place where), *n*: slavery, luminary, mortuary _____

_____

3. *-ic(al)* (like, characteristic of), *a*: orthopedic, astronomical _____

_____

4. *-ing* (causing, caused by, resulting from), *a*: humbling _____

_____

WORD LIST

1. chimer*ical* (ki-MER-i-kəl), *a*: like a terrible monster, and thus absurdly or fantastically unreal; hugely fantastic; impossible
2. cut*lery* (KUT-lər-ee), *n*: various implements used for cutting, especially in the preparation of food
3. debilitat*ing* (di-BIL-ə-*tay*-tiŋ), *a*: causing weakness or an inability to function
4. dot*age* (DOWT-ij), *n*: a feeble and childish state caused by old age; senility; also, a state of excessive or foolish fondness
5. gran*ary* (GRAN-ər-ee), *n*: a place where grains are either grown (in great abundance) or stored after being harvested
6. impend*ing* (im-PEND-iŋ), *a*: about to happen; imminent or threatening
7. inhibit*ing* (in-HIB-ə-tiŋ), *a*: holding back or restraining
8. inim*ical* (in-IM-i-kəl), *a*: like an enemy, and thus hostile or unfriendly; in opposition
9. nostalg*ic* (nah-STAL-jik), *a*: characteristic of a sometimes painful homesickness for the past, as embodied in one's childhood or hometown
10. patron*age* (PAY-trən-ij), *n*: the act of supporting, sponsoring, or encouraging someone or an enterprise

---

a (f*a*t); ay (f*a*te); ah (f*a*r); au (d*ou*bt); ch (*ch*urch); e (*e*lf, b*e*d, c*a*re); ee (*e*qual); ə (*a*bout); hw (*wh*ile); i (f*i*t); iy (k*i*te); ŋ (li*n*k, si*ng*); o (*au*dio, c*o*rn); ow (*o*cean); oo (b*oo*k); oi (*oi*l); sh (*sh*oe, ambi*ti*on); th (*th*ink); u (*u*p, de*te*r); uw (*oo*ze); y (*y*es, on*i*on); yu (b*u*reau, c*u*re); yuw (*you*th, *u*nity); zh (plea*s*ure)

FILL-IN AND PART-OF-SPEECH IDENTIFICATION

_____ 1. Ian's wife gave him an expensive set of _____ for his birthday, along with a cookbook and a map of the kitchen.

_____ 2. Lies are _____ to the truth, its worst enemy.

_____ 3. Any law _____ freedom of the press increases the government's control over the people.

_____ 4. I have managed to achieve my _____ without ever passing through a prime.

_____ 5. We took a _____ trip back to our hometown and discovered that everything seemed to have shrunk.

_____ 6. _____ monsters appear in many Japanese disaster films.

_____ 7. My _____ of the corner delicatessen has lasted for more than twenty years.

_____ 8. In the summer of 1988, the American _____, the Midwest, suffered through the worst drought in many years.

_____ 9. Constant criticism from a parent can have a _____ effect on children, making them feel worthless.

_____ 10. The _____ collapse of the stock market had millions of people in a state of panic.

MATCHING

_____ 1. granary   a. like an enemy, and thus in opposition to

_____ 2. patronage   b. a place where grains are grown or stored

_____ 3. chimerical   c. cutting implements used in food preparation

_____ 4. inimical   d. the act of supporting, as with money

_____ 5. debilitating   e. holding back or restraining

_____ 6. nostalgic   f. a state of foolish fondness

_____ 7. inhibiting   g. like a hugely fantastic monster

_____ 8. cutlery   h. about to happen; imminent

_____ 9. dotage   i. characteristic of homesickness for the past

_____ 10. impending   j. causing weakness or an inability to function

Completion Exercise for Suffixes 1 through 4

1. An *absentee* is a person who is not _____.

2. *Celibacy* is practiced by people who _____.

3. *Demonstrative* individuals often show their _____.

4. A *designee* has not yet been _____.

5. *Dissimilar* items are not _____.

6. A *fallacy* is a mistake in the _____.

7. An *insular* person will likely be _____.

8. *Remunerative* activities are ones that _____.

9. A *tentative* agreement has not yet been _____.

10. A *titular* position always has a(n) _____.

11. *Bovine* movements or thoughts are _____.

12. *Commiseration* always involves feelings of _____.

13. *Culinary* skills are best demonstrated in _____.

14. *Fragmentary* evidence will likely be _____.

15. To *pacify* is to make _____.

16. A *pristine* setting has not been _____.

17. A *reformation* results in a(n) _____.

18. A *savory* flavor will likely be _____.

19. *Sedentary* people prefer to _____.

20. To *vilify* someone is to _____.

21. An *aggrandizement* makes something appear _____.

22. A *detriment* causes _____.

23. A *disclosure* results in something being _____.

24. *Docile* students are easily _____.

25. The *habiliments* of a knight included _____.

26. A *portly* individual is _____.

27. *Puerile* behavior is typical of _____.

28. One is likely to experience *rapture* when _____.

29. *Surly* individuals are often _____.

30. A *virile* man is anything but a(n) _____.

31. A *chimerical* happening will likely be _____.

32. *Cutlery* is used to _____.

33. Anything *debilitating* may result in _____.

34. A state of *dotage* includes _____.

35. A *granary* is a place where _____.

36. An *impending* event is about to _____.

37. An *inhibiting* circumstance will likely _____.

38. Anything *inimical* to fair play is _____.

39. *Nostalgic* situations sometimes make us _____.

40. To offer *patronage* is to _____.

Words with Suffixes (5)

SUFFIXES

1. *-acity* (the quality of), *n*: veracity _____

2. *-al, -ial* (like, related to), *a*: maternal, convivial _____

   _____

3. *-istic* (with the quality of), *a*: futuristic _____

4. *-ize* (to cause to be, to act), *v*: fraternize _____

WORD LIST

1. autumn*al* (o·TUM·nəl), *a*: in any way characteristic of fall: colorful, mature, declining, nostalgic, and so on

2. cauter*ize* (KO·tə·riyz), *v*: to burn or sear, as with an iron or needle; to kill dead tissue to prevent infection

3. chauvin*istic* (*show*·və·NIS·tik), *a*: excessively (mindlessly) devoted to one's country or to one's race, group, sex, and so on

4. fatal*istic* (*fayt*·əl·IS·tik), *a*: characteristic of the notion that all things are controlled by fate and are thus beyond human influence; willing to accept every event as inevitable; often pessimistic

5. fil*ial* (FIL·ee·əl), *a*: like, related to, or befitting a son or daughter—usually in a good sense

6. galvan*ize* (GAL·və·niyz), *v*: to startle (electrically) into action; to excite; to spur

7. plagiar*ize* (PLAY·jə·riyz), *v*: to steal the words, writings, or ideas of another and present them as one's own

8. plural*istic* (*ploor*·əl·IS·tik), *a*: having more than one part or form; characteristic of a society with many different bases of political, economic, and social power

9. sag*acity* (sə·GAS·ə·tee), *n*: the quality of wisdom and good judgment; the type of wisdom that comes with age and experience

10. ten*acity* (tə·NAS·ə·tee), *n*: the quality of holding on firmly, as to beliefs or long-range goals; persistent toughness

a (*fat*); ay (*fate*); ah (*far*); au (*doubt*); ch (*church*); e (*elf, bed, care*); ee (*equal*); ə (*about*); hw (*while*); i (*fit*); iy (*kite*); ŋ (*link, sing*); o (*audio, corn*); ow (*ocean*); oo (*book*); oi (*oil*); sh (*shoe, ambition*); th (*think*); u (*up, deter*); uw (*ooze*); y (*yes, onion*); yu (*bureau, cure*); yuw (*youth, unity*); zh (*pleasure*)

FILL-IN AND PART-OF-SPEECH IDENTIFICATION

_____ 1. Nell is such a _____ person; her favorite line is "In the end, we're all dead."

_____ 2. You may _____ a wound against further discomfort, but not a broken heart.

_____ 3. The youthful lawyer displayed a _____ beyond her years in questioning the witnesses.

_____ 4. A dozen quick break-ins will _____ most neighborhoods into some protective action.

_____ 5. The ambassador's obviously _____ statements displeased the visiting delegation from Japan.

_____ 6. America is indeed a _____ nation, having a great variety of power bases.

_____ 7. Orphans have little chance to demonstrate _____ affection.

_____ 8. Hodge, a person of great _____, will simply not give up on anything he starts.

_____ 9. Do not _____ the words of others; write your own paper.

_____ 10. On such an _____ afternoon, the mountains were a kaleidoscope of bright colors.

MATCHING

_____ 1. chauvinistic   a. characteristic of the fall of the year

_____ 2. galvanize   b. having many bases of power

_____ 3. filial   c. to use another's words as one's own

_____ 4. sagacity   d. to spur, as into action

_____ 5. autumnal   e. persistent toughness

_____ 6. plagiarize   f. viewing all events as inevitable

_____ 7. cauterize   g. the wisdom of age

_____ 8. pluralistic   h. due from a son or daughter to parents

_____ 9. tenacity   i. to burn or sear, as to kill dead tissue

_____ 10. fatalistic   j. excessively devoted to one's own group

Words with Suffixes (6)

SUFFIXES

1. *-eer, -ier* (a person who), *n*: mountaineer _____

2. *-ility* (the quality of), *n*: civility _____

3. *-less* (without, lacking), *a*: colorless _____

4. *-ose* (possessing qualities of), *a*: verbose _____

WORD LIST

1. comat*ose* (KOW-mə-*tows*, KAHM-ə-*tows*), *a*: almost unconscious; in a stupor; lethargic or torpid

2. feck*less* (FEK-lis), *a*: without vitality or purpose; careless, irresponsible, or ineffectual

3. financ*ier* (*fin*-ən-SEER), *n*: an expert or one clever at handling stocks, bonds, investments, and other money matters

4. fut*ility* (fyuw-TIL-ə-tee), *n*: the condition or quality of hopelessness or uselessness; a useless act or gesture

5. hap*less* (HAP-lis), *a*: without much luck; unfortunate, as if by nature

6. joc*ose* (jow-KOWS), *a*: given to good-natured joking; playful, merry, and humorous

7. mor*ose* (mə-ROWS), *a*: sullen, gloomy, fretful, peevish, and generally unpleasant

8. profit*eer* (*prahf*-ə-TEER), *n*: one who takes unfair advantage of a market shortage to charge very high prices and thus make large profits

9. relent*less* (ri-LENT-lis), *a*: persistent; never letting up; harsh and pitiless in pursuing anything

10. sen*ility* (si-NIL-ə-tee), *n*: the condition or quality of mental deterioration that often accompanies old age

a (f*a*t); ay (f*a*te); ah (f*a*r); au (d*ou*bt); ch (*ch*urch); e (*e*lf, b*e*d, c*a*re); ee (*e*qual); ə (*a*bout); hw (*wh*ile); i (f*i*t); iy (k*i*te); ŋ (li*n*k, si*n*g); o (*au*dio, c*o*rn); ow (*o*cean); oo (b*oo*k); oi (*oi*l); sh (*sh*oe, ambi*ti*on); th (*th*ink); u (*u*p, de*te*r); uw (*oo*ze); y (*y*es, on*i*on); yu (b*u*reau, c*u*re); yuw (*you*th, *u*nity); zh (plea*s*ure)

FILL-IN AND PART-OF-SPEECH IDENTIFICATION

_____ 1. Of all the nerve, to call me _____ just because I am careless and irresponsible.

_____ 2. No one can be _____ all the time; sometimes there is nothing to joke about.

_____ 3. The small-town _____ was charging five dollars for a bottle of Pepsi.

_____ 4. From a blow to the head, the victim was _____ for several days.

_____ 5. _____ is a dirty trick that time plays on the aging.

_____ 6. Bruno is a _____ character, an accident always about to happen.

_____ 7. With _____ effort, the brigade continued to fight the fire day after day.

_____ 8. After winning the lottery, Laura needed a _____ to manage her money.

_____ 9. The very climate of the northern islands seemed _____—gloomy, fretful, and generally unpleasant.

_____ 10. There is a degree of _____ in trying to teach those who do not want to learn.

MATCHING

_____ 1. futility   a. an expert in money matters

_____ 2. jocose   b. almost unconscious

_____ 3. relentless   c. one making excessive profits

_____ 4. feckless   d. consistently having bad luck

_____ 5. morose   e. mental deterioration of old age

_____ 6. financier   f. a condition of hopelessness

_____ 7. senility   g. gloomy, sullen, and fretful

_____ 8. comatose   h. joking, playful, and merry

_____ 9. profiteer   i. never letting up; persistent

_____ 10. hapless   j. careless, irresponsible, or ineffectual

Words with Suffixes (7)

SUFFIXES

1. *-able, -ible* (able to be), *a*: inalterable, audible _____

_____

2. *-escent* (being, becoming), *a*: phosphorescent, convalescent _____

_____

3. *-esque* (in the manner of), *a*: picturesque _____

4. *-ion,* (action, condition, result of), *n*: oblivion, incursion _____

_____

WORD LIST

1. allus*ion* (ə-LUW-shən), *n*: a passing, indirect, or casual mention of something; an indirect reference to

2. contrit*ion* (kən-TRISH-ən), *n*: the feeling of sorrow and remorse resulting from having done something wrong

3. fluor*escent* (fluw-RES-ənt), *a*: giving off light, as mercury vapor in a tube; radiant

4. grot*esque* (grow-TESK), *a*: unnaturally strange or bizarre; markedly different from that which is considered normal and natural

5. intang*ible* (in-TAN-jə-bəl), *a*: not able to be touched, seen, or easily defined; not concrete

6. laud*able* (LO-də-bəl), *a*: worthy of praise; commendable

7. profus*ion* (prə-FYUW-zhən), *n*: a pouring forth, as of some great quantity; a great abundance

8. qui*escent* (kwiy-ES-ənt), *a*: (becoming) still, quiet, or inactive; dormant

9. statu*esque* (*stach*-uw-ESK), *a*: like a statue, and thus possessing a well-proportioned and graceful physical appearance

10. vi*able* (VIY-ə-bəl), *a*: able to live, as a newborn infant; workable, as a plan or system

a (f*a*t); ay (f*a*te); ah (f*a*r); au (d*ou*bt); ch (*ch*urch); e (*e*lf, b*e*d, c*a*re); ee (*e*qual); ə (*a*bout); hw (*wh*ile); i (f*i*t); iy (k*i*te); ŋ (li*n*k, si*ng*); o (*au*dio, c*or*n); ow (*o*cean); oo (b*oo*k); oi (*oi*l); sh (*sh*oe, ambi*ti*on); th (*th*ink); u (*u*p, det*er*); uw (*oo*ze); y (*y*es, on*i*on); yu (b*u*reau, c*u*re); yuw (*you*th, *u*nity); zh (plea*s*ure)

FILL-IN AND PART-OF-SPEECH IDENTIFICATION

_____ 1. A _____ monster, horrible and unnatural, came out of the swamp one night and ate the sleeping village.

_____ 2. Few actions are more _____ than taking care of one's aging parents.

_____ 3. Do you think that a _____ fetus, one that could live outside the mother's body, should be considered a citizen?

_____ 4. Only one student caught the speaker's _____ to Shakespeare's _Hamlet._

_____ 5. The autumnal mountain scene presented a _____ of bright colors, each flowing into all the others.

_____ 6. It is the _____ quality of leadership that we most prize in elected officials.

_____ 7. The lake becomes _____ at dusk when all the boats come in, and campers begin their fires.

_____ 8. Because the accused demonstrated no _____, the judge gave a harsh sentence.

_____ 9. By lifting weights, Michelle has developed a very _____ physical appearance.

_____ 10. The _____ bulb buzzed and crackled before exploding.

MATCHING

_____ 1. laudable   a. a passing or indirect reference to something

_____ 2. allusion   b. a great abundance

_____ 3. statuesque   c. not concrete or touchable

_____ 4. grotesque   d. able to live; workable

_____ 5. profusion   e. giving off light; radiant

_____ 6. quiescent   f. well-proportioned or physically graceful

_____ 7. contrition   g. unnaturally strange or bizarre

_____ 8. viable   h. worthy of praise; praiseworthy

_____ 9. fluorescent   i. inactive or dormant

236 _____ 10. intangible   j. a feeling of sorrow, remorse, or shame

Words with Suffixes (8)

SUFFIXES

1. *-ant, -ent* (a person who, that which), *n*: emigrant, solvent _____

2. *-ed* (having, characterized by), *a*: perverted, bearded _____

3. *-ish* (to make, to do), *v*: diminish _____

4. *-ity* (quality, condition, state), *n*: amity _____

WORD LIST

1. compon*ent* (kəm-POW-nənt), *n*: a constituent part; an element or ingredient of a larger apparatus or system

2. fetter*ed* (FET-ərd), *a*: restricted from doing what one wants to do; restrained or shackled

3. flour*ish* (FLUR-ish), *v*: to blossom; to thrive, grow, and prosper; to become successful

4. gratu*ity* (grə-TUW-ə-tee), *n*: a gift (generally money) given beyond the usual payment; a tip

5. longe*vity* (lahn-JEV-ə-tee), *n*: the length of life, especially a long life; the span of time spent in a specific activity, such as a job

6. mut*ed* (MYUWT-id), *a*: made quieter or less offensive; toned down

7. par*ity* (PAR-ə-tee), *n*: an equality or resemblance of value, rank, or power; the state of being equal

8. propon*ent* (prə-POW-nənt), *n*: a person who makes a proposal or supports a cause of any sort; an advocate

9. refurb*ish* (ri-FUR-bish), *v*: to freshen up and make like new again; to renovate

10. rever*ed* (ri-VIRD), *a*: viewed with great respect, even awe; venerable

---

a (*fat*); ay (*fate*); ah (*far*); au (*doubt*); ch (*church*); e (*elf, bed, care*); ee (*equal*); ə (*about*); hw (*while*); i (*fit*); iy (*kite*); ŋ (*link, sing*); o (*audio, corn*); ow (*ocean*); oo (*book*); oi (*oil*); sh (*shoe, ambition*); th (*think*); u (*up, deter*); uw (*ooze*); y (*yes, onion*); yu (*bureau, cure*); yuw (*youth, unity*); zh (*pleasure*)

FILL-IN AND PART-OF-SPEECH IDENTIFICATION

_____ 1. The waiter was insulted by a _____ of only a dollar.

_____ 2. I am a _____ of a national health system. That means I am in favor of it.

_____ 3. A few minor repairs will never _____ this old house.

_____ 4. Feminists seek wage _____, or equality, between men and women.

_____ 5. _____ by poor study habits, Ed had a tough time during his first year in college.

_____ 6. Surprisingly, the most _____ person I ever met was Chuck Yeager, the first man to break the sound barrier.

_____ 7. Free enterprise does not _____ in a communist state.

_____ 8. My great-grandparents are proud of their health and _____.

_____ 9. A _____, or muffled, sound came from the closet.

_____ 10. The first _____ of altruism is concern for one's fellow creatures.

MATCHING

_____ 1. muted   a. to blossom, thrive, or prosper

_____ 2. flourish   b. a part, element, or ingredient

_____ 3. revered   c. to make like new again

_____ 4. parity   d. the length of life

_____ 5. component   e. an advocate or supporter

_____ 6. longevity   f. equality of value

_____ 7. refurbish   g. a tip

_____ 8. fettered   h. toned down

_____ 9. proponent   i. held in great respect

_____ 10. gratuity   j. restrained or shackled

Completion Exercise for Suffixes 5 through 8

1. *Autumnal* breezes will likely be _____.

2. To *cauterize* a wound is to _____.

3. *Chauvinistic* individuals are sometimes _____.

4. A *fatalistic* attitude is not very _____.

5. *Filial* responsibilities always involve _____.

6. To *galvanize* people is to _____.

7. To *plagiarize* ideas is to _____.

8. *Pluralistic* societies include _____.

9. *Sagacity* is more common among _____.

10. The quality of *tenacity* includes _____.

11. A person in a *comatose* state is not very _____.

12. A *feckless* reaction is without _____.

13. A *financier* should know all about _____.

14. To experience *futility* is to feel _____.

15. *Hapless* characters do not have much _____.

16. A *jocose* disposition is generally _____.

17. *Morose* individuals are often _____.

18. A *profiteer* is much interested in _____.

19. A *relentless* attack seemingly never _____.

20. *Senility* is more common among _____.

21. If you make an *allusion* to something, you _____.

22. A feeling of *contrition* is evidence of _____.

23. Anything *fluorescent* gives off _____.

24. A *grotesque* situation will likely be _____.

25. *Intangible* things cannot actually be _____.

26. A *laudable* act is worthy of _____.

27. A *profusion* of anything is _____.

28. When anger becomes *quiescent*, it _____.

29. A *statuesque* physique displays _____.

30. That which is *viable* can _____.

31. A stereo's *components* are its _____.

32. To be *fettered* by something is to be _____.

33. If a bush *flourishes*, it _____.

34. To receive a *gratuity* is to receive _____.

35. The *longevity* of an idea is its _____.

36. *Muted* colors or sounds are not very _____.

37. When there is *parity*, there is _____.

38. A *proponent* of peace is one who _____.

39. To *refurbish* a building is to _____.

40. A *revered* person is one who is _____.

Words with Suffixes (9)

SUFFIXES

1. *-ious, -ous* (having, characterized by), *a*: commodious, hazardous _____

2. *-ish* (like, related to), *a*: foolish _____

3. *-ist* (a person who), *n*: anarchist _____

4. *-ive* (having the quality of), *a*: creative _____

WORD LIST

1. amor*ous* (AM·ər·əs), *a*: having or showing love; suggestive of lovemaking or sexual desire
2. apolog*ist* (ə·PAHL·ə·jist), *n*: an individual who speaks or writes in defense or support of something, as a doctrine or political action
3. apprehens*ive* (ap·ri·HEN·siv), *a*: fearful, uneasy, or anxious—especially about the future or some future event
4. boor*ish* (BOOR·ish), *a*: like a boor, and thus rude, impolite, ill-mannered, socially awkward, and so on
5. cop*ious* (KOW·pee·əs), *a*: full of; plentiful or abundant; in large numbers
6. fopp*ish* (FAHP·ish), *a*: characteristic of a foolish person, especially a vain man who pays too much attention to his appearance and clothing
7. incis*ive* (in·SIY·siv), *a*: keenly penetrating; cutting into
8. nihil*ist* (NIY·ə·list), *n*: a person who denies the existence of any rational basis for truth or knowledge as well as any meaning or purpose in life; also, one who wishes to destroy established institutions; sometimes, a terrorist
9. punit*ive* (PYUW·nə·tiv), *a*: having the quality of punishment; intended to discipline
10. sad*ist* (SAY·dist), *n*: a person who gets (sexual) pleasure from inflicting pain on others

---

a (*fat*); ay (*fate*); ah (*far*); au (*doubt*); ch (*church*); e (*elf, bed, care*); ee (*equal*); ə (*about*); hw (*while*); i (*fit*); iy (*kite*); ŋ (*link, sing*); o (*audio, corn*); ow (*ocean*); oo (*book*); oi (*oil*); sh (*shoe, ambition*); th (*think*); u (*up, deter*); uw (*ooze*); y (*yes, onion*); yu (*bureau, cure*); yuw (*youth, unity*); zh (*pleasure*)

FILL-IN AND PART-OF-SPEECH IDENTIFICATION

_____ 1. Only a hippo could have _____ feelings for another hippo; the beast is too ugly for anything else to love.

_____ 2. It is sometimes difficult to distinguish between a _____ and a terrorist who claims to act out of patriotic or religious zeal.

_____ 3. Once again the village had a _____ harvest, and everyone's barn was filled.

_____ 4. This _____ character spends too much time on his appearance.

_____ 5. The American Libertarian Party sent a political _____ to the symposium to explain the party's philosophy.

_____ 6. _____ measures are intended to punish someone.

_____ 7. Ralph is so _____ that he is rude even when he talks in his sleep.

_____ 8. I am not really a _____; I just like to watch people crawl.

_____ 9. Coming from a friend, such _____ criticism can cut one deeply.

_____ 10. The villagers were _____ about the government's grand scheme to build a dam on the local trout stream.

MATCHING

_____ 1. apprehensive   a. a defender, as of a doctrine or teaching

_____ 2. foppish   b. plentiful or abundant

_____ 3. punitive   c. suggestive of lovemaking

_____ 4. boorish   d. intended to punish

_____ 5. nihilist   e. keenly penetrating; pointed

_____ 6. amorous   f. rude, impolite, and ill-mannered

_____ 7. incisive   g. paying too much attention to one's appearance

_____ 8. apologist   h. one who enjoys inflicting pain

_____ 9. sadist   i. fearful, uneasy, or anxious

_____ 10. copious   j. one who denies any purpose to life

Words with Suffixes (10)

SUFFIXES

1. *-en* (to make), *v*: weaken _____

2. *-escence* (the quality of), *n*: adolescence _____

_____

3. *-ice* (condition, state, quality), *n*: malice _____

_____

4. *-id* (like, marked by, showing), *a*: pellucid, candid _____

_____

WORD LIST

1. chast*en* (CHAY-sən), *v*: to punish or discipline in order to make better; to correct
2. conval*escence* (*kahn*-və-LES-əns), *n*: the period of time or state during which one is recovering from an illness; a regaining of strength
3. coward*ice* (KAU-ər-dis), *n*: a shameful lack of courage, especially when in danger
4. enlight*en* (in-LIYT-ən), *v*: to deliver the "brightness" of truth and knowledge; to broaden the mind
5. liv*id* (LIV-id), *a*: lead-colored or bluish-gray, as with rage or hostility
6. lumin*escence* (*luw*-mə-NES-əns), *n*: the quality of giving off much light but little heat; cool brilliance
7. morb*id* (MOR-bid), *a*: marked by disease or a diseased state of mind, and thus grim, gruesome, grisly, or gloomy
8. nov*ice* (NAHV-is), *n*: a person new at any task or activity; a beginner or neophyte
9. obsol*escence* (*ahb*-sə-LES-əns), *n*: the quality of being out of fashion or no longer in practice or use
10. torp*id* (TOR-pid), *a*: marked by diminished activity; slow, dull, or sluggish

---

a (*fat*); ay (*fate*); ah (*far*); au (*doubt*); ch (*church*); e (*elf, bed, care*); ee (*equal*); ə (*about*); hw (*while*); i (*fit*); iy (*kite*); ŋ (*link, sing*); o (*audio, corn*); ow (*ocean*); oo (*book*); oi (*oil*); sh (*shoe, ambition*); th (*think*); u (*up, deter*); uw (*ooze*); y (*yes, onion*); yu (*bureau, cure*); yuw (*youth, unity*); zh (*pleasure*)

FILL-IN AND PART-OF-SPEECH IDENTIFICATION

_____ 1. _____ with rage, Martin looked as if he might faint.

_____ 2. I am only a _____ at golf, and I doubt that I will ever be a scratch player.

_____ 3. Major surgery usually requires a period of _____.

_____ 4. At the college level, should teachers _____ students?

_____ 5. The reporters seemed to take a _____ delight in detailing the grisly crime.

_____ 6. Technological _____ can happen very quickly in some high-tech industries; innovations occur rapidly.

_____ 7. It is sometimes difficult to distinguish between _____ and discretion or prudence.

_____ 8. Many animals sink into a _____ state during hibernation.

_____ 9. A strange _____ surrounded the swamp after the electrical storm.

_____ 10. Copious reading can _____ even a lazy mind.

MATCHING

_____ 1. livid

_____ 2. torpid

_____ 3. luminescence

_____ 4. cowardice

_____ 5. convalescence

_____ 6. morbid

_____ 7. obsolescence

_____ 8. chasten

_____ 9. novice

_____ 10. enlighten

a. cool brilliance

b. grim, gruesome, or grisly

c. to discipline or correct

d. slow, dull, or sluggish

e. to broaden the mind

f. a period of time during which strength is regained

g. lead-colored or bluish-gray

h. a beginner or neophyte

i. a shameful lack of courage

j. the quality of being out of fashion

Words with Suffixes (11)

SUFFIXES

1. *-ance, -ence* (quality, state, action), *n*: tolerance, benevolence _____

_____

2. *-ate* (to make, to act), *v*: alienate _____

3. *-ism* (practice, state, quality, action), *n*: altruism, archaism _____

_____

4. *-some* (tending to be), *a*: burdensome _____

WORD LIST

1. barbar*ism* (BAHR-bə-*riz*-əm), *n*: the state or condition of primitive incivility; a brutal or savage act
2. conflu*ence* (KAHN-*fluw*-əns), *n*: the act of coming or flowing together, as rivers or ideas; a place of joining
3. denigr*ate* (DEN-ə-*grayt*), *v*: literally, to make black or to blacken, and thus to tarnish the reputation of; to defame
4. femin*ism* (FEM-ə-*niz*-əm), *n*: the principle or movement holding that women and men should enjoy the same social, political, and economic rights
5. ful*some* (FOOL-səm), *a*: offensive to either the senses or one's moral sensibilities; beyond the bounds of good taste; excessive to the point of being disgusting
6. nepot*ism* (NEP-ə-*tiz*-əm), *n*: the practice of a person in public office giving political positions to relatives or friends; favoritism
7. procrastin*ate* (prow-KRAS-tə-*nayt*), *v*: to put off doing until a later time; to postpone, as doing some unpleasant task
8. retic*ence* (RET-ə-səns), *n*: the state of being habitually silent or uncommunicative; an unwillingness to speak
9. vigil*ance* (VIJ-ə-ləns), *n*: a state of purposeful watchfulness, as at one's post; the quality of being alert, as to danger or trouble
10. win*some* (WIN-səm), *a*: charming in a sweet, engaging way; innocently charming

a (fat); ay (fate); ah (far); au (doubt); ch (church); e (elf, bed, care); ee (equal); ə (about); hw (while); i (fit); iy (kite); ŋ (link, sing); o (audio, corn); ow (ocean); oo (book); oi (oil); sh (shoe, ambition); th (think); u (up, deter); uw (ooze); y (yes, onion); yu (bureau, cure); yuw (youth, unity); zh (pleasure)

FILL-IN AND PART-OF-SPEECH IDENTIFICATION

_____ 1. Such black deeds _____ the characters of everyone taking part in them.

_____ 2. The mayor was accused of _____ when she appointed her nephew as building inspector.

_____ 3. Jacqueline's _____ manner makes it difficult not to like her.

_____ 4. The _____ of ideas should be a natural part of university life.

_____ 5. Tom's _____ makes it almost impossible for him to speak in public.

_____ 6. _____, the movement for equality for women, is really a natural part of the American dream.

_____ 7. Most of us _____ a little when it comes to doing an unpleasant task.

_____ 8. Such _____ flattery offends everyone of taste and sensibility.

_____ 9. It takes more than academic _____ to earn good grades; you must also have some brain power.

_____ 10. _____ thrives on brutality and savagery.

MATCHING

_____ 1. fulsome   a. a coming or flowing together

_____ 2. nepotism   b. the quality of being alert

_____ 3. barbarism   c. the movement for equal rights for women

_____ 4. reticence   d. favoritism toward relatives

_____ 5. confluence   e. to tarnish the reputation of

_____ 6. procrastinate   f. an unwillingness to speak

_____ 7. vigilance   g. innocently charming

_____ 8. feminism   h. a savage act

_____ 9. winsome   i. to postpone or put off doing

_____ 10. denigrate   j. beyond the bounds of good taste

Words with Suffixes (12)

SUFFIXES

1. *-ent, -ant* (doing, showing, having), *a*: eminent, extravagant _____

_____

2. *-ette, -et* (little, small), *n*: cigarette, piglet _____

_____

3. *-ful* (full of), *a*: graceful _____

4. *-tude* (quality, state, result), *n*: fortitude, magnitude _____

_____

WORD LIST

1. corpul*ent* (KOR-pyə-lənt), *a*: having a stout body; fleshy and obese
2. dole*ful* (DOWL-fəl), *a*: deeply sorrowful and melancholy; causing sadness
3. gain*ful* (GAYN-fəl), *a*: full of gain, and thus producing profit or sustenance
4. insolv*ent* (in-SAHL-vənt), *a*: not solvent, and thus unable to meet one's financial responsibilities; broke
5. isl*et* (IY-lit), *n*: a small island
6. multi*tude* (MUL-tə-*tuwd*), *n*: a great mass, as of people or objects; the people collectively
7. plenti*tude* (PLEN-tə-*tuwd*), *n*: the state or condition of abundance, fullness, or completeness
8. poign*ant* (POIN-yənt), *a*: pointedly affecting the senses; sharply painful to the feelings; emotionally moving
9. trench*ant* (TREN-chənt), *a*: keen, sharp, and penetrating; clear-cut and distinct
10. vign*ette* (vin-YET), *n*: a brief (sometimes flowery) artistic piece of writing; a story or sketch, usually quite short

a (fat); ay (fate); ah (far); au (doubt); ch (church); e (elf, bed, care); ee (equal); ə (about); hw (while); i (fit); iy (kite); ŋ (link, sing); o (audio, corn); ow (ocean); oo (book); oi (oil); sh (shoe, ambition); th (think); u (up, deter); uw (ooze); y (yes, onion); yu (bureau, cure); yuw (youth, unity); zh (pleasure)

FILL-IN AND PART-OF-SPEECH IDENTIFICATION

_____ 1. The company was _____, unable to pay its bills.

_____ 2. An occasional descriptive _____ will not spoil an otherwise tightly written novel.

_____ 3. The _____ expressions on the faces of the defeated team suggested sorrow and sadness.

_____ 4. A _____ of people, hundreds of them, gathered outside the church.

_____ 5. The speaker's _____ remarks moved many in the audience to tears.

_____ 6. The drought has reduced nature's usual _____.

_____ 7. _____ employment is the ultimate goal of most college students today.

_____ 8. A comic's _____ wit can be very cutting to the people at whom the barbs are directed.

_____ 9. The recluse lives on a tiny _____ in the middle of Lake Woebegone.

_____ 10. Grown _____ from years of overeating, I have decided not to participate in the sack race.

MATCHING

_____ 1. gainful   a. stout

_____ 2. plentitude   b. unable to meet one's financial responsibilities

_____ 3. trenchant   c. producing substantial profits

_____ 4. insolvent   d. a brief sketch or story

_____ 5. multitude   e. deeply sorrowful and melancholy

_____ 6. vignette   f. emotionally moving

_____ 7. corpulent   g. the state of abundance

_____ 8. poignant   h. a great mass of people

_____ 9. islet   i. clear-cut and distinct

_____ 10. doleful   j. a small island

Completion Exercise for Suffixes 9 through 12

1. An *amorous* expression suggests _____.

2. An *apologist* is a person who _____.

3. If you are *apprehensive*, you are _____.

4. A *boorish* individual is often _____.

5. A *copious* reader is one who _____.

6. A *foppish* fellow is one who spends a lot of time on _____.

7. An *incisive* observation will likely be _____.

8. A *nihilist* sees little _____.

9. *Punitive* remarks are intended to _____.

10. *Sadists* get pleasure from _____.

11. To *chasten* a child is to _____.

12. The goal of *convalescence* is to _____.

13. A person guilty of *cowardice* lacks _____.

14. To *enlighten* the mind is to _____.

15. A *livid* appearance might suggest _____.

16. Intellectual *luminescence* might be called _____.

17. *Morbid* fears are likely to be _____.

18. A *novice* at anything is a person who _____.

19. *Obsolescence* can make the value of something go _____.

20. A person *torpid* from overwork will likely be _____.

21. An act of *barbarism* is not evidence of _____.

22. The *confluence* of two rivers is the place where they _____.

23. To *denigrate* a person is to _____.

24. Contemporary *feminism* promotes _____.

25. *Fulsome* praise can be _____.

26. *Nepotism* is favoritism involving _____.

27. To *procrastinate* is to _____.

28. *Reticence* inhibits one's ability to _____.

29. Without *vigilance,* one is not _____.

30. People with *winsome* ways will likely be _____.

31. A *corpulent* appearance suggests _____.

32. A *doleful* melody may make listeners _____.

33. *Gainful* activities usually result in _____.

34. If I am *insolvent,* I cannot _____.

35. *Islets* are usually surrounded by _____.

36. A *multitude* of mistakes is a(n) _____.

37. When there is a *plentitude,* there is _____.

38. *Poignant* words can be _____.

39. A *trenchant* remark may be intended to _____.

40. Narrative *vignettes* are sometimes quite _____.

Answers to Odd-Numbered Sequences

WORDS FROM ROOTS (1)

True-False: 1-T, 2-F, 3-F, 4-T, 5-F, 6-T, 7-T, 8-F, 9-T, 10-F

Definition Replacement: 1. millennium, 2. superannuated, 3. biennial, 4. perennial, 5. centennial, 6. annuity, 7. annals, 8. semiannual, 9. gregarious, 10. per annum

Fill-in: 1. (a) centennial, 2. (n) biennial, 3. (a) gregarious, 4. (a) superannuated, 5. (n) annuity, 6. (a) perennial, 7. (n) millennium, 8. (n) annals, 9. (a) semiannual, 10. (adv) per annum

Matching: 1-g, 2-c, 3-f, 4-i, 5-j, 6-h, 7-b, 8-d, 9-a, 10-e

WORDS FROM ROOTS (3)

True-False: 1-F, 2-T, 3-T, 4-F, 5-T, 6-F, 7-F, 8-T, 9-F, 10-T

Definition Replacement: 1. biogenesis, 2. bionics, 3. symbiotic, 4. autobiography, 5. biopsy, 6. cyclical, 7. biodegradable, 8. biomass, 9. biosphere, 10. biofeedback

Fill-in: 1. (a) symbiotic, 2. (n) biogenesis, 3. (n) biosphere, 4. (n) autobiography, 5. (n) biopsy, 6. (n) bionics, 7. (a) biodegradable, 8. (a) cyclical, 9. (n) biomass, 10. (n) biofeedback

Matching: 1-j, 2-c, 3-g, 4-f, 5-i, 6-a, 7-d, 8-h, 9-b, 10-e

WORDS FROM ROOTS (5)

True-False: 1-T, 2-F, 3-F, 4-T, 5-T, 6-F, 7-T, 8-T, 9-F, 10-F

Definition Replacement: 1. cursory, 2. precursor, 3. concourse, 4. discursive, 5. incursion, 6. toxic, 7. recurrent, 8. concurrent, 9. incur, 10. courier

Fill-in: 1. (a) discursive, 2. (n) courier, 3. (n) incursion, 4. (n) concourse, 5. (a) recurrent, 6. (a) cursory, 7. (v) incur, 8. (a) toxic, 9. (n) precursor, 10. (a) concurrent

Matching: 1-b, 2-e, 3-j, 4-a, 5-g, 6-i, 7-d, 8-f, 9-c, 10-h

WORDS FROM ROOTS (7)

True-False: 1-T, 2-F, 3-F, 4-F, 5-F, 6-T, 7-F, 8-T, 9-T, 10-F

Definition Replacement: 1. convene, 2. despicable, 3. specious, 4. speculate, 5. aspect, 6. introspection, 7. specter, 8. auspicious, 9. retrospect, 10. conspicuous

Fill-in: 1. (a) conspicuous, 2. (n) retrospect, 3. (a) despicable, 4. (n) specter, 5. (n) aspect, 6. (a) specious, 7. (v) convene, 8. (n) introspection, 9. (v) speculate, 10. (a) auspicious

Matching: 1-h, 2-c, 3-i, 4-a, 5-g, 6-j, 7-d, 8-f, 9-b, 10-e

WORDS FROM ROOTS (9)

True-False: 1-F, 2-T, 3-F, 4-F, 5-T, 6-F, 7-T, 8-T, 9-F, 10-T

Definition Replacement: 1. pedagogue, 2. pyromaniac, 3. expedient, 4. sesquipedalian, 5. pedantic, 6. expedite, 7. Pyrotechnics, 8. impediment, 9. pedestrian, 10. orthopedics

Fill-in: 1. (n) Orthopedics, 2. (a) pedestrian, 3. (v) expedite, 4. (n) pyrotechnics, 5. (n) pedagogues, 6. (n) pyromaniac, 7. (a) expedient, 8. (a) sesquipedalian, 9. (a) pedantic, 10. (n) impediment

Matching: 1-c, 2-f, 3-e, 4-g, 5-j, 6-a, 7-h, 8-d, 9-i, 10-b

WORDS FROM ROOTS (11)

True-False: 1-T, 2-T, 3-F, 4-T, 5-F, 6-F, 7-F, 8-T, 9-F, 10-F

Definition Replacement: 1. hierarchy, 2. patriarch, 3. Archaeology, 4. anarchist, 5. archenemy, 6. sinecure, 7. archaism, 8. archives, 9. oligarchy, 10. archetype

Fill-in: 1. (n) archetype, 2. (n) sinecure, 3. (n) archaeology, 4. (n) patriarch, 5. (n) anarchist, 6. (n) archenemy, 7. (n) oligarchy, 8. (n) archives, 9. (n) archaism, 10. (n) hierarchy

Matching: 1-e, 2-i, 3-f, 4-j, 5-b, 6-a, 7-c, 8-g, 9-d, 10-h

WORDS FROM ROOTS (13)

True-False: 1-T, 2-F, 3-F, 4-F, 5-T, 6-F, 7-T, 8-T, 9-T, 10-F

Definition Replacement: 1. sensory, 2. terrestrial, 3. apogee, 4. presentiment, 5. terrarium, 6. disinter, 7. subterranean, 8. geopolitical, 9. perigee, 10. geocentric

Fill-in: 1. (n) geopolitics, 2. (a) subterranean, 3. (n) presentiment, 4. (n) terrarium, 5. (a) geocentric, 6. (n) apogee, 7. (a) sensory, 8. (n) terrestrials, 9. (n) perigee, 10. (v) disinter

Matching: 1-h, 2-d, 3-f, 4-b, 5-i, 6-c, 7-e, 8-j, 9-g, 10-a

WORDS FROM ROOTS (15)

True-False: 1-T, 2-F, 3-F, 4-T, 5-F, 6-F, 7-T, 8-F, 9-F, 10-T

Definition Replacement: 1. interminable, 2. affinity, 3. terminology, 4. finite, 5. terminate, 6. definitive, 7. vacuous, 8. infinite, 9. terminal, 10. finale

Fill-in: 1. (a) vacuous, 2. (n) terminology, 3. (a) finite, 4. (a) terminal, 5. (n) affinity, 6. (a) interminable, 7. (n) finale, 8. (v) terminate, 9. (a) infinite, 10. (a) definitive

Matching: 1-c, 2-i, 3-a, 4-h, 5-f, 6-j, 7-d, 8-g, 9-b, 10-e

WORDS FROM ROOTS (17)

True-False: 1-T, 2-F, 3-T, 4-F, 5-T, 6-F, 7-F, 8-T, 9-T, 10-F

Definition Replacement: 1. epigram, 2. nondescript, 3. ascribe, 4. graphic, 5. postscript, 6. anagram, 7. vivacity, 8. transcribe, 9. Calligraphy, 10. monograph

Fill-in: 1. (a) graphic, 2. (v) transcribe, 3. (n) vivacity, 4. (n) monograph, 5. (n) epigrams, 6. (v) ascribe, 7. (n) postscript, 8. (n) calligraphy, 9. (a) nondescript, 10. (n) anagram

Matching: 1-e, 2-h, 3-a, 4-f, 5-i, 6-b, 7-j, 8-d, 9-g, 10-c

WORDS FROM ROOTS (19)

True-False: 1-T, 2-T, 3-F, 4-T, 5-T, 6-F, 7-F, 8-F, 9-T, 10-F

Definition Replacement: 1. urbanize, 2. politic, 3. inurbane, 4. synonymous, 5. urbanite, 6. suburban, 7. megalopolis, 8. metropolitan, 9. urbanity, 10. cosmopolitan

Fill-in: 1. (a) inurbane, 2. (n) urbanite, 3. (a) synonymous, 4. (n) megalopolis, 5. (v) politic, 6. (a) cosmopolitan, 7. (v) urbanize, 8. (n) urbanity, 9. (a) metropolitan, 10. (a) suburban

Matching: 1-j, 2-f, 3-i, 4-g, 5-h, 6-b, 7-c, 8-a, 9-e, 10-d

WORDS FROM ROOTS (21)

True-False: 1-T, 2-F, 3-T, 4-F, 5-T, 6-F, 7-T, 8-F, 9-T, 10-F

Definition Replacement: 1. mentation, 2. psychic, 3. commentary, 4. psyche, 5. dementia, 6. sophisticated, 7. mentality, 8. sophomoric, 9. psychosomatic, 10. psychedelic

Fill-in: 1. (n) mentality, 2. (a) psychosomatic, 3. (n) psyche, 4. (a) psychic, 5. (a) sophisticated, 6. (n) dementia, 7. (a) sophomoric, 8. (a) psychedelic, 9. (n) mentation, 10. (n) commentary

Matching: 1-d, 2-i, 3-g, 4-h, 5-j, 6-c, 7-a, 8-f, 9-e, 10-b

WORDS FROM ROOTS (23)

True-False: 1-F, 2-T, 3-F, 4-T, 5-F, 6-T, 7-F, 8-T, 9-F, 10-T

Definition Replacement: 1. emigrant, 2. Genocide, 3. vagary, 4. aberration, 5. immigrant, 6. erroneous, 7. concise, 8. vagrant, 9. erratic, 10. extravagant

Fill-in: 1. (n) immigrants, 2. (n) aberration, 3. (a) extravagant, 4. (a) erratic, 5. (n) vagary, 6. (n) emigrants, 7. (a) erroneous, 8. (a) vagrant, 9. (n) genocide, 10. (a) concise

Matching: 1-j, 2-e, 3-g, 4-b, 5-i, 6-c, 7-h, 8-a, 9-d, 10-f

WORDS FROM ROOTS (25)

True-False: 1-F, 2-T, 3-F, 4-T, 5-T, 6-F, 7-T, 8-T, 9-F, 10-F

Definition Replacement: 1. contemporary, 2. fortify, 3. corroborate, 4. firmament, 5. affirmative, 6. infirmity, 7. fortitude, 8. extemporaneous, 9. forte, 10. robust

Fill-in: 1. (a) robust, 2. (n) forte, 3. (a) extemporaneous, 4. (n) fortitude, 5. (a) affirmative, 6. (v) fortify, 7. (v) corroborate, 8. (n) infirmity, 9. (n) firmament, 10. (a) contemporary

Matching: 1-h, 2-c, 3-g, 4-i, 5-j, 6-b, 7-a, 8-e, 9-d, 10-f

WORDS FROM ROOTS (27)

True-False: 1-T, 2-T, 3-F, 4-F, 5-T, 6-F, 7-F, 8-F, 9-T, 10-T

Definition Replacement: 1. divulge, 2. populist, 3. inanimate, 4. populace, 5. demagogue, 6. vulgarism, 7. endemic, 8. plebeian, 9. plebiscite, 10. Demographic

Fill-in: 1. (a) endemic, 2. (n) plebiscite, 3. (a) Demographic, 4. (a) populist, 5. (a) inanimate, 6. (n) vulgarism, 7. (n) demagogue, 8. (n) populace, 9. (a) plebeian, 10. (v) divulge

Matching: 1-e, 2-j, 3-d, 4-h, 5-b, 6-i, 7-c, 8-f, 9-g, 10-a

WORDS FROM ROOTS (29)

True-False: 1-F, 2-F, 3-T, 4-F, 5-T, 6-T, 7-T, 8-F, 9-T, 10-F

Definition Replacement: 1. patrician, 2. fraternize, 3. confraternity, 4. veracity, 5. fratricide, 6. patron, 7. alma mater, 8. matriarch, 9. paternalism, 10. matriculate

Fill-in: 1. (n) Fratricide, 2. (v) matriculate, 3. (n) alma mater, 4. (a) patrician, 5. (n) veracity, 6. (n) confraternity, 7. (n) Paternalism, 8. (n) matriarch, 9. (n) patron, 10. (v) fraternize

Matching: 1-c, 2-g, 3-i, 4-f, 5-h, 6-a, 7-e, 8-j, 9-d, 10-b

WORDS FROM ROOTS (31)

True-False: 1-T, 2-F, 3-F, 4-T, 5-T, 6-F, 7-T, 8-F, 9-F, 10-F

Definition Replacement: 1. genial, 2. incorporate, 3. genesis, 4. homogenize, 5. genre, 6. congenital, 7. ingenuous, 8. eugenics, 9. progeny, 10. generic

Fill-in: 1. (n) eugenics, 2. (a) ingenuous, 3. (n) genesis, 4. (n) progeny, 5. (v) incorporate, 6. (v) homogenize, 7. (a) genial, 8. (a) congenital, 9. (n) genre, 10. (a) generic

Matching: 1-c, 2-f, 3-g, 4-i, 5-b, 6-j, 7-e, 8-a, 9-h, 10-d

WORDS FROM ROOTS (33)

True-False: 1-F, 2-T, 3-F, 4-T, 5-F, 6-T, 7-F, 8-F, 9-T, 10-T

Definition Replacement: 1. lustrous, 2. pellucid, 3. verisimilitude, 4. elucidate, 5. translucent, 6. phosphorescent, 7. illustrative, 8. photogenic, 9. luminary, 10. photomural

Fill-in: 1. (n) luminary, 2. (a) phosphorescent, 3. (a) translucent, 4. (a) lustrous, 5. (n) photomural, 6. (v) elucidate, 7. (n) verisimilitude, 8. (a) pellucid, 9. (a) photogenic, 10. (a) illustrative

Matching: 1-c, 2-e, 3-i, 4-g, 5-j, 6-h, 7-a, 8-d, 9-b, 10-f

WORDS FROM ROOTS (35)

True-False: 1-F, 2-F, 3-F, 4-T, 5-F, 6-T, 7-T, 8-T, 9-T, 10-F

Definition Replacement: 1. incredulous, 2. ostensible, 3. distraction, 4. pretentious, 5. détente, 6. protracted, 7. intractable, 8. contentious, 9. retract, 10. distended.

Fill-in: 1. (a) pretentious, 2. (a) distended, 3. (a) contentious, 4. (n) distraction, 5. (a) ostensible, 6. (a) incredulous, 7. (v) retract, 8. (a) Intractable, 9. (n) détente, 10. (a) protracted

Matching: 1-g, 2-d, 3-j, 4-a, 5-i, 6-h, 7-c, 8-f, 9-e, 10-b

WORDS WITH PREFIXES (1)

Fill-in: 1. (n) admixture, 2. (v) aggrandize, 3. (n) ally, 4. (v) accede, 5. (v) alleviate, 6. (a) affable, 7. (a) Affluent, 8. (v) acclimate, 9. (n) aggregation, 10. (v) admonish

Matching: 1-g, 2-d, 3-i, 4-f, 5-a, 6-h, 7-c, 8-j, 9-e, 10-b

WORDS WITH PREFIXES (3)

Fill-in: 1. (n) ambiance, 2. (a) catatonic, 3. (a) aboriginal, 4. (n) cataclysm, 5. (a) abstruse, 6. (a) antebellum, 7. (n) amphitheater, 8. (a) antediluvian, 9. (a) ambiguous, 10. (v) abdicate

Matching: 1-c, 2-j, 3-i, 4-h, 5-g, 6-b, 7-d, 8-a, 9-f, 10-e

WORDS WITH PREFIXES (5)

Fill-in: 1. (a) commodious, 2. (n) colleague, 3. (v) correlate, 4. (n) collusion, 5. (n) correspondence, 6. (a) Coeval, 7. (a) convivial, 8. (n) consensus, 9. (a) Cogent, 10. (a) commensurate

Matching: 1-c, 2-g, 3-e, 4-i, 5-h, 6-b, 7-d, 8-a, 9-j, 10-f

WORDS WITH PREFIXES (7)

Fill-in: 1. (a) escapist, 2. (a) effervescent, 3. (v) exhume, 4. (a) eccentric, 5. (a) efficacious, 6. (v) exonerate, 7. (a) ecstatic, 8. (v) eradicate, 9. (a) effete, 10. (n) escapade

Matching: 1-d, 2-f, 3-i, 4-g, 5-d, 6-j, 7-e, 8-a, 9-h, 10-c

WORDS WITH PREFIXES (9)

Fill-in: 1. (a) Hypothetical, 2. (n) occupant, 3. (a) oblique, 4. (n) Hypertension, 5. (a) occluded, 6. (a) opprobrious, 7. (a) hypocritical, 8. (n) oblivion, 9. (a) opportune, 10. (n) hyperbole

Matching: 1-j, 2-i, 3-h, 4-f, 5-c, 6-b, 7-e, 8-a, 9-g, 10-d

WORDS WITH PREFIXES (11)

Fill-in: 1. (v) retrofit, 2. (a) sedulous, 3. (v) transcends, 4. (n) prospectus, 5. (v) transpose, 6. (n) telekinesis, 7. (a) retroactive, 8. (a) telegenic, 9. (v) seduce, 10. (a) profuse

Matching: 1-f, 2-i, 3-g, 4-h, 5-a, 6-e, 7-b, 8-j, 9-c, 10-d

WORDS WITH PREFIXES (13)

Fill-in: 1. (a) antagonistic, 2. (v) countermands, 3. (n) anomaly, 4. (v) controvert, 5. (a) atypical, 6. (a) amoral, 7. (n) contretemps, 8. (a) antisocial, 9. (n) anecdotes, 10. (n) contraband

Matching: 1-d, 2-i, 3-g, 4-f, 5-j, 6-h, 7-a, 8-c, 9-b, 10-e

WORDS WITH PREFIXES (15)

Fill-in: 1. (a) illicit, 2. (a) irrational, 3. (a) immutable, 4. (n) incognito, 5. (a) ignoble, 6. (a) inclement, 7. (a) Immoderate, 8. (a) incredible, 9. (a) irresolute, 10. (a) illegible

Matching: 1-e, 2-i, 3-g, 4-h, 5-a, 6-j, 7-c, 8-b, 9-f, 10-d

WORDS WITH PREFIXES (17)

Fill-in: 1. (n) malcontent, 2. (v) malign, 3. (n) malice, 4. (a) maladroit, 5. (n) malfeasance, 6. (a) malignant, 7. (n) malady, 8. (a) maladorous, 9. (n) malaise, 10. (a) malevolent

Matching: 1-j, 2-e, 3-d, 4-f, 5-i, 6-h, 7-b, 8-a, 9-g, 10-c

WORDS WITH PREFIXES (19)

Fill-in: 1. (n) dilemma, 2. (a) bicameral, 3. (a) dubious, 4. (n) hemiplegia, 5. (a) bilateral, 6. (a) semi-literate, 7. (n) duplicity, 8. (a) binary, 9. (n) semiconductors, 10. (n) demitasse

Matching: 1-c, 2-j, 3-f, 4-h, 5-g, 6-a, 7-i, 8-d, 9-e, 10-b

WORDS WITH SUFFIXES (1)

Fill-in: 1. (a) demonstrative, 2. (a) remunerative, 3. (a) dissimilar, 4. (a) titular, 5. (n) absentees, 6. (a) tentative, 7. (n) designee, 8. (n) fallacy, 9. (a) insular, 10. (n) celibacy

Matching: 1-e, 2-i, 3-a, 4-g, 5-j, 6-c, 7-d, 8-f, 9-b, 10-h

WORDS WITH SUFFIXES (3)

Fill-in: 1. (n) aggrandizement, 2. (n) rapture, 3. (n) habiliments, 4. (a) virile, 5. (n) detriment, 6. (a) Puerile, 7. (n) disclosure, 8. (a) portly, 9. (a) surly, 10. (a) docile

Matching: 1-f, 2-i, 3-a, 4-c, 5-j, 6-h, 7-d, 8-e, 9-b, 10-g

WORDS WITH SUFFIXES (5)

Fill-in: 1. (a) fatalistic, 2. (v) cauterize, 3. (n) sagacity, 4. (v) galvanize, 5. (a) chauvinistic, 6. (a) pluralistic, 7. (a) filial, 8. (n) tenacity, 9. (v) plagiarize, 10. (a) autumnal

Matching: 1-j, 2-d, 3-h, 4-g, 5-a, 6-c, 7-i, 8-b, 9-e, 10-f

WORDS WITH SUFFIXES (7)

Fill-in: 1. (a) grotesque, 2. (a) laudable, 3. (a) viable, 4. (n) allusion, 5. (n) profusion, 6. (a) intangible, 7. (a) quiescent, 8. (n) contrition, 9. (a) statuesque, 10. (a) fluorescent

Matching: 1-h, 2-a, 3-f, 4-g, 5-b, 6-i, 7-j, 8-d, 9-e, 10-c

WORDS WITH SUFFIXES (9)

Fill-in: 1. (a) amorous, 2. (n) nihilist, 3. (a) copious, 4. (a) foppish, 5. (n) apologist, 6. (a) Punitive, 7. (a) boorish, 8. (n) sadist, 9. (a) incisive, 10. (a) apprehensive

Matching: 1-i, 2-g, 3-d, 4-f, 5-j, 6-c, 7-e, 8-a, 9-h, 10-b

WORDS WITH SUFFIXES (11)

Fill-in: 1. (v) denigrate, 2. (n) nepotism, 3. (a) winsome, 4. (n) confluence, 5. (n) reticence, 6. (n) Feminism, 7. (v) procrastinate, 8. (a) fulsome, 9. (n) vigilance, 10. (n) Barbarism

Matching: 1-j, 2-d, 3-h, 4-f, 5-a, 6-i, 7-b, 8-c, 9-g, 10-e

Index of Roots, Prefixes, and Suffixes

Index of Words

irrational, 203
irresolute, 203
irritant, 185
islet, 247
isomagnetic, 201
isometric, 201

jocose, 233

kilowatt, 215

laudable, 235
lexicographer, 119
lexicon, 119
literati, 151
livid, 243
localism, 15
locality, 15
localize, 15
locomotion, 15
locus, 15
logorrhea, 119
longevity, 237
loquacious, 160
luminary, 147
luminescence, 147, 243
lustrous, 147

macrobiotics, 211
macrocosm, 211
maladjusted, 209
maladroit, 209
malady, 209
malaise, 209
malcontent, 209
malevolent, 209
malfeasance, 209
malice, 209
malign, 209
malignant, 209
malingerer, 209
malnutrition, 209
malodorous, 209
malpractice, 209
maritime, 119

matriarch, 131
matriculate, 131
mediate, 15
mediocrity, 15
megalith, 205
megalomania, 205
megalopolis, 83
megaton, 205
memento, 23
memento mori, 23
memoirs, 23
memorabilia, 23
memorandum, 23
mentality, 99
mentation, 99
metronome, 127
metropolitan, 83
microcosm, 211
microfiche, 211
migrant, 107
migratory, 107
millennium, 11
millisecond, 215
minacious, 55
minatory, 55
minuscule, 55
minutia, 55
minutiae, 55
misanthrope, 143
misanthropic, 143
misconstrue, 205
miscreant, 205
misogamist, 205
missive, 39
mnemonic, 23
mnemonics, 23
monochromatic, 205
monograph, 75
monologue, 215
monopoly, 215
monopsony, 215
morbid, 243
moribund, 23
morose, 233
multilateral, 215

multitude, 247
muted, 237

neocolonialism, 63
neolithic, 63
neologism, 63
neonatal, 63
neophyte, 63
neoteric, 63
nepotism, 245
nihilist, 241
nonchalant, 211
nonconformist, 211
nondescript, 75
nonego, 80
nonentity, 211
nostalgic, 227
novantique, 63
novelty, 63
novice, 64, 243

oblique, 189
obliterate, 151
oblivion, 189
obsolescence, 243
occluded, 189
occupant, 189
oligarchy, 52
omnibus, 71
omnidirectional, 71
omnipotent, 71
omnipresent, 71
omniscient, 71
omnivorous, 71
opportune, 189
opprobrious, 189
orthodox, 55
orthography, 55
orthopedics, 43
ostensible, 155

pacify, 223
panacea, 71
panchromatic, 71
pandemic, 71, 123